HOLD ON, MR. PRESIDENT!

HOLD ON, MR. PRESIDENT!

SAM DONALDSON

Random House New York

Published in the United States by Random House, Inc., New York, and
simultaneously in Canada by Random House of Canada Limited, Toronto.

Library of Congress Cataloging-in-Publication Data
Donaldson, Sam.
Hold on, Mr. President—.

1. Donaldson, Sam. 2. Journalists—United States—
Biography. 3. Television broadcasting of news—United
States. 4. Presidents—United States—History—20th
century. I. Title.
PN4874.D66A3 1987 070′.92′4 [B] 86-10132
ISBN 0-394-55393-4

Manufactured in the United States of America
897

FOR MY MOTHER, CHLOE HAMPSON DONALDSON,

AND MY FATHER, SAMUEL ANDREW DONALDSON

Acknowledgments

This is the story of how I got into the news business, got into the White House press room, and got under the skin of presidents and other public figures.

The fact is, I'm a television news reporter who loves politics and politicians. With few exceptions, I have liked and respected the people I've covered. But my job is to hold their feet to the fire of public accountability. To be honest, I have never actually said "Hold On, Mr. President" to Jimmy Carter or Ronald Reagan in the line of duty. But in thinking about what to call this book, it seemed to me those words captured the essence of how I see my job. In doing the job that way I've made a few enemies. That's all right with me.

I don't intend this book to be a definitive work on the news business or White House reporting or for that matter the last word on anything. I've simply recounted some of the things I've seen and done in more than a quarter century in Washington that were fun, even exciting. I've tried to explain why I cover the White House beat the way I do and why I ask the questions I ask. I've thrown in a little about myself, including a few of my skeletons (not all, mind you). And, naturally, I've seized the opportunity to tell you what I think about certain people, places, and things.

You may wonder why I didn't hire a really good ghostwriter like William Novak (look what he did for Iaccoca). The answer is I've always thought it wrong for a writer to hire another writer to write the first writer's book. Consider: Piano Concerto in D Minor by Wolfgang Amadeus Mozart as hummed to Salieri. Somehow it smacks of the wrong motivation, and seems a little lazy to boot. However, to write all this by myself and still hold down a job required the understanding and cooperation of my employer. I am grateful to the management of ABC News for giving me both, particularly to Executive Vice-President David Burke. I called Burke one day to ask for some time off in order to write. "How much time do you have in mind?" he inquired. I had six weeks in mind, but I can be extraordinarily timid at times, believe it or not. I found myself answering, "How about every Thursday for two months." Request granted. I am grateful also to ABC's Washington bureau chief, George Watson, and news coverage manager, Dean Norland, for looking the other way when I stole a few extra hours here and there to complete the project.

I drew most of what follows from memory rather than from a comprehensive review of my reporter's notes on the theory that if it hadn't stuck in my mind in some form, it must not have been as interesting as the things that did. Then, too, my notes aren't all that complete. I admire those reporters who have file cabinets of cross-indexed material covering every moment of their professional lives, but I'm not one of them. Oh, yes, I have box after box of papers, scripts, notebooks, press releases, and old press passes piled up in my attic and someday someone may paw through them. But not me and not now.

Once I got down what memory had retained, my hard-working researcher, Donna Paine, checked it all to see that the facts were correct and helped me proof the numerous drafts of the manuscript. She did a terrific job and believe me there was a lot to do. All reporters know that memory is fallible but I was shocked to discover how often I recalled things just a little bit off. Close doesn't count in the news business.

My thanks to my colleagues and acquaintances whose stories I've included. Many of them have been kind enough to confirm details of events; others have successfully denied my recollections and spared themselves and me the embarrassment of seeing it come out wrong.

I'm grateful to Random House and my editor, Peter Osnos, for taking me on. Other publishers I talked to about this project told me how much they would like to publish this book, but it was Osnos who had the most faith in me. He may have soon regretted it. He must have been bewildered by the disorganized stream of consciousness pouring from my word processor. Thank goodness he was there to help prune and shape it. I am also grateful for the suggestions of my wife, Jan, and of my friends Dorrance Smith, executive producer of *This Week with David Brinkley*; John Weisman, Washington bureau chief of *TV Guide*; and Robert Barnett, partner in the Washington law firm of Williams & Connolly.

Most of all I am indebted to my wife, Jan, for putting up with my long stretches at the word processor and with my mood swings. Sometimes I would stare at the keyboard for hours without writing a word for keeps, then get up and denounce all the people who had driven me to make a fool of myself by encouraging me to take on this project. At other times I would punch away with self-delight, chuckling at my own wit, nodding at my own perspicacity, acting as if I were writing *Moby Dick* or some other masterpiece. Jan never complained and always encouraged me to press on.

Finally, my thanks to the two presidents I've known best, Jimmy Carter and Ronald Reagan. Their public utterances and conduct as observed by me provided a good deal of the material in this book, although they might claim not to recognize it and should not be held responsible for my interpretations. When Carter left the presidency he said he wished only two things on his successor: That the irascible Menachem Begin would remain prime minister of Israel and that Sam Donaldson would remain ABC's White House correspondent. Reagan may have come to know what he meant by that. If I've vexed Carter and Reagan in doing my job as I think it ought to be done—my mail tells me I've certainly vexed a lot of their supporters—I want them to know I didn't mean it personally. I'd like to think they understand.

Contents

HOLD ON, MR. PRESIDENT!

Chapter One

CHALLENGING PRESIDENTS

"Ladies and gentlemen, the president of the United States," intones an offstage announcer. We reporters, gathered in the White House East Room for a prime-time televised presidential news conference, rise. From a doorway halfway down the main first-floor hall emerges Ronald Reagan, dressed in a dark gray suit. He is as prepared as a lifetime of stage appearances, political experience and last-minute rehearsal with his staff can make him to handle the questioning that is about to begin. Reagan is in deep trouble over the secret sale of arms to Iran. And on this night—November 19, 1986—it is widely believed that how he fields the thirty minutes or so of questions may profoundly affect the remainder of his presidency.

Reagan does not like to hold press conferences. He much prefers to communicate with the public by reading a carefully written speech delivered on his own terms. But in this case, a canned response is no longer an option. He has already done that. The previous week, the man called the Great Communicator had gone on television with one of his patented Oval Office addresses in which he acknowledged he had been selling arms to Iran and tried to explain it. But he failed to convince the country that his secret policy was a proper exercise in improving contacts with moderate Iranians. The immediate post-speech polls indicate a disapproving majority of the public believes he has actually been engaged in paying a ransom of arms for help in freeing U.S. citizens held hostage in Lebanon. Now he is holding a press conference in a second attempt to keep his public support from slipping further. That is what Ronald Reagan is doing in the East Room.

But why am I there? What is my purpose, and the purpose of the other reporters present? The answer is simple. Our job is to challenge the president, challenge him to explain policy, justify decisions, defend mistakes, reveal intentions for the future, and comment on a host of matters about which his views are of general concern. On that night, topic A was clearly the president's Iranian arms sale policy and the impact of disclosure on his presidency. When he called on me I stood and asked: "Mr. President, when you had the arms embargo on [Iran] you were asking other nations, our allies in particular, to observe it publicly, but at the same time privately, you concede, you were authorizing a breaking of that embargo by the United States. How ean you justify this duplicity?"

"I don't think it was duplicity," he insisted hotly, reeling off several reasons for the policy without ever addressing why he had engaged in the dictionary definition of *duplicity*: "pretending to act one way while acting another."

I followed up. "Sir, if I may, the polls show that a lot of American people just simply don't believe you; that the one thing that you've had going for you more than anything else in your presidency, your credibility, has been severely damaged. Can you repair it and what does it mean for the rest of your presidency?"

"Well, I imagine I'm the only one around who wants to repair it," said Reagan in a swipe at the rest of us in the room. Then in a rejoinder that strained his credibility further, he said, "And I didn't have anything to do with damaging it."

A number of viewers wrote me to complain about my questions. They said they were disrespectful and should not have been put to the president. I disagree. Let me tell you how I see my job, and how I go about challenging presidents.

I'm a reporter who goes to work every morning to cover the president of the United States. I have one goal: to find out what's *really* going on at the White House. That involves a lot more than just writing down what the President and his aides say. Sometimes they don't say. And when they do, they often don't say it all.

In twenty-six years of reporting from Washington, I've never heard a president admit he had made a mistake, never heard a White House press secretary go on the record to say the boss was confused about how to proceed. That is understandable. Presidents and their aides want to put their best foot forward, emphasize their successes, minimize or hide their blunders, send only the messages they think will advance their interests—to Congress, to the Soviets, to the American people—and generally use the press to the extent they can as a tool for governing and retaining power.

There's nothing illegal or even immoral in wanting to do all that.

If I were president, I certainly wouldn't come out to the press room to announce I had just made a mistake in dealing with the Soviets, and if my press secretary told reporters, "Boy, the boss really botched that one," why, I'd fire him in an instant.

But I'm not president. I'm a reporter trying to find out who did botch what, where, when, why, and how and what's on the front burner for possible botching tomorrow. If you think I ought to stand by waiting for the president to tell the country only what he wants when he wants, you've picked up the wrong book. What's more, you ought to apply for a job on the White House press staff; they're looking for people like you. Reporters are not part of the White House team of cheerleaders. Not for Jimmy Carter, not for Ronald Reagan, not for any president.

Now, I'm happy to talk to the president's assistants and get their views. A reporter learns a lot that way. But they weren't elected to run the country. I'm assigned by ABC News to the White House to cover the one person who was—the president. In order to do that, I need to talk to him directly every chance I get.

Many people find it extremely difficult to talk to presidents.

They get nervous. They are tongue-tied, intimidated by the larger-than-life quality we've built up around presidents, particularly, I think, in this television age. Jimmy Carter once told me he found it strange and disconcerting to have people from his hometown whom he'd known all his life stammer with awestruck admiration when they visited him in the Oval Office.

But reporters can't afford to remain in awe of those they cover. People expect the press to hold the mayor's feet to the fire and to bore in on the city council and to make sure the governor doesn't get away with a thing. It doesn't make any sense to let up on the one public servant whose official conduct affects us all the most. Presidents have a greater responsibility than other public servants and deserve a compassionate understanding of the difficulty of discharging that responsibility. But they are not due worship.

I know that's easier said than done. I trembled with nervousness when I met my first president, John F. Kennedy. But you get over it and come to realize that presidents put their pants on one leg at a time like everyone else. I think you talk to presidents just the way you talk to anyone else. And reporters can't be timid about it.

Nine months into his administration, I asked Jimmy Carter to defend himself against charges that "your administration is inept" and to comment on the recurring Washington undercurrent that "as a Georgian, you don't belong here."

Two years into his administration, I asked Ronald Reagan to comment on the perception that "disarray is here in the White House, that you have been out of touch, that you have had to be dragged back by your staff and friends on Capitol Hill to make realistic decisions on the budget. There was even a newspaper column saying that your presidency is failing."

I suppose neither man liked hearing those things. But those things were being said about them, and it was legitimate to ask them to respond.

A lot of people want to know what I'm after when I ask questions of the president. Well, it's simple. I'm looking for straight answers on topics the public has an interest in, most of them important, some of them not. With a nod to Will Rogers, I've never heard a question I didn't like. Sure, some are more relevant, important, interesting, more artfully or tactfully phrased than others. But I don't believe there's any such thing as a bad question, only bad answers.

So when I ask questions, I think it's important to challenge the president, challenge him to explain policy, justify decisions, defend mistakes, reveal intentions for the future, and comment on a host of matters about which his views are of general concern. I try to put my questions in a courteous manner, but I try also to make them specific, and pointed.

"Mr. President," I asked Ronald Reagan in October 1983, "Senator [Jesse] Helms has been saying on the Senate floor that Martin Luther King, Jr., had communist associations, was a communist sympathizer. Do you agree?" The president replied, "We'll know in about thirty-five years, won't we [a reference to the fact that certain records that might shed light on the subject would be sealed for that length of time]?" In the same answer, the president went on to defend Senator Helms's sincerity for wanting to unseal the records. He had not delivered a direct reply to my question "Do you agree?" But he had nevertheless spoken volumes about his feelings.

Reagan later called Dr. King's widow, Coretta Scott King, to apologize for what he said was the press's distortion of his remark. There was no distortion, just an embarrassing insensitivity, and that was his, not the press's.

The wording of questions is very important. If you say to a president, "Would you care to comment on *X*," he can always answer, "No, thanks," or he can say anything he wants to and call it a comment. As Reagan mounted the stairway of *Air Force One* in Texas one day in July 1986, we tried to get his reaction to the razor-thin victory he'd won that day in the Senate on confirmation of one of his judicial nominees.

"What about [Daniel] Manion?" someone yelled.

"He's going to be a judge," replied Reagan with a smile, which was hardly a reaction, only a statement of fact. But having established that he could hear us above the noise, I sang out, "What about Tutu?" an obvious reference to Bishop Desmond Tutu's criticism the day before that "the West, for my part, can go to hell" because of its reluctance to embrace economic sanctions against the white minority government of South Africa.

"He's not going to be a judge," replied the president solemnly as he disappeared through the doorway of his plane. All right, pretty funny, but then in neither case had we asked the president a specific question, so it's fair to say we had only ourselves to blame.

Once I cried out in exasperation as Reagan retreated across the White House lawn, "What about the Russians?"

"What about them?" he shot back. As he ducked into his helicopter, I could only stammer that I'd ask the questions around here.

To be effective, questions must be specific and, preferably, short. They should invite a direct answer. I once asked Jimmy Carter, referring to former CIA director Richard Helms, "Mr. President, Mr. Helms's attorney says that his client will wear his conviction on charges of failing to testify fully before Congress as a badge of honor. Do you think it's a badge of honor, and do you think a public official has a right to lie in public about his business under any circumstances?"

Carter replied, "No, it is not a badge of honor, and a public official does not have a right to lie . . ." Direct question. Direct answer.

Of course, presidents don't always agree with the way questions are framed as Carter did in that one, but when they don't, that too can be most revealing.

In March 1985, I asked Reagan about the death of seventeen South African blacks who were shot by government authorities the day before, in what I said "appears to be a continuing wave of violence by the white minority government against the black majority population." Reagan was having none of my characterization. ". . . I think to put it that way—that they were simply killed and that violence was coming totally from the law-and-order side—ignores the fact that there was rioting going on in behalf of others there," he corrected me, making it perfectly clear who he thought was right and who was wrong in South Africa.

Reagan is always looking for a way to support existing authority, no matter whose, unless, of course, it is communist authority. So his attitude about the unrest in South Africa may not spring from racism. But, of course, to blacks the effect is the same as if Reagan meant it personally.

Occasionally, I'm told I ask mean questions, that I'm always trying to "trap the president," and trying to make him "look bad." Not so. Consider the question I asked Reagan at his first press conference as president; there were no barbs, no hooks: I said, "Mr. President, what do you see as the long-range intentions of the Soviet Union? Do you think, for instance, that the Kremlin is bent on world domination that might lead to a continuation of the cold war, or do you think that under other circumstances détente is possible?" And out came his view that the Soviets "reserve unto themselves the right to commit any crime, to lie, to cheat, in order to attain" their goal of world revolution. That answer created an uproar, not matched until his speech two years later in which he called the Soviet Union an "evil empire."

And why did I ask him the question in the first place? After all, there was nothing startling about hearing such a view from Ronald Reagan. He had been offering it for years. But he hadn't been president then, and now that he was, it was important for people to know where the president stood. In fact, one of the main objectives in questioning a president is to put him on the record. Of course, sometimes presidents don't want their views on the record. Let me give you an example:

In February 1985, I asked Ronald Reagan at one of his infrequent news conferences, "Mr. President, on Capitol Hill . . . Secretary Shultz suggested that a goal of your policy now is to remove the Sandinista government in Nicaragua. Is that your goal?"

From the beginning of his presidency, Reagan has been working to overthrow the Sandinista government—officials of his administration freely admit it when they know their names will not be used—but for reasons of international law, foreign relations, and domestic politics, no one wants to admit it on the record. Following the advice of his aides, Reagan had always publicly denied any intention of "overthrowing" the Sandinistas.

But when I asked Reagan that night about "removing" the

Sandinista government, he replied, "Well, remove in the sense of its present structure, in which it is a communist totalitarian state and it is not a government chosen by the people . . ." Ah, I thought: It's out at last! The word *remove* had not triggered the same warning bell in Reagan's mind that the word *overthrow* would have, and he had delivered the unvarnished truth about his policy.

I pursued it.

"Well, sir," I followed up. "When you say *remove* . . . aren't you then saying that you advocate the overthrow of the present government of Nicaragua?" Now, the alarm bells went off in Reagan's head. He threw up a massive barrage of familiar rhetoric about the Sandinistas having betrayed the original revolution.

I pressed on, violating the one follow-up rule.

"Is the answer yes, sir?" I asked.

"To what?" replied the president.

"To the question 'Aren't you advocating the overthrow of the present government if you substitute another form of what you say was the revolution,' " I answered.

Cornered. But when Ronald Reagan is cornered, he stands and fights. "Not if the present government would turn around and say, 'All right,' if they'd say 'uncle' . . ." he replied. That seemed clear enough to me. The choice for Nicaragua was on the record: surrender or die. Reagan's zealous pursuit of the Sandinistas led to the illegal diversion of funds from his Iranian arms sales to supply the anti-Sandinista contra rebels. Presidents set direction for those who serve under them through many channels. Sometimes they give direct orders; other times subordinates get the message by simply listening to their public declarations. "Cry uncle," indeed!

Getting presidents to put their policy on the record is very important. Lyndon Johnson increased U.S. participation in Vietnam from a military advisory force of 16,000 to a full-scale battlefield force of about 542,000 men while maintaining throughout that there had been no change in policy. Given that reminder, reporters now try very hard to get presidents to keep the record straight about policy changes and the reasons for those changes.

Take the case of the U.S. Marines and Lebanon. In the fall of 1983, with U.S. Marines dying in Lebanon, Reagan declared that the "credibility of the United States would suffer on a worldwide scale" if the U.S. peace-keeping force of marines were withdrawn.

And one Friday in early 1984, the *Wall Street Journal* published an interview with Reagan in which he told the paper's Washington bureau chief Albert Hunt, when asked about House Speaker Thomas P. ("Tip") O'Neill's call for the marines to be brought home, ". . . he may be ready to surrender [in Lebanon], but I'm not."

You can imagine the consternation in some quarters when the *very next Tuesday*, Reagan announced the withdrawal from Lebanon of the U.S. Marines.

At his April press conference, I asked him about it.

"Mr. President," I said. "Last October you said the presence of U.S. Marines in Lebanon was central to our credibility on a global scale. And now you've withdrawn them . . . to what extent have we lost credibility?"

"We may have lost some with some people," replied the president, ". . . but situations change, Sam. . . . I can, I think, explain." And off he went with the patented Ronald Reagan version of the history of the Middle East conflict. It always takes him several minutes to recite it, and he tells it differently each time.

When the recitation was over, I pressed him.

"You began your answer by saying we lost some credibility. Are you to blame for that? Or, like Secretary Shultz, do you blame Congress?"

I had made a tactical mistake. I had given him an out instead of simply asking, "Are you to blame for that?"

He seized it. ". . . they must take a responsibility . . . with the Congress demanding—'Oh, take our, bring our men home. Take them away'—all this can do is stimulate the terrorists and urge them on to further attacks because they see a possibility of success in getting the force out which is keeping them from having their way . . ." said the president, thus shifting all blame, escaping my question, but at the price of provoking a fearful row with Congress.

Sometimes, people say that my questions reflect a political bias. It may seem hard to believe, but reporters' questions are not necessarily indicative of their own point of view. A lot of people thought I was personally opposed to Jimmy Carter because of the questions

I asked him, and a lot of people think I'm opposed to Ronald Reagan because of the questions I ask him. It's a reporter's job to challenge a president—every president—to explain and defend his policies whether you agree with them or not. Still, a lot of people, including presidents, seem to think the questions are personal.

In the summer of 1980, at a news conference devoted to Billy Carter's business relationship with the Libyan government, I asked President Carter to respond to an underlying widespread criticism "that this Billy Carter case is another example of a general aura of incompetence that hangs over your presidency . . ." Carter began his response by saying, "I've heard you mention that on television a few times, but I don't agree with it . . ." If he had heard me mention that on television, it was because I had often reported what *others* were saying. As a rule, critics should be named when asking for a response, which helps to make it clear the reporter isn't expressing a personal view. But if I had tried that day to name all the people who were accusing the Carter administration of being incompetent, there would not have been a 1980 election; we would all still be in that room listening to me recite names.

Loyal admirers of the chief executive in office frequently demand that I stop asking critical questions and "support our president." Well, if I ever do decide to try to "get" a president, one way to do it would be to stand up and inquire, "Sir, please tell us why you are such a great man," and then watch the "great man" try desperately to keep from making a fool of himself as he tried to handle that softball. Good politicians, like any good batter, want something they can swing at.

Consider the hardball from House Speaker Tip O'Neill I tossed at Reagan in June 1981. "Tip O'Neill says you don't know anything about the working people, that you have just a bunch of wealthy and selfish advisers," I told him. Reagan, who had already started from the room because the press conference had officially ended, turned back to the microphone with relish. "I'm trying to find out something about . . . [Tip's] . . . boyhood," said Reagan. ". . . I grew up in poverty and got what education I got all by myself and so forth, and I think it is sheer demagoguery to pretend that this economic program which we've submitted is not aimed at helping the great cross section of people in this country . . ." Now, you may or may not agree with O'Neill's assessment of Ronald Reagan, but it's hard not to agree that Reagan took that question and hit it out of the ball park.

Not only do good politicians like to swing at tough questions, but they also use them for their own purposes. Reagan did this once in Tokyo even before any questions had been asked.

He and leaders of other industrialized non-communist nations meeting at one of their yearly economic summits were trying to hammer out a statement on terrorism in May of 1986. Everyone was against state-sponsored terrorism but some of the leaders did not want to specifically identify Libya as one of the chief culprits. Reagan told them that if Libya wasn't named, the very first question the press would ask would be Why not? And in light of Libya's highly spotlighted activities that would be a hard question to answer. Reagan's argument carried the day. Libya was put in but, of course, those of us waiting outside didn't know it.

Sure enough, when the leaders emerged I sang out as if on cue, "Mr. President, your statement on terrorism does not mention Libya by name. Why not?" Reagan's face lit up in a wide smile. "Read the final statement," he replied triumphantly, and, I was told later, once out of earshot of the press he turned to the other leaders and crowed, "See, didn't I tell you, the very first question!" Oh, well. I'm always glad to be of service.

No matter how such questions are handled, getting the president to respond to the criticism of others is one of our main jobs in the White House press room. And sometimes, not often enough in my view, reporters ask questions that zero in on people who are not important figures but are still deserving of his attention. The champion of this calling is the legendary Sarah McClendon, who has been badgering, some would say terrorizing, presidents for forty years. Once, Sarah sharply berated Reagan for pulling back a promised appointment because the candidate for the job had criticized cutting the budget for an agency that protects consumers. ". . . Did you mean to give a signal to other Republicans that if they don't conform, that off would go their heads?" asked Sarah. Reagan, looking properly chastened, began his reply, "How can you say that about a sweet fellow like me? . . ." That drew a laugh, but then, he had to go on and answer the question. Sarah, more power to her, is always sticking up for the underdog and asking presidents to explain why they are not.

That seems to me the right approach for a reporter. It's the people who don't have the power or whose thinking isn't in the mainstream who most need help in being heard.

When I said earlier that you ought to talk to presidents the way you talk to anyone else, I wasn't referring only to asking questions. I think that also applies to light banter at appropriate times.

Once, in the Oval Office, Ronald Reagan signed a congressional spending resolution and thanked senators Baker and Hatfield and congressmen Conte and "Michelle" for their "strong leadership" on this.

There is no Congressman Michelle. Reagan was clearly referring to Bob Michel of Illinois, the Republican leader in the House. So I said to the president, "That's Michel, sir, Michel."

"Oh, Michel, yes," he said. "Don't tell anyone, will you?" This while five television cameras were shooting away.

"No deals, Mr. President," I replied sternly.

"Now, Sam, haven't you ever made a mistake?" he pleaded.

"Sir," said I, "The last time I called someone Michelle, she was blond."

He laughed.

Later, I was told one of the VIP's present from Capitol Hill thought it outrageous that a mere reporter had dared to banter with the president of the United States. To his credit, Reagan doesn't seem to share this attitude. Whereas others around Reagan often seem to be striving to put him on some kind of imperial pedestal, he seems to have his feet on the ground. In fact, he can even be a little pixieish. Once, as he stood on the pavement at Checkpoint Charlie looking into communist East Berlin, I yelled out to him to be careful not to cross the line. "You don't want to get captured by the commies," I admonished with a grin.

On hearing this, Reagan lifted his leg and, with a devilish smile on his face, swung it in the air across the line. Fortunately for the safety of the free world, he didn't fall over.

And he laughed loudly at himself when, having fulminated to newspaper editors against the Shiite Muslim leader he identified as Nabih Berra, I later told him out of their earshot, "Listen here, Berra was a catcher for the New York Yankees. The man you're after is named Berri."

Reagan spars better with reporters than Carter did, because of this ability to laugh at himself. Carter preferred to laugh at the other fellow. We noticed this trait early in the Carter campaign. Curtis Wilkie, a reporter for the *Boston Globe*, brought it up on the press plane one day. "Why don't you ever engage in any self-deprecating humor?" Wilkie asked. The next day, Carter tried to poke fun at himself at every stop. Somehow, he didn't manage to sound convincing. But Carter does have a quick wit when it comes to casting humor in an outward direction. And one day in the Rose Garden he got me good. As I sat relaxing on one of the lawn chairs at the back of the garden waiting for a scheduled presidential appearance, Carter, suddenly and early, came out of the Oval Office, walked up to the rope line behind which other reporters were waiting, and started talking.

I ran up as quickly as I could, but by the time I got there, Carter had turned away and headed back inside. "What did he say, what did he say?" I asked a little frantically.

"He said," replied one of the reporters, "he just wanted to see if he could get Donaldson off his lawn chair."

On another occasion, Carter hit home in a brief exchange in India. We had been taken to a small village near New Delhi (renamed Carterpuri by the Indians for the occasion) to see how the village solved its energy problem. This was at the height of concern over the energy crisis. Carterpuri solved its energy problem by throwing all the cow manure from its herds into a large pit, then siphoning off the methane gas to light the village lamps. So it came to pass that we all stood on the lip of the manure pit inspecting the process.

"If I fell in, you'd pull me out wouldn't you, Mr. President?" I joked.

"Certainly," Carter replied—pause—"after a suitable interval."

It's not every day that presidents take reporters to the lip of a manure pit (literally, that is), but when they do, that's all right: It's our job to follow them wherever they go. And when presidents try to give us the slip, it's war.

A week or so after Jimmy Carter took office, he let it be known that he didn't see the need to take along a press pool in his motorcade every time he left the White House grounds, as had been the custom for years. We in the press were alarmed. We think there is a great, overriding public interest in covering the president when he's out and about, including in motorcades and on airplane rides. Consider the day James Salamites, a young man out on the town, accidentally drove through an unguarded intersection in Hartford, Connecticut, and slammed into the side of the limousine carrying President Gerald R. Ford. Fortunately, no one was seriously hurt (one of Ford's aides suffered a broken finger), but it was one of those unplanned events that make the case for full-time press coverage of the president.

Jody Powell, Carter's press secretary, set up a meeting in the cabinet room, and I was chosen by lot as one of the press representatives to argue the case with Carter. The president opened by saying he understood the public interest in his activities, but he saw no need to take the press along on purely personal outings, such as taking his daughter, Amy, to the Washington zoo, for instance.

The headline flashed through my mind: "President Mauled by Runaway Lion, *It Is Suspected.*"

So I told him in so many words that he was wrong; that he no longer could expect to be left alone as an ordinary citizen might, because of the overriding interest in him as president, a position, I reminded him politely, no one had forced him to seek.

"You can take us along in your motorcade or we can stake out every one of the gates twenty-four hours a day and chase you through the streets, but we're going to cover you one way or the other," I told him. After all, no one dragged Carter or Reagan to the Oval Office and made them serve in the presidency. They fought long and hard for that job and the publicity glare that goes with it. Presidents must understand they live in a glass house when they move to the White House. Carter took the point and agreed to continue the motorcade press pool.

The fact is, the public is curious about everything presidents do, even when no great public issues are involved. A reporter once asked John F. Kennedy why he had a bandage on his finger and he replied he had cut it with a knife down in the White House kitchen the night before as he was slicing sandwich bread. People found it fascinating.

During the Carter presidency, much of the copy turned out by news organizations and avidly gobbled up by readers had to do with Carter's family—his mother, Lillian, his sister Gloria, who rode a motorcycle, his sister Ruth, who was a faith healer, and of course his brother, Billy. And the comings and goings of young Amy Carter were chronicled and commented on unrelentingly. The same goes, of course, for Reagan's family.

One morning after the serious questioning at one of Reagan's mini-press conferences in the White House briefing room had ended and he was leaving the podium, I asked him, "Are you and your son Michael closer to resolving your differences?" He ducked the question by replying that he would give me the same answer his wife, Nancy, had given me the day before, when I had put the question to her during a Christmas tree photo op: "Merry Christmas."

Well, you would have thought by the outrage registered in some quarters that I had inquired as to the First Couple's sex life—something *Los Angeles Times* reporter George Skelton once did in an interview with Reagan (more power to you, George). A Nixon appointee on the Federal Communications Commission, James Quello, thundered that I had asked the nastiest, most underhanded, most vicious question ever heard. I thought Quello's nomination of my humble effort a little too generous, as well as ham-handed, coming from the FCC.

But balanced against Quello's blast came a flood of letters from ordinary citizens wanting more information on the First Family's domestic dispute. They said they had been reading about the dispute (it was in all the papers and news magazines) and wondered why the president hadn't answered the question. And when Patti Davis, the Reagans' daughter, wrote a novel that reflected an unflattering view of her parents, it was natural for me to ask Reagan if he had read his daughter's book and what he thought about it.

Reagan replied he found it "interesting fiction." Quello has yet to weigh in on that exchange.

I have a reputation for putting uncomfortable questions to presidents, but I am certainly not alone. One of the most relentless interrogators is the White House bureau chief for United Press International, Helen Thomas, the dean of the White House press corps. Helen has been taking dead aim at the First Magistrate of the land since Kennedy's days. Two of my favorite examples of Helen's technique are: to Jimmy Carter, ". . . was it worth it to you to cause some destabilization of the dollar and demoralization of the federal government, spreading doubt through the land, in order to repudiate much of your Cabinet?"; and to Ronald Reagan, ". . . how high does unemployment have to go and how much does the economy have to deteriorate before you are willing to accept cuts in the defense budget?"

Thomas is particularly effective because she is always working. I found that out one day early in the Carter administration, when I stumbled onto a birthday party for deputy press secretary Rex Granum in Granum's office, right off the press room. Carter himself was there having a piece of cake with Rex and other staff members. A moment later, Ed Bradley of CBS discovered the group. Bradley and I began reminiscing with Carter about his presidential campaign, which we had both covered. Suddenly, Thomas appeared. And after the polite hellos, she immediately whipped out her notebook and began asking Carter about the details of his forthcoming energy program. Carter fled. At first, I was unhappy that Thomas had ruined the light conversation. But upon reflection, I realized she was absolutely right to do it. Reporters are there to get information and to do it at every opportunity. That principle, noble though it may be, once almost cost me my job, however. It came about this way.

In November 1981, the ABC News Washington bureau moved into a new building, and Reagan came to dedicate it. All the top executives of the company were there, led by ABC board chairman Leonard Goldenson. Roone Arledge, president of ABC News, presided at the ceremony in our news room. President Reagan delivered a short speech, after which I started shooting questions at him. I'm sure it came as no surprise to him, because he had seen me standing ten feet away with a microphone in my hand.

"Can David Stockman continue to be effective after saying such damaging things about your economic program?" I asked, referring to the Office of Management and Budget director's famous admission to William Greider in *The Atlantic* that the administration had cooked the budget figures and really didn't know what it was doing.

The president began dodging and weaving in his answers but did reveal that he would be seeing budget director Stockman right after he returned to the White House—it turned out to be the famous meeting in which Stockman said Reagan had taken him to the "woodshed."

I kept on, and Helen Thomas joined me in popping questions.

"I was only joking when I said the first question would be by Sam Donaldson," Roone Arledge snapped in a decidedly non-joking voice, aware that the majesty of the dedication ceremony was rapidly disappearing.

"So, fire me," I interjected in what I hoped was a lighthearted tone.

"You know, that's not a bad idea," replied Arledge in a tone he may have meant to be similarly lighthearted but somehow sounded more like the whistle of a Katyusha rocket about to crash through the roof.

The official party moved backstage. I am told that Michael Deaver, then White House deputy chief of staff, immediately turned on Arledge. "You mouse trapped us," said Deaver. "We agreed to come here to dedicate the building, and you tried to turn this into a press conference." It was a terribly embarrassing moment for the top management of the American Broadcasting Company and a terribly dangerous moment for me.

Before Arledge could reply—thank God, before he could reply—another voice interrupted. "Oh, that's all right, that's just the way Sam is," said Ronald Reagan with a chuckle.

Reagan may regret that moment of generosity. The give and take of years of intense and often critical press coverage can change a president's feeling toward the press. Carter, whose national career was made possible by early favorable press coverage, left the presidency convinced that many Washington reporters had been viciously unfair to him. By early 1986, Reagan publicly spoke of reporters as "sons of bitches" and by the end of the year, as his Iranian arms sale policy collapsed about him, he complained that we were circling like "sharks . . . with blood in the water." Such reactions are regrettable but understandable. No one likes to be criticized, especially presidents who are surrounded by people telling them they are beyond reproach.

Let me sum up my philosophy of covering presidents. It's important work, and it never stops. Neither the press nor the president is ever off duty. I want to put questions to presidents directly, not just to their press secretaries and other aides. As to what questions are appropriate and how they should be asked, well, let's put it this way: If you send me to cover a pie-baking contest on Mother's Day, I'm going to ask dear old Mom whether she used artificial sweetener in violation of the rules, and while she's at it, could I see the receipt for the apples to prove she didn't steal them. I maintain that if Mom has nothing to hide, no harm will have been done. But the questions should be asked. Too often, Mom, and presidents—behind those sweet faces—turn out to have stuffed a few rotten apples into the public barrel.

So when I cover the president, I try to remember two things: First, if you don't ask, you don't find out; and second, the questions don't do the damage. Only the answers do.

Chapter Two

EARLY YEARS

Some viewers accuse me of putting on an act for purposes of self-promotion when I push to get the story at the White House. But that's no act. I've always been aggressive, have always gone all out to come in first. My World War II record proves it.

I was seven years old when the United States entered World War II. But you're never too young to defend your country. I managed to do it by blowing up the family truck. One night at dusk, I crept past the hay barn on the farm in southern New Mexico where I lived with my mother. I saw in the gloom a German tank. Of course, it looked like nothing more than our farm truck, but then that could have just been enemy camouflage. I rushed the vehicle, pretended to throw up the hatch, and hurled a grenade inside. Since a truck has no hatch, I had to be content with unscrewing the gas cap and dropping a lighted match down the gas pipe—a minor detail when there's a war to be fought.

The truck gave a *whoosh* and I was thrown back unharmed—that is, until my mother took a switch to me. Oh, injustice! President Reagan, with his love for heroes, probably would have pinned a medal on me, maybe even ordered a full dress South Lawn ceremony.

My mother did her best. And if there's any credit for the way I turned out, it belongs to her because my father, who was born in 1871, died of a heart attack in July 1933, eight months before I arrived. I never knew him, but I have his name, Samuel Andrew Donaldson.

He had been from a poor Tennessee family that moved from the Knoxville area to Texas when he was a boy. First he worked on a cattle ranch as a cowboy. Then he got a job on the Galveston, Houston & San Antonio railroad (the Southern Pacific today), first as a fireman, then an engineer. He saved his money and bought farmland in the Mesilla valley of New Mexico, below Las Cruces and just across the line from Texas. Judging from what everybody said about him when I was growing up, he must have been a very good man.

My brother, Tom, used to tell stories about how he and Dad would go walking in downtown El Paso and my father would say, "See that block where the Mills Building is located? I could have bought that whole block in 1912 for a hundred dollars."

Tom's mouth would begin to water, and he'd ask, "Why didn't you, Dad?"

"Who had a hundred dollars?" my father would reply with a shrug. In 1933, he was negotiating to buy a big ranch in New Mexico, but he died before the deal could go anywhere. Think of the riches that slipped through my fingers. But I can't complain. Thanks to my mother, I learned enough to make it on my own.

My mother was born in 1894. She, too, came from a poor family and was raised on a small farm near Tipton, Missouri. Her name was Chloe Hampson. She was the eldest of seven children and a very pretty girl when she was young. But she probably didn't have much time for fun, since she had to help her mother take care of the other children as they came along. The Hampson family's main social life was centered around the local Baptist church.

After getting a teaching degree, my mother came to Dona Ana County in southern New Mexico to teach school. The schoolhouse was just across the road from my father's dairy and cotton farm. He was forty-seven, she was twenty-four, and before long they were courting. They were married in 1918, and the next year my brother, Tom, was born.

Tom died of cancer in 1969, but my mother is alive, at the age of ninety-two, as I write this. She still lives on the farm alone, by her own choice, and still carries water in a milk pail to the chicken pen every day. Many years ago, Tom put in a water line from the deep well to the chicken pen to save her the work. She wouldn't use it; the work ethic is too strongly embedded in her. Don't laugh. The water line has long since rusted; my mother is still going strong.

Mother sacrificed a lot to give me the best. Every morning she drove me twenty-five miles to school in El Paso, Texas, because she thought the schools there were better than those in the nearest little town, Anthony, New Mexico. And every night she drove us back to the farm. I should explain that I am a native Texan, having been born in the old Masonic hospital in El Paso. But I was taken home to the family farm in New Mexico at age three days. I claim dual citizenship and hold forth as a loyal son of whichever state the people I'm with happen to be from.

The very first school in which my mother enrolled me was, I blush to report, Radford School for Girls in El Paso. It took boys in its kindergarten, and there were several of us four-year-olds there. Sometimes students in the upper classes of the elementary school would come down to the playground to join in the games and I have a picture of myself with one of them, Sandra Day O'Connor, who is now an associate justice of the U.S. Supreme Court. Later, I went to Dudley Grade School in El Paso.

During those years, my mother would read to me from the Bible and many other good books. Then, she encouraged me to read on my own. I remember so many of those classics, from Aesop's fables to *Moby Dick*. She also encouraged me to speak in public. First came my annual reading of Luke 2, the Christmas story, on Christmas Eve at the Anthony Baptist church, then later came lessons from Myrtle Ball, a voice coach in El Paso.

I was fascinated by the radio from the moment we first got one, just after the Japanese attack on Pearl Harbor. We would sit in the kitchen by the coal stove on cold winter nights and listen to the war news. I would sometimes pretend to be delivering it. As I got older, I discovered amateur radio. There was a fellow in Anthony who was a ham operator. W5GVX was his call sign. He used to let me come over every couple of weeks and sit with him as he called up other hams around the world. He had a Morse code key, but from the beginning I liked talking into his condenser microphone.

I got a Hallicrafters S-42 short wave radio receiver for my eleventh birthday. It had a button on its face that said "send/transmit." I would flip it and, holding a cheap microphone, pretend I was carrying on conversations around the world.

Eventually, I took the examination for a ham license. I failed it, and that almost broke my heart. I was twelve. Looking back, I realize I didn't study hard enough for the exam because I wasn't that interested in circuits and Ohm's law. I was interested in talking on the radio.

I enjoyed growing up on a farm. But I was clearly a trial to those around me. One noontime when I was seven, I playfully shot out a front tooth of one of the Mexican workers with my bb gun. No one was amused. When I was twelve, I got a kick out of letting the horses out of their corral so I could chase after them on a farm tractor. Ride 'em, cowboy! I also discovered that one could get "high" on gasoline fumes. Just open the cap on a tractor's gas tank and sniff away.

None of this was reform school-brand conduct, I suppose, but my mother clearly thought she needed some help in instilling discipline in me so she sent me to New Mexico Military Institute (NMMI) in Roswell, New Mexico, at the earliest moment possible. My brother had gone there, and I went when I was fourteen.

New cadets were called rats by the old cadets, who lorded over them. There may have been a worse rat than I was, but I doubt it. I disliked the discipline, I disliked the hard work of shining shoes and brass, of making beds and cleaning rooms. I disliked having to call all the old cadets sir as I responded to their every whim (new cadets had to "brace" stiffly at attention against the wall when they entered the room). And I hated the toothbrush.

The toothbrush. Let me tell you a secret. If anyone ever enters your room and yells, "Grab your ankles, rat, and name your punishment," do not choose the toothbrush. Demand a paddle, plead for a rifle stock, volunteer for a wire coat hanger. But a toothbrush, bent back, then released to spring forward against a bare bottom, can raise the kind of welt that stays for days. There, don't say this book isn't teaching you anything.

At the noon formation each day, just before marching off to the mess hall, the list of infractions was read over the loudspeakers. Last names and initials. "Donohue, W.B., dirty room, two demerits; Donaldson, S.A., late to class, two demerits, two tours . . ." To this day, I can remember my classmates mainly by last names and initials.

I can also remember marching around the quadrangle on Saturday afternoons with my M-1 rifle at right shoulder arms, working off those disciplinary "tours." That's my nine-and-a-half-pound gas-operated, semiautomatic shoulder weapon, sir. Serial number 24-74-84-6, sir. Ronald Reagan is right. You remember things from fifty years ago with absolute clarity; yesterday is up for grabs.

By the time my first year ended, I decided I didn't like being laughed at as the worst cadet in the corps. Something clicked. I went back after the summer vacation and knuckled down. I was the hardest working cadet in the corps. I was sharp and it paid off. My squad, led by cadet Sgt. Jose Ortiz y Pino, was judged best squad in my company. At the end of my second year I was promoted to sergeant, the highest rank that anyone in my class could attain. I discovered how much more enjoyable life was when you are doing well.

My experience at New Mexico Military Institute taught me something I've preached ever since: Never give up. Never decide that you can't succeed or that the book is already in on you. As a matter of fact, the person who comes up from the bottom in a big way is often noticed more favorably than someone who has always been in the safe but unspectacular middle.

My first year at NMMI I fell in love with flying. Instruction in a Piper Cub (stick control, sixty-five horsepower engine) cost seven dollars an hour at Callens' Flying Service at the Roswell municipal airport. I went up every chance I got. Now, seven dollars may not seem like a lot today. But in 1948, it was a fortune. So I kept telling my mother that I needed blankets for my bunk to ward off the arctic air that swept down on the New Mexico plains. She'd send me the money and I'd buy some more flying lessons.

Of course, I couldn't go up alone. You could solo at age sixteen with your parents' permission, but when I turned sixteen, my mother wouldn't grant it. So I didn't solo until I was twenty-one.

Once I did get my private pilot's license, flying alone was both an adventure and an escape. The adventure was to fly in any weather, land on any surface (ditch bank levees, sandy desert roads, alfalfa fields newly mown), the escape was to fly over mountains and desert listening to the quiet engine hum and thinking all alone of doing great and heroic things someday.

I went to college in the fall of 1951 at a small school in El Paso called Texas Western and majored in telecommunications. It would be nice if I could say that I had already come to an understanding of the importance of the news business in ensuring an enlightened citizenry and I had come to an appreciation of the First Amendment. It would be nice, but it wouldn't be true.

It would also be nice if I could say that I studied hard and made excellent grades. That, too, wouldn't be true. I pledged a fraternity, Kappa Sigma, whose illustrious ranks included Edward R. Murrow, and set about having fun. I wasn't much different in that respect from many of my contemporaries. Anyone could get in to college in those days, and it didn't cost much. But I did work very hard when it came to broadcasting.

Early in the fall of my freshman year, I went to work for KELP, a small 250-watt radio station in El Paso, as a teenage disc jockey. The studio-transmitter was located in a field belonging to the El Paso stockyards. Many of those who heard me thought the location fitting, I'm sure. I wanted to work as many hours as I could, but I didn't think of it as work; I was having a great time. I got a kick out of being on the radio. And in those days, if you couldn't be a football hero, the next best thing you could do to attract girls was be a radio disc jockey. I was even earning a little money. I had pumped gas over the summer for the minimum wage of seventy-five cents an hour, but at KELP I was making the magnificent sum of a dollar twenty-five an hour. Soon, I switched to a bigger station, KEPO, which had a real studio, separate from its transmitter building.

At KEPO I had my own hour-long disc jockey show, called Sam's Show, the theme music (you guessed it), Sam's Song as sung by Bing and Gary Crosby. During the summers, I would often open up the place at six A.M. as the morning man and sometimes also close it up in the evening as the night announcer. Long hours, but I got to do it all, playing records, reading the news wires, interviewing the famous people who came to town, such as newscaster Paul Harvey and country singer Eddie Arnold.

By my last year in college, television had come to El Paso and I got a job at KROD-TV as an announcer. I didn't like it as well. I didn't get to do as much, and I sensed the lack of that magic link with the audience radio provides. Ask anyone who has worked in both, and they'll tell you the real freedom and romance in broadcasting is to be found in radio.

When I turned twenty-one, I came into a few thousand dollars' inheritance provided in my father's will. On my birthday, my brother came to the campus to see me.

"I've got the inside track on a silver mine in the Superstition Mountains of Arizona," said Tom, "and if you'll put up five thousand dollars, I'll double it for you in ninety days." Ninety days; why would it take so long? I thought. But something told me not to put in the entire five, so I only gave him thirty-five hundred dollars. I never saw the money again.

Tom was always trying to get rich quickly. He was a friendly guy whom everybody liked. Not a mean bone in his body. But, brother, it was a mistake to lend him money. I watched him try to build roads in northern New Mexico, run the Lone Star Beer distributorship in El Paso, clear farm land in Dell City, and make countless deals on crops of onions and lettuce that never came in. If he had only stuck to farming, slow and steady, he might have eventually made his million dollars.

I loved Tom and I'm very sorry he's gone. But the lesson I learned from watching him fail in his business ventures is that it's better to work hard at one thing even though there are a lot of early lean years rather than flit from deal to deal in an effort to make it quick. Coming up slowly also gives you the experience you can't get quickly. In the news business, when a story breaks, there isn't time to call up the research department and read a lot of background. You'd better have it in your head, or you won't be able to compete.

After getting my B.A., I went to the University of Southern

California for a year of postgraduate work. This time I worked hard but didn't stick to it. Instead, I started a magazine in Hollywood called *Television Film* with five thousand dollars and a friend named Al Preiss. We went first-class, letter press printing instead of offset, four-color ads instead of black and white. It soon became evident that we needed fifty thousand dollars, not five. I sold my car to raise cash and took a job for a couple of weeks typing invoices at the Catalina Swim Suit factory, but it wasn't enough. Finally, I sold out to Al and went back to spend the summer in El Paso before going into the army, as I was obligated to do. Al is still publishing the magazine under the name *Television International Magazine*.

That fall of 1956, I had my first brush with a political VIP. Along with a fraternity brother, Gale Grose, I had organized the Young Republicans club of El Paso. My forefathers fought for the Union in the Civil War; since then, all Donaldsons and Hampsons had been Republicans.

Moreover, I was brought up in the Southwest and learned as a young man the same things that Ronald Reagan learned in California. Like Reagan, I was taught that if a man was able-bodied and out of work, he was obviously a bum. After all, you could always get a job on a farm in our valley, chopping weeds or picking cotton, and if you were hard-working, you might even earn five or six dollars a day. What more could anyone ask for?

I still believe in hard work and the free enterprise system. But I've now learned that a lot of able-bodied men and women can't get a job because they don't speak the language or have any training and sometimes because of racial discrimination. But in those days it was natural for me to help organize the campaign stop in El Paso of Vice President Richard M. Nixon.

I persuaded the A. B. Poe motor company to loan us some Chrysler automobiles for the motorcade. Nixon campaign advance men said the Republican ticket didn't want to ride in Cadillacs. Voters, they explained, might think the ticket represented the wealthy corporations. I also helped make the banners and signs. The same advance men explained that the signs should be hand-lettered in order to make it appear they were the spontaneous handiwork of ordinary voters.

Grose and I and a few others worked all night spontaneously lettering signs in support of Ike and Dick. Nixon's appearance was actually a bit of an anticlimax. He came and went and I can't remember a thing he said. But I got to shake his hand. The next time I shook his hand, sixteen years later, I had a microphone in my other hand; but that's a story I'll tell later on.

The day after Nixon left town in 1956, I reported for active duty in the army at Ft. Bliss in El Paso as an ROTC commissioned second lieutenant of air defense artillery.

The normal tour of duty for ROTC officers was two years, but the Pentagon was trying to save money and several of us were called up for only six months. I was outraged. Six months suggested to me that I wasn't really needed, so when my time was up, I extended my active duty service for two more years. For half my time in the army, I was a training officer; first in basic training for new recruits, then in a battery that trained units in the deployment and operation of Nike anti-aircraft missiles.

In those days, major American cities and military installations were ringed with Nikes to protect against Soviet air attack. It is ludicrous now to think that in the 1950s, when this country had such massive nuclear superiority over the Soviets and they had such a modest long-range bomber force, we could seriously believe they might suddenly attack American cities. But we did. I have ever since been skeptical of arguments for new weapons systems that have no clearcut rational mission. But in the late fifties, while in the army, I was mainly doing what I was told.

A few days after the Soviets put up Sputnik I (the first satellite to orbit the globe) in October 1957, the new secretary of defense, Neil McElroy, who had been the president of Procter and Gamble, came for an inspection tour of Ft. Bliss, escorted by the then Army Chief of Staff Maxwell Taylor. Taylor was the general who as chairman of the Joint Chiefs in later years helped talk Presidents Kennedy and Johnson deeper into Vietnam. But on this day, I did the talking. I was the briefing officer.

Using a sand table and pointer, I explained to McElroy and his entourage how the Nike system worked. Then I invited the secretary to look toward the launching area a distance away, where four Nike Ajax missiles pointed skyward, ready for launching. I had done my part, but somebody else hadn't done his. Two missiles never got off the pad. A third broke up some ninety thousand feet overhead at the 7-G dive point, and the fourth struggled down range for a few miles, only to fail-safe short of the target. The battery commander received a reprimand. I went on to my reward: a transfer to the post information office, where I spent the last half of my army tour. While there, I did my first network radio report. I offered a thirty-second telephone description of a ceremony transferring a Nike battery to Italy to NBC News and they ran it on an hourly newscast anchored from the Pentagon by Peter Hackes. I waited for a phone call from NBC telling me I had a job waiting, but it didn't come.

If the Nike system taught me something about costly weapons, another experience in the army shaped my thinking about nuclear war. In the summer of 1957, my friend Lt. Dick Fene and I wangled temporary duty orders to Camp Desert Rock, Nevada, to observe an atomic test code-named Kepler. It was a thrilling and terrifying experience.

We crouched in a deep slit trench six thousand yards from a tower on which an atomic device was set. It contained half the destructive power of the bomb that destroyed Hiroshima. Ten seconds short of H-hour, we were told to lower our heads to our chests and cover our eyes with our hands.

H-hour. Suddenly there was a blinding light even though our eyes were closed and covered. In an instant the ground shook violently, then an ear-splitting crash came with the sound wave. Desert sand and debris rained down on us. We continued to huddle in the bottom of the trench. Finally, the reverse wave crashed around us as air rushed back into the vacuum the bomb's explosion had created. Then, we were told to get out of the trench and look around.

The tower was gone. The rapidly rising mushroom cloud was just losing its glow. In a few minutes, white ash debris began to fall on us. We were rushed off in trucks to a huge water tanker parked some distance away and hosed off. Later, the army informed me the device I was wearing to detect radiation showed I had not gotten a dangerous dose, even though those tests that summer were the dirty ones.

So, what did I learn? I learned that those people who argue that nuclear war is acceptable have never seen the force of those weapons firsthand. The atomic bomb is not just another weapon. Ronald Reagan says a nuclear war can never be won and must never be fought. I hope he means it. I know some of those around him seem to think otherwise. They wouldn't if they had been with Dick and me in that slit trench in Nevada.

My army service ended with an honorable discharge in April 1959. I emerged with a good deal of self-confidence. I was ready to start on the long path to the White House press room. So, of course, I decided to do something else. I decided to get rich.

You can't have been born on America's frontier—among the cattlemen, the oil men, the copper barons, the bankers—without feeling the lure of riches. The Southwest was a place to make a fortune. I went down to Dallas and tried to learn the stock brokerage business.

My sister-in-law's brother, David Munson, who was an investment banker in Dallas, put me to work selling mutual funds. I hated it. Now, I'm not afraid to argue ideas with someone. I can push people to do their job at work. And I am certainly not shy in selling myself. In fact, Marty Schram, who reports for the *Washington Post*, once said if there were no television, Donaldson would go door to door. But believe me, Marty, it wouldn't be to sell mutual funds.

Trying to make sales calls in those days was terribly depressing. Often, David would come by looking for me in the morning and I'm sure he knew when he got no response to the doorbell that I was cowering inside. I suppose he thought me lazy. Not true. I just couldn't sell mutual funds, and for weeks couldn't work up the courage to tell him so. In the meantime, I played bridge with my friend Al Woods.

Al was an expert and I was merely okay. But we did battle at the Texas Bridge Club with Jim Jacoby and occasionally his celebrated father, Oswald, with Dr. John Fisher and other stars of the contract and rubber bridge world. Aside from Al, my favorite bridge partner was his mother, Effie Woods.

Effie had taught Al, and together they taught me. Effie lived in El Paso, and when I would go back there for a visit, I would often stay at her house. We would stay up and play bridge or gin rummy all night long, both of us chain smoking and sipping vodka. She's dead now, but I will always treasure her memory.

I was clearly getting nowhere in the mutual funds business and hating myself for it when one day, reading the want ads, I spotted an advertisement for a writer to work for HLH Products.

H. L. Hunt was the legendary wildcatter who, with a fifth-grade education and a lot of guts, had struck it rich in the Permian basin of West Texas. I saw big money. I applied and discovered that, yes indeed, Hunt wanted to write down his political philosophy. I made the rounds of his department heads and impressed them. Finally, Hunt's secretary called to say the boss himself would see me on Friday, and she added, "I don't mind telling you, you are the leading candidate."

I was ushered into Hunt's office in the Mercantile National Bank building. There he was, an undistinguished looking man of seventy, dressed in a nondescript suit that looked like it could have come from Robert Hall, sitting behind an ordinary office desk. After a few routine questions, he asked sharply, "How cheap will you work?"

My answer, I thought, was brilliant. "I'm not married," I replied, "and I have a small farm income. I want very much to work for you, so I'll work for whatever you think the job is worth to start." Within moments, Hunt dismissed me.

The next Monday, his secretary called to tell me I would not get the job. "When Mr. Hunt asked you how cheap will you work, he expected you to name your price," she explained. "Mr. Hunt believes that if a man doesn't know his own worth, he isn't worth anything." I've never forgotten that. In negotiations since, I've sometimes settled for less than I thought I was worth, but it hasn't been because I didn't name my price.

So there you are. How did I get where I am today? By saying the wrong thing to H. L. Hunt among other reasons. Of course if I had said the right thing, this book might be titled *My First Billion*.

I saw H. L. Hunt one more time. I was in a crowd of onlookers in the lobby of the Waldorf-Astoria Hotel in New York City one night in September 1960, watching Soviet premier Nikita Khrushchev and foreign minister Andrei Gromyko walk through the door and up some steps to a reception. People in the crowd were booing Khrushchev, that "godless commie." Suddenly I realized the undistinguished looking man standing next to me in a cheap seersucker suit was H. L. Hunt.

"Ugly devil, isn't he, Mr. Hunt," I said in a whisper. Hunt just nodded. By that time, someone else had written his book for him. It was titled *Alpaca* and advocated such things as extra votes for the wealthy and as lopsided a view of how the state should protect property rights over human rights as any poor boy made good could hope to see.

One week after I failed to get the ghostwriter's job with Hunt, I threw in the towel on getting rich and went back to what I knew best. I applied for work at KRLD-TV, the CBS affiliate in Dallas, and was hired. I've been in this business ever since.

At KRLD-TV, I performed general television announcing chores and read the news at noon. I was glad to be back at work, but after a year, decided I had learned as much as I was going to learn there. I thought I was hot stuff. So in September 1960, I resigned, got in my car, and drove to New York City. I was twenty-six years old and had never been east of the Mississippi River in my life; but I thought I was ready for the big time. I soon found out the big time wasn't ready for me.

When I got to New York, I subscribed to an answering service, rented a one-room apartment in Queens, bought a fold-up cot, a card table, and two chairs, printed up some résumés, and started making the rounds: CBS, NBC, ABC, Mutual, and, eventually, almost all the television and radio stations in New York City.

Much to my chagrin, no one was the slightest bit interested in me. The man I saw at NBC News looked over my résumé and quickly said, "I'm sorry, we don't consider anyone who hasn't had three years' print experience; we prefer five." I said I'd be glad to write something on the spot to prove I could do it notwithstanding my lack of print background, but he wasn't interested.

In those days, news broadcasters had an enormous inferiority complex. If print—what we call newspapers and magazines—did something, we automatically considered it right. And when print reporters criticized us, we were often too eager for their acceptance to argue with them.

That's changed now. Print experience provides an excellent background for broadcast reporters. But it's not essential. Today, bright young people are coming into broadcast news rooms directly from college, learning it all there. And no one is embarrassed about it anymore.

But that was 1960. The immediate issue for me was survival. I wasn't working. My money was almost gone. In desperation, I turned for help to the one person I knew in New York, Sherry Varon. I had met Sherry on a flight from Dallas to El Paso once and was thrilled to discover that she was Alfred Levy's secretary. Levy was David Susskind's partner in Talent Associates, Ltd., the production firm that at that time was doing many hot television shows. Sherry lined up two days of work for me as an extra in a Family Classics drama produced by her firm. I wore a seventeenth-century period costume and pretended to be one of the players around a gaming table. I made a hundred sixty dollars, less taxes; it was the most welcome paycheck I've ever received.

I made another daily scale of ninety-five dollars on one other occasion. I was hired to make a pilot television commercial for German Chocolates. I looked into a camera as a female model's hand thrust a bar of German Chocolate under my nose. I looked down and said, "Um, good." We did it scores of times. Thrust bar, say, "Um, good," until we got it right. Unfortunately, the client must have thought it looked "um, bad" since the commercial never went on the air. My fault, I'm sure; the model's hand was beautiful.

I had nearly reached the end of my rope when WTOP-TV, the CBS affiliate in Washington, owned by the Washington Post Company, called to ask if I wanted to audition for the job of summer relief announcer (I had applied there some time before). Boy, did I! I got the job and moved to Washington, where I rented a room from Jose Cruz Salvador and family on Macomb Street for thirty-five dollars a month.

At work, I "announced" as hard as I could, making station breaks, reading commercials and, because the CBS network news bureau was located in the WTOP-TV building in those days, signing off the network radio newscasts that were delivered by the likes of Paul Niven, Bill Downs, George Herman, and Lou Cioffi.

One day, the management came to me and said, "Congratulations, you are going to be the All Night Texaco Satellite."

"What's that?" I stammered, wondering whether I was about to learn what it feels like to hit the Nike Ajax 7-G dive point.

It turned out that I was being given the privilege of driving out to the WTOP radio transmitter in the Washington suburbs six nights a week to play records all night on behalf of the Texaco gas stations in the Washington area. During the day, I got to drive around to the Texaco stations and slap the owners on the back. On occasion, I also got a little sleep—but not much.

But I did more than play records. I read the news, which I ripped from the wire machines. And I began to comment on it; a comment here about Khrushchev's breaking of the voluntary nuclear test ban moratorium, some words there about the civil rights-related violence in the South.

By the end of the summer, the WTOP management offered me a job in the news department. I took the spot that opened up when Roger Mudd left the station in August 1961 to join CBS. Ed Ryan was the news director, the late Jack Jurey, the editorial director. Ryan was a World War II veteran who had come back to his job as a reporter on the *Washington Post* severely wounded. The *Post* sent him out to organize the WTOP newsroom. Jurey was an ex-newspaperman from the steel mills of Ohio who didn't have the background of the icons of the news business but made up for it with plenty of guts. He did the on-air editorials for WTOP-TV and once opined in an editorial: "What Mr. Lippmann fails to understand . . ." Believe me, in 1961, any local reporter in Washington who took on the legendary Walter Lippmann had to have guts.

I was very lucky to work for WTOP, which led the way in Washington in expanding local newscasts from the traditional fifteen minutes of news, weather, and sports to an hour or more. Not only did I get in on the ground floor of expansion of local television news, I did it in the nation's capital. One day I would cover the Montgomery County Court House in Rockville, Maryland; the next I would cover the United States Senate. One day I would chase a fire in northeast Washington, the next day I would chase President Kennedy as he gave the Veterans Day address at Arlington Cemetery.

It was all great training and great fun. And when I wasn't working in those early days in Washington, I was back at the bridge table, playing rubber bridge at the Dupont Bridge Club or tournament bridge someplace in town with my favorite Washington partner, Agnes Fischer.

Aggie, who has since gone on to her reward, was then sixty-eight years old, a little old woman who smoked and drank and loved to play bridge. Along with Stella Kaplan and Sam Lucks, we would often play all night long. Sometimes we would go over to her daughter's house and baby-sit and play bridge there.

I'm not sure Aggie's son-in-law approved of us. I can see him now, coming home and nodding from the hall a little stiffly as we sang out, "Four spades," "Double," "Redouble." I might have taken the initiative to get to know him better, but I have to confess, as a junior reporter at WTOP-TV, I was a little in awe of Aggie's son-in-law, David Brinkley, already one of the biggest names in television news. But the good times at the bridge table finally broke up. Wedding bells broke up that old gang of mine, and those bells, they tolled for me.

On November 17, 1962, I went out to cover President John F. Kennedy dedicating Dulles Airport. One of the pretty girls representing the U.S. Immigration and Naturalization Service at the ceremony was Billy Kay Butler. She has a photograph taken that day of John F. Kennedy leering at her cleavage. But Kennedy had to go home. I didn't. And a year later, Billy Kay and I were married.

Things were going well for me at WTOP. I reported from the field, I anchored from the studio, I even wrote and delivered commentary nightly for a year. The commentary spot was called "The Second Look." My commentaries were not very tough. Believe it or not, in those days I was so careful not to offend anyone that I wound up never really saying anything. But bland as my commentaries were, one of them did offend someone: Vice President Lyndon Johnson, who promptly went after my scalp.

One night in late 1962, I reviewed the fact that Austin, Texas, capital of the Lone Star State, had only one television station, KTBC-TV. Lots of people had applied to the FCC for permission to construct additional stations, but for some reason the FCC wouldn't grant anyone permission. Why? KTBC-TV was owned by Lyndon Johnson's wife, and a lot of people thought they could figure out why the FCC wouldn't act. Moreover, when cable companies competed for permission to wire the city, LBJ turned out to have a fifty-one percent interest in the winning company. All I did was outline the facts of the situation, not a word of condemnation did I deliver. But LBJ was so thin-skinned that he called up my boss and complained anyway.

"Johnson wanted me to fire you," John S. Hayes, the president of Post-Newsweek stations, told me later, "but I assured him you meant no harm and wouldn't do it again."

Actually, it was because of my boss's relationship with Lyndon Johnson that I got to cover Senator Barry Goldwater's presidential campaign of 1964, even though I worked for a local station.

Hayes was one of Johnson's unofficial television advisers in the 1960 campaign, and when Johnson became president, Hayes wanted very much to be an insider and perhaps secure an ambassadorship. So he assigned Tony Sylvester, our 11 P.M. anchorman, to cover Johnson's 1964 campaign and, out of fairness, had to assign someone to cover Goldwater, the Republican candidate. I was the one.

I followed Goldwater around, but had no camera crew. So I would phone in my reports and they would go on the air over a still picture of me, or if CBS had aired a report by Robert Pierpoint, their man covering Goldwater, we would rerun their pictures with my telephone narration. It was great fun, and an easy way to learn how to cover a national campaign without having your mistakes matter much. And I learned a valuable lesson about reporting.

Goldwater was giving a speech one day, saying things that seemed to be poorly thought out, at least poorly explained, when a man came hurrying up to the press area, visibly agitated. He was clearly a Goldwater supporter and he was worried about what reporters were writing down. "Listen here," he told us. "Write what he means, not what he says."

At first I thought that was the silliest thing I'd ever heard. Our job was to report what people said. But the more I thought about it, the more I realized we should do both. It's certainly always more important to understand what politicians mean.

In the end, Goldwater lost, John S. Hayes went on to become ambassador to Switzerland, and I went back to covering the Montgomery County Court House, the U.S. Senate, and my other haunts.

One of the most interesting public figures of those days was Everett McKinley Dirksen, the Senate Republican leader. He was colorful and fun to listen to and he taught me something about successful politicians. He had a reputation as a dyed-in-the-wool conservative, yet he ended up lending crucial support to most of the progressive legislation of the sixties.

Dirksen would stake out an early position of opposition to, say, the Test Ban Treaty of 1963 or the Civil Rights Act of 1964, then one day emerge from his office to announce that he had struck a compromise with the bill's proponents that would enable him to support it. Watching Dirksen operate, I decided the people who get the most done are those who know when to compromise and get something of what they want rather than those who are forever demanding it all be done their way. Ronald Reagan is like Dirksen. He will put up a fierce front, but if it's clear he can't win it all, he'll gladly take half a loaf. Then, of course, he'll be back tomorrow for a quarter of what's left and gobble up the rest, if he can, the day after.

For all the good times, I did have a few sinking spells at WTOP-TV. The most serious one came over my union activity. Along with Julian Barber, our top anchorman, I helped organize the news department into the American Federation of Television and Radio Artists (AFTRA). It wasn't that WTOP-TV was a bad place to work. It was just that WTOP-TV didn't want to pay much money to reporters.

There has always been this notion that says you can't be a serious news reporter unless you are willing to starve to death. I think it must be managements everywhere that try to perpetuate the idea that low wages are a sign of professionalism. What rot. Some salaries today are high, but in those days we were agitating for a hundred fifty dollars a week.

So we organized the WTOP-TV news room for AFTRA. The management was not pleased, and suddenly I lost my commentary slot and went back to the second team. But I kept on with my union activity, even winning election as president of the Washington/Baltimore local for two terms, 1967–68. I owed my election not to any personal popularity but to the fact I had the confidence of our local's executive secretary, Evelyn Freyman.

Freyman really ran the local. We were lucky to have her. "Dawling," she would say to management's negotiator across the table in her best Tallulah Bankhead style. "You are a rotten, miserable human being. What you are asking these people of yours to do is *immoral.*" More often than not, management swallowed hard and came across with a hefty raise in the contract.

My union activity didn't keep me behind the eight ball for very long, however. I soon began getting good assignments again, including anchoring duties. Much of the time I was at WTOP-TV, I anchored weekend newscasts, but finally, in September 1967, I was given the plum assignment of anchoring our 6 P.M. weekday newscast. It was the payoff for all the hard work. I was set for life. So naturally, a few weeks later I quit and took another job.

Chapter Three

ABC NEWS

I was hired by ABC News in October 1967. It was an act of faith on both our parts.

Whereas NBC and CBS had been around since before World War II, ABC News really came to life in 1961, when James Hagerty, just out of the White House, where he had been Dwight Eisenhower's press secretary, was hired to set up a full-scale news department. In the fifties, John Charles Daly (when he was not moderating *What's My Line*), John Cameron Swayze (when he was not selling Timex watches), and a few other people put some news on the air at ABC, but it wasn't much.

Hagerty hired reporters. He mainly knew print journalists; he had been one himself in his earlier days. The late William Lawrence, the *New York Times* White House correspondent, got so fed up when the paper didn't send him on President Kennedy's first foreign trip that he told press secretary Pierre Salinger that if he had another job to go to, he'd quit. Salinger called Hagerty with the tip, and Hagerty hired Lawrence. He also hired John Scali from the Associated Press, Bob Clark from the *Washington Star*, and others. Scali, who acted as an unofficial go-between when

Moscow and Washington faced nuclear war in the Cuban missile crisis in 1962, is perhaps the television correspondent who has had the most high-level sources in Washington (he served a stint as U.S. ambassador to the United Nations in the Nixon/Ford administrations). Clark was the most knowledgeable Capitol Hill reporter for any network when he covered the Hill for ABC. Roger Mudd had a well-deserved reputation, but Bob Clark dug the deepest.

Hagerty knew the news business, but he didn't know the television news business, so two years after he was hired, Hagerty got kicked upstairs and Elmer Lower, who had been a top news executive at NBC, was brought on board to be the president of the news department. Lower had about one tenth the budget of CBS's and NBC's news departments. He also was stuck with a fifteen-minute dinner-hour news show—while the others were going to a thirty-minute broadcast—that more than one third of the ABC affiliates were routinely refusing to carry. Well into the late 1960s, our evening news program wasn't carried anywhere in the entire state of Ohio, for instance. In short, Lower found that he was presiding over an outfit that was, indeed, a pound light, a day late, and a dollar short.

In those days ABC News had one indisputable heavyweight broadcast veteran, Howard K. Smith, and he was considered damaged goods. Smith had left CBS in a bitter dispute over the issue of what constituted fair comment by news correspondents. He had narrated for *CBS Reports* a documentary titled "Who Speaks for Birmingham?" that showed how Public Safety Commissioner Eugene "Bull" Connor, his dogs, cattle prods, and water hoses were trying to hold back the tide of racial equality. Smith wanted to end the show with a quotation attributed to Edmund Burke: "The only thing necessary for the triumph of evil is for good men to do nothing." The CBS management insisted that was improper commentary and said he couldn't do it. Write something else, they said. Smith refused and simply signed off by saying, "Good night." Shortly thereafter, he quit CBS.

When he came to ABC, Smith was given his own show, and he did good, controversial broadcasts, including one titled, prematurely, *The Political Obituary of Richard M. Nixon.* Nixon had lost the gubernatorial race in California in 1962 and had held his famous last press conference ("You won't have Nixon to kick around anymore"). Smith had been planning to do a show on the American soldier that week, but he switched topics at the last moment to discuss the demise of Nixon's political career. To make matters worse, one of those he put on to discuss it was Alger Hiss, the State Department official who had been convicted of perjury after Nixon went after him in congressional hearings.

ABC was deluged with complaints from American Legionnaires who had been expecting the show originally scheduled. The John Birch Society organized a mass letter-writing campaign. Protestors thought what that liberal Smith and convicted felon Hiss had said about that patriot Nixon was just awful. The Kemper Insurance Company, which had nothing to do with Smith's broadcast but sponsored the *ABC Evening News*, tried to cancel its advertising contract out of patriotic fervor. Before long, Smith was rushed into the doghouse of television oblivion (temporarily, because he later bounced back to become one of ABC's main news anchors).

So when Lower took over, ABC's star heavyweight was on the bench. Lower started hiring nobodies. He hired Frank Reynolds, Peter Jennings, Ted Koppel, Steve Bell, Tom Jarriel and Sam Donaldson, among others. I shall always be grateful to Lower for giving me my network break.

It was really John Lynch, then ABC's Washington bureau chief, who brought me to Lower's attention. ABC was looking for reporters who could also act as their own producer (when you're operating on a tight budget, you look for such ways to cut corners), and having seen me on WTOP-TV, Lynch thought I filled the bill.

I had dreamed about getting a recruitment call from CBS or NBC. I would have jumped at the chance to work for either of them. But when Lynch called, I hesitated. At thirty-three, I had begun to give up my dreams of glory and settle in at WTOP-TV. It was a good place to work. We were number one. The *Washington Post*, which owned the station, was a good company to be with. Its profit-sharing plan was generous. I had just been given a weeknight anchor job after years of weekend work. And ABC simply wasn't very impressive.

I hesitated for two weeks. Then Lynch called me one night and said, "I can't wait, I've got to have an answer." There it was, no more time to procrastinate; I said yes without another moment's thought. The rest of that sentence usually reads, "And I've never had a moment's regret." But that's not true. For the first three months, I wasn't sure I'd made the right decision.

I went to work on a Monday, and after being shown around and meeting the few people who worked in the small and cramped offices on Connecticut Avenue, the assignment manager told me I could go home and he'd call me when he had an assignment for me.

I was incredulous. Here I had come to work in the big time and was being told I could stay home every day except on those occasions when I was needed for a specific assignment. I refused to do it. I came in every day and read the wires and newspapers and called around to places whether I had an assignment or not.

Now, before I get carried away being too hard on the old ABC, I must tell you that all the news departments in those days left a lot to be desired when it came to aggressive, enterprising reporting; that is, going out and getting stories and digging up information instead of simply covering news conferences and other pre-planned events.

For instance, on the morning after the 1968 New Hampshire primary, Senator Robert Kennedy got on an airplane in New York and flew to Washington. It was not hard to find out Kennedy's schedule. Senator Eugene McCarthy had racked up an impressive number of votes against a president of his own party the day before, and it was suddenly clear that the Vietnam War might bring down Lyndon Johnson. It was also clear under these changed circumstances that Kennedy might reconsider his decision not to run against Johnson.

The same assignment manager who had told me to stay home sent me to National Airport with a film crew to meet Kennedy's plane, I'll give him credit for that. How many other film crews would you guess were there? None. How many other reporters, with or without crews? None.

Today, ordinary travelers wouldn't be able to get in the door at

National Airport, there would be such a crush of reporters and photographers blocking the passageways waiting for that airplane to land.

Kennedy got off the plane, told me he was reconsidering his decision not to run, and ABC had a big scoop. Except we managed to keep the news to ourselves—we didn't bother to tell our viewers. We didn't break into network programming, we didn't phone the wires to tell them what we had. We put the story on radio. Nothing more until our evening news broadcast, by which time Kennedy had talked to everyone else.

I was astounded. I was learning that a lot of people at ABC simply didn't have an instinctive competitive urge.

The real low point came early in 1968, when ABC announced it was not going to carry that summer's political conventions gavel to gavel. We put out a press release explaining that we would broadcast a nightly ninety-minute wrap-up, including packaged reports of the day's activities and some live programming of the main evening events. I was in despair. I went home and told my wife I had ruined our lives by going to ABC. I cursed the name of Elmer Lower—until I discovered what had happened.

Lower had literally saved the news department's ability to compete on a daily basis by taking that action. He had received an ultimatum from Leonard Goldenson, chairman of the board and the man who had built ABC. After a planned merger with International Telephone and Telegraph Company fell through, Lower was given a week to cut the news department's budget by a whopping twenty-five percent. In order to have enough money to keep the evening news broadcast on the air to compete against Walter Cronkite and Huntley-Brinkley, Lower cut back on convention coverage.

Goldenson likes to say that he has always believed that ABC could not be number one as a network unless it had a first-class news department. But as a businessman looking at the bottom line in 1968, survival was his first consideration, not funding a first-class news department.

I didn't stay in despair for very long, however. It dawned on me that since we were so small, and so poor, it meant that I had a greater chance to advance. I took all the late and dirty assignments no one wanted. Had the Silver Bridge over the Ohio River collapsed during rush hour, hurling almost fifty people to their death? Yes indeed, and I would go gladly. Cancel the dinner party, dear, you'll hear from me later. Would I want to anchor the two late-night fifteen-minute weekend news broadcasts from New York, requiring me to work seven days a week? Absolutely. Put my picture on the mantel, dear, and remind the children to look at it once in a while.

From August 1969 to August 1970, I anchored the ABC weekend network news reports on Saturday and Sunday nights at 11 o'clock from New York. That meant that I worked Monday through Friday in Washington, flew to New York at noon on Saturday, spent Saturday and Sunday nights in a hotel there, then flew back to Washington on Monday morning to go to work. Except for the four or five national holidays, I don't recall having a day off during that entire year.

Things eased slightly after August 1970. For the next three years, I only anchored the Saturday night news from New York. That meant I could take Sunday afternoon off at home.

Almost every reporter who has gone on to greater responsibilities and recognition in this business can tell you similar stories about long periods of intense, sometimes grubby work. It pays off, though.

I began getting good assignments that would probably not come the way of a newcomer to the news department today. Also, because we had so few good producers, I was given great latitude in shooting and airing my own reports.

One day during the 1968 Republican National Convention in Miami Beach, I supervised the filming of the Idaho delegation as it caucused to thrash out its position on something or other. I expected to turn over the raw material to a producer for evaluation, but when I got back, the senior producer for our ninety-minute special, David Jayne, told me to whip up a piece on my own. Minutes before air time, Jayne came running into the edit room, where I was working with a film editor, and asked how long the piece was. I told him I didn't know yet. "That's all right," he said. "When you finish, just rack it up and we'll put it on." I must have done it right. The piece on the Idaho caucus drew one of the few mentions of critical praise for our coverage that we got during that convention. But what a gamble Jayne took.

That method of doing business would not happen at ABC now, as it didn't happen at CBS and NBC then. No neophyte correspondent would be entrusted with three or four minutes of air time on a critically important broadcast sight unseen. There would be field producers, senior producers, executive producers and, perhaps, department vice-presidents involved in making judgments every step of the way. I agree, that is generally a better way to do it. But we didn't have the resources then. And I'm very fortunate that we didn't. Thanks to the situation, and people who trusted me—like David Jayne, who died in a chartered plane crash in 1977 while on assignment for ABC—I was able to move forward rapidly.

Why, I was in such demand after we put on that Idaho caucus piece that when one of the assignment editors at the convention suggested I go up to the Deauville Hotel to cover the governor of California, Ronald Reagan, who was making noises about challenging Nixon for the nomination, the management decided I was too important to be spared for such a fool's errand.

If the Republican convention of 1968 gave me the opportunity to show what I could do on my own, the Democratic convention that year gave me the opportunity to participate in the great Chicago riot. The Walker Commission, convened to investigate the disturbances, called it a "police riot." I agree. I spent a good deal of my time in Grant Park or out on Michigan Avenue getting teargassed by the police and trying to dodge their night sticks.

I'm not going to excuse the antiwar demonstrators who hurled bottles and human excrement at police. But the police excesses in combating the demonstrators were inexcusable, also. The late Jim Burnes, one of our best correspondents in that period, turned in a blistering report one night of demonstrators being clubbed to the ground. It was all right there, on film. It provoked such passionate debate from our duo of hired commentators, Gore Vidal and William Buckley, that right on the air Vidal called Buckley a "crypto-Nazi" and Buckley replied, "Listen, you queer, stop calling me a crypto-Nazi or I'll sock you in your goddamn face . . ." There was more, but you get the general idea.

In 1971, I volunteered to go to Vietnam. Having run out of people who were logical candidates to send, ABC news management let it be known it would begin three-month tours for any correspondent who wanted to go. Don Farmer was the first to volunteer; I was the second. Three months is not a long time. In no way could it be compared to the years that many of my colleagues spent covering the war. But it was enough for a taste. And the taste was different from what I expected.

By 1966 or '67, I was already convinced we were fighting the wrong war. By 1971, the Nixon policy was withdrawal. Still, what I thought about policy didn't matter once I was there. I reported what I actually observed: American doctors at the 91st evacuation hospital at Chu Lai trying to save the life of a North Vietnamese lieutenant; South Vietnamese helicopter teams bravely flying into enemy fire to resupply firebases on "Rocket Ridge" near Tan Canh. And when napalm is dropped on a nearby tree line from which rockets are being fired at you, you cheer. Arguments over policy seem far away.

Working with our ABC camera teams in Vietnam, all of whose members were Orientals at this stage of the war, was quite an experience—particularly for them, since they were working with a ninety-day wonder from Washington who didn't know the territory. Once in Cambodia, a reporter for a rival network claimed I had jeopardized the lives of my crew, not to mention my own, by persisting in going down a road alone for several kilometers near Phnom Penh looking for a firefight reportedly under way nearby. I angrily pointed out that I had told Terry Koo, my cameraman, I realized I didn't have much experience and would rely on his judgment as to when it might be unsafe to continue. The problem with doing that, my accuser pointed out just as angrily, was that Koo would never want to lose face by appearing to be too cautious and might therefore feel he had to press on since I had left the decision up to him.

Koo was a brave man. Steve Bell, ABC's longtime *Good Morning America* news anchorman, credits Koo with saving his life when their car was stopped on another Cambodian road by Viet Cong soldiers one day. The Viet Cong offered to let Koo go, but said they would keep Bell. Koo refused on the grounds that Bell was his leader, and miraculously, they were all allowed to drive on. Finally, though, things caught up with Terry Koo. He walked off a road above Hue in 1972, trying to get better pictures of a combat area, and a North Vietnamese unit ambushed him and shot him dead.

Learning the territory in Vietnam meant learning more than how to stay alive. You were often working with a different value system. Once at Camranh Bay I got a tip that one of the Vietnamese commanding general's aides was actually one of the general's nephews. The position of general's aide is a highly coveted one and nepotism clearly should not be involved. I explained to my cameraman, Tony Hirashiki, why we needed to get pictures of the two men as they came out of the headquarters building, telling him that if the tip turned out to be true, it would be quite a scandal and a good story for us.

"I don't want to do it," said Hirashiki. "I'll feel dirty if you make me do it." I was nonplussed. What was the problem? Hirashiki explained to me that in Vietnam, taking care of one's family was the right thing to do. The scandal would be if the general, having a deserving nephew in the army, did *not* make him his aide. I finally convinced him to shoot the film. It turned out the tip was wrong so I never used it, but the lesson—that other cultures' values are different and must be taken into consideration—has not been forgotten.

Vietnam, as I said, was the wrong war for us. Our national interest did not require that we fight it at the loss of fifty-eight thousand Americans killed doing their duty. They were sacrificed to an obsession with fighting communism wherever we found it, regardless of whether it constituted a clear and present danger to us.

Did the news media lose the war for the United States? Of course not. We reported what we found. And we reported on the gap between the optimistic official line and reality. What changed public opinion was not the press but the body bags coming home, with no end in sight. The public was right.

When U.S. participation in the Vietnam War ended, Watergate was heating up. The Watergate story kept me going for the next year and a half, until Richard Nixon resigned.

Watergate was the most intense story I've covered. And Watergate proved to be the most difficult story I've covered when it came to keeping my own emotions and feelings from coloring my reporting. As the facts of Watergate accumulated, I became convinced that Richard Nixon was participating in a criminal conspiracy to obstruct justice and ought to be punished for it through the constitutional and legal process. I tried to keep this personal view out of my reporting, but in retrospect, I didn't always succeed.

Professionally, the story helped me reach a wider audience and flex my wings, thanks to the fact that the networks rotated live coverage of the Senate Watergate hearings in the summer of 1973, and every third day, if you wanted to watch, you had to watch me.

Frank Reynolds anchored from our Connecticut Avenue studios, and I reported from the hall outside the old Senate Caucus Room, where Senator Sam Ervin presided over the hearings. Frequently, the bells would ring on the Senate floor for a vote and the committee would recess for twenty minutes or so while its members went over to vote. During that time, Frank and I would talk back and forth about the testimony and the story, and I would grab whomever I could to interview.

On the day the Nixon enemies list was revealed in committee testimony, I grabbed Mary McGrory, the *Washington Post* columnist, who was then with the now-defunct *Washington Star*.

"It says here that you write daily 'hate Nixon' articles," I told her, reading from the enemies list, which Nixon speechwriter Patrick J. Buchanan had helped compile—the same man, who's back at the White House now as Reagan's communications director.

"That's not true," replied McGrory in that-ever-so-gentle, sweet manner of hers that masks the instincts of a barracuda. "I only write three days a week."

The competition inside and outside the caucus room was fierce. Carl Stern, NBC's veteran law and court correspondent, covered for that network, and Daniel Schorr covered for CBS. Schorr was a very controversial reporter. He was tough and aggressive and would do almost anything to get a story and then get it on the air. I marveled at the way Schorr could sharpen his information to make it sound more important or more exclusive than it was.

Once, while covering a session of the AFL-CIO executive committee mapping its opposition to the wage-and-price controls imposed by Nixon in 1971, we all picked up copies of the union federation's contract expiration list. There was nothing secret about it, but that night Schorr closed his report by saying in an arresting tone, "To understand the intransigence of organized labor, one has to read its internal working papers . . ." That night, I too talked about the contracts that would be affected by the wage freeze, but my producer wanted to know how come I hadn't gotten hold of the "internal working papers" of the federation, like Schorr had.

But if Schorr often took the lead in Watergate, I got in my licks as well. One of them, unfortunately, hit Schorr's number two in covering the Ervin committee for CBS, Lesley Stahl. Stahl has always been aggressive and hard-working, traits I strongly admire. Today she is one of the best reporters around, having fought her way to the top despite the discrimination that still plagues women in this business. But there came a day in 1972 when she had some bad luck and the way she reacted to it almost got her slugged by David Schoumacher, a former CBS reporter who was then with ABC.

I covered the Ervin committee, and Schoumacher covered the special Watergate prosecutor, Archibald Cox. Shortly after Cox was appointed, I spotted him one noontime coming out of the elevator on the third floor near the Senate caucus room and going down to Senator Stuart Symington's office. I called for Schoumacher, who came running over with a film crew, which he posted outside the building's side exit. No one else had spotted Cox, and we thought we had a "clean kill" coming up, that is, a noteworthy triumph over the competition.

When Cox emerged from Symington's office, Stahl spotted him and jumped in the elevator with us. When we emerged from the building, she almost had a fit. She saw the ABC camera crew, waiting, alone, and she knew she had been beaten. Schoumacher stepped up, took the microphone that was waiting for him, and asked Cox a question.

Stahl, horrified, gave a strangled shout. *"No!"* She jumped forward and put her hand out to block our camera lens. Schoumacher took his free arm and pushed her back hard. The interview proceeded without further interruption.

ABC did score clean kills over the competition in those days. But who knew it? We had the smallest audience of the three networks; more importantly, the Washington insiders and the television critics didn't watch us. Frank Reynolds, during an early period when he was the principal ABC anchorman, liked to joke that if you ever got on the FBI's ten most wanted list, the best place to hide was to take the job of anchoring of the *ABC Evening News*.

It's not that our fate in those days wasn't to a great extent self-made. Consider what happened on October 20, 1973, the date of the Saturday Night Massacre, when Nixon ordered special prosecutor Cox fired and Attorney General Elliot Richardson and his deputy, William Ruckelshaus, refused to do it and resigned. Late in the afternoon, knowing that Richardson had visited the White House, I caught Ruckelshaus in the Justice Department courtyard as he was leaving. He wouldn't tell me what was happening, but when I took a shot in the dark and asked him if an expected White House statement might be an announcement of Richardson's resignation, Ruckelshaus replied to camera, "It just might be."

That was big news, and it was exclusive. Today, we probably would be hooked up live at that moment. At the very least, we would rush that comment onto the air. What did we do at ABC that night? Nothing. We had no early evening news broadcast on Saturday in those days. No one who had the power to order up a network bulletin, except for the most obvious emergency, was on duty, and when an executive who did was called, he took no action.

I just stewed until it was all announced at the White House that evening. Then the other networks went live from the White House lawn; ABC had an announcer in New York read a bulletin over a slide.

The Saturday Night Massacre made the impeachment investigation inevitable. And I moved on to cover it. Which meant covering Peter Rodino, chairman of the House Judiciary Committee. Most of us didn't know much about Rodino but suspected he might not be up to the job of organizing the first serious impeachment investigation of a president since Andrew Johnson. Rodino proved us wrong. Of course, he had help. John Doar, who had been an official in JFK's Justice Department, did an excellent job directing the staff. And Francis O'Brien, who took over as Rodino's administrative assistant, handled the press expertly.

In the beginning, Rodino was sort of overwhelmed and intimidated by the media. But O'Brien had the sure touch. He knew that if reporters realize you think they are serious about their work and their coverage and if you do not resent the adversary relationship that exists between them and you, then things will usually work out to your advantage. Moreover, O'Brien further understood what reporters needed for their stories, whether print or TV, and tried to make sure they had it whenever he could. Finally, he resisted the temptation to try to punish reporters or news organizations that didn't tell it the way he would have liked.

One noontime, Jack Nelson and Paul Houston of the *Los Angeles Times* and I were in O'Brien's office talking over the events of the morning when Chairman Rodino opened the door from his own office and came in. We started talking to him about the upcoming impeachment vote on Richard Nixon in the committee. Nelson asked him how he thought the vote was shaping up on Article One. Without hesitating, Rodino said he was confident all twenty-one committee Democrats would vote for impeachment, and while less confident about the Republicans, thought five or six of them would vote aye also.

It was certainly injudicious for Rodino to make such a prediction, since the committee had not yet reached the point of deliberation. But the ground rules for such informal sessions, whether in Rodino's office or the White House press office, are always "guidance" or "background," meaning in the first instance, no direct disclosure of the information, in the second instance, the information may be reported but not attributed to the source by name. The ground rules that day were not clear because no one had set them in so many words.

The next morning, Nelson had the story on the front page of the *Times*. Nelson wrote that "Rodino was quoted as saying that all twenty-one Democrats on the House Judiciary Committee are prepared to vote to impeach President Nixon . . ." Nelson did not attribute the information directly to Rodino, but said that visitors to Rodino's office had relayed his views. I hadn't done the story at all. I should have.

All hell broke loose. The White House attack team, led by Kenneth Clawson, insisted that this proved Rodino was biased against Nixon, had no intention of judging the evidence fairly, and was simply leading a partisan Democratic lynch mob.

Speaker Carl Albert called Rodino and told him he had to deny the story before the House or the consequences would be incalculable. Rodino took to the House floor and denied flatly that he had ever said the Democrats "are prepared" to vote for impeachment. He said he didn't know how committee members would vote, and he had never made the prediction ascribed to him.

Reporters everywhere that day were doing the story. They could say that the *Los Angeles Times* reported Rodino was predicting all the Democrats would vote for impeachment but that Rodino said he had never made such a prediction. Reporters everywhere could say that except for one: me. I had been there. I *knew* Rodino had said it. And Francis O'Brien knew I knew it.

As the afternoon wore on, O'Brien kept trying to get me to agree to do the story in the same way all the other reporters would have to do it. He said it was clear Rodino was not reporting a Democratic plot to prejudge the evidence, but giving an estimate based on what committee members were freely saying about their feelings and intentions in the privacy of the cloakroom. To let this candid observation by the chairman jeopardize the entire investigation would be wrong, argued O'Brien.

I thought about it. O'Brien was right. Rodino had told us that he *thought* the Democrats would vote that way, not that he knew it for a certainty. Furthermore, by this time I was personally convinced that Richard Nixon was guilty as hell and that he should be removed from office. I was tempted. But having done the wrong thing by not reporting the story in the first instance, I was not about to make things worse by fudging the truth. If you can't say to your audience you're telling them the truth the best you know it, you aren't saying anything that matters to them.

So that night I reported what the *Times* said. I quoted Rodino as telling the House that he wanted to state ". . . unequivocally and categorically that this statement is not true . . ." After which, I concluded, "This reporter was present when Rodino made his remarks yesterday. . . . It is true as he says, he did not state that he had specific individual knowledge that all the Democrats would vote for impeachment. But he did say it was his sense of the mood and of the way members were reacting to the evidence that he thought all twenty-one Democrats would most likely reach that conclusion."

O'Brien never said another word about it.

When Committee Clerk Garner "Jim" Cline began calling the role on Article One of the Bill of Impeachment at 7:03 P.M., July 27, 1974, Frank Reynolds and I were both there. I can still call the roll from memory: Mr. Donohue, "Aye"; Mr. Brooks, "Aye"; Mr. Kastenmeier, "Aye"; Mr. Edwards, "Aye" . . . When it was over, chairman Rodino had gotten his twenty-one Democrats plus six Republicans. Article One was adopted, twenty-seven to eleven.

It was a thrilling moment and the most unique experience any political reporter can imagine. What Judge John J. Sirica started, with his pressure on the Watergate burglars, and the Supreme Court expedited, with its unanimous decision forcing Nixon to turn over his tapes, culminated in that committee room as thirty-eight men and women wrestled with the evidence and their consciences over whether to vote to recommend impeachment of a president. With one or two exceptions, I respect every one of them.

A lot of people say Richard Nixon has been rehabilitated. Not for me. Richard Nixon disgraced himself and the presidency, and that stain can't be wiped away.

I've spent some time talking about the Vietnam War and Watergate because these two events left a lasting impression on reporters in my generation and convinced many of us that we should adopt a new way of looking at our responsibilities.

When I first came to town in February 1961, many reporters saw themselves as an extension of the government, accepting, with very little skepticism, what government officials told them. Everyone in Washington seemed to be in the club. Reporters loved to brag about their social connections with presidents and members of his cabinet, they loved being consulted and made to feel that while the secretary of state might eventually have stumbled on the right policy, he certainly wouldn't have done it as quickly without their help. But then along came Vietnam and Watergate. In both those two great events, the highest officials in our government pursued policies harmful to this country, in the course of which they persistently lied and attempted to cover up the truth. And to some extent they were able to do it initially, because the press wasn't skeptical enough.

Along with many others, I concluded that a reporter's role ought to be one of continuing, unrelenting skepticism about government's actions. Not hostility, but a continuing eyes-open look at what the establishment is doing.

This skepticism I'm advocating should also be extended to the *conventional wisdom* about things. If everyone says we'll bring North Vietnam to its knees in ninety days of bombing, be skeptical. If it's clear that Edmund Muskie has the 1972 Democratic nomination locked up or that Ronald Reagan is too far to the right ever to be elected president, take it with several grains of salt. If world oil prices can do nothing but go up and up, watch out. The conventional wisdom isn't *always* wrong, but wrong just often enough to make it dangerous for reporters to accept it and stop doing their job. The time to really question something strongly is when everyone says it's true. Today, some members of the press still instinctively rally to the side of the establishment no matter who's in power or what the issue.

But I think in order to do their job, reporters should keep their distance from the powerful people they cover. I think we should consider ourselves outsiders. I'm not saying you can't ever have a drink with a politician or occasionally go to dinner with members of the cabinet. But I don't think a reporter's goal ought to be to get in *The Green Book*, the Washington social register. The goal ought to be to keep tabs on those who are.

When the Watergate story ended with Nixon's resignation, on August 9, 1974, I went through the greatest period of decompression I've experienced in my professional life. Every reporter goes through decompression after a long story is over, particularly after political campaigns, where you eat and sleep and travel with the rest of the press corps and campaign staff. The story becomes your life. Then, suddenly it's over.

So, shortly after Nixon resigned, I went to Av Westin and told him I needed something to do that would jolt me out of the doldrums.

Westin, an ABC News vice-president now in charge of *20/20* and other major programs, was then the executive producer of the evening news broadcast. He has one of the quickest, most creative minds in television. Perhaps I'm a bit prejudiced because he has always liked my work. Ever notice how difficult it is to dislike someone who goes around saying nice things about you? Westin, who made his reputation as a wunderkind producer at CBS News, then went to PBS to produce its first major news effort, was hired by ABC in early 1969 to produce our evening news broadcast. While watching ABC shortly before coming over to his new job with us, he saw me participate in live questioning of Lyndon Johnson and Richard Nixon as they got out of a limousine at the Capitol for the 1969 inaugural ceremony. Mike Wallace was there for CBS, Nancy Dickerson for NBC. Westin's recollection is that I dominated the questioning, beating my two competitors. Actually, I had done no more than get my fair share. But I think in those days to see an ABC correspondent stand toe to toe with Wallace and Dickerson was considered nothing short of miraculous. So when I came to him looking for something to do after Watergate, Westin was receptive. He suggested I go out and do a "mood of America" story. Where?

"I see you standing under the arch in St. Louis," said Westin, and off I went to Missouri. We went to Fulton, where Churchill had delivered his Iron Curtain speech. We went to Carthage to a hog barn auction. We went to Hannibal and sat on Mark Twain's riverbank. I came back with nine thousand feet of film and told Westin, There is no mood. The truth is, I was in no mood to discover a mood. I couldn't do a story. Westin was understanding enough of an emotional cripple not to recommend firing me.

Still, after seven years of being on the "fast track" at ABC, I was clearly in the doldrums. Careers in this business, as in others, follow an up and down path. Correspondent George Herman, who started with CBS in 1944, once said he'd been "discovered" five times, each time slipping back onto the shelf until the next time.

(Herman's luck ran out at the end of 1986 when CBS, in a staff cutback to save money, let him go.) I've been pretty lucky in that I've never gone through a long stretch of shelf-sitting at ABC. But there have been valleys as well as peaks, and during this period right after Watergate I almost got dropped into the bottomless abyss.

Ernest Leiser, a veteran producer who has spent most of his career at CBS, was producing the ABC evening news broadcast at that time. Leiser and I didn't get along very well. And he didn't think I was all that good. Leiser advanced the idea that we should put our limited air time in the hands of just a very few correspondents, build them, and let the audience get to know them without diluting that effort by putting on everybody. I was not on Leiser's preferred list. He presented the idea to the news management and it was touch and go. But the management rejected the idea and Leiser returned to CBS. I also had to contend with low marks from the Frank Magid consulting firm, which ABC had hired to advise it on who the audience liked to see on the air.

Now, I have a "minimum high regard" (as the senator likes to say about another senator whom he positively loathes) for most consulting firms. These firms don't give advice on the most responsible way to report and cover the news but on how to "gimmick up" coverage and presentations, how to select the sexy stories, keep the bouncing ball bouncing, how to clothe and coiffure the anchors, and so forth. Their "happy talk" formats often win ratings, but that approach is in direct opposition to my feeling about what's really important in the news business.

Anyway, Magid seemed to have the same minimum high regard for my talents as I had for his advice. I found that I was no longer being called on to anchor special broadcasts or to be the center of any other high-visibility assignment. In fact, I went through a period of about a year and a half of residing in this purgatory and only came out of it with the assignment to Jimmy Carter's presidential campaign.

While I was in this trough, Av Westin came to my rescue once again, letting me produce an hour-long "ABC News Close Up" documentary. He didn't say so at the time, but he was running over budget for the year and expected me to produce an hour for pennies. I didn't know enough about documentaries to object.

The subject of this documentary was government regulation: how it costs you money. Jimmy Carter and Ronald Reagan have both worked since then to decrease regulation by the federal government, but I was there before them. We zeroed in on the Interstate Commerce Commission (ICC) and the Civil Aeronautics Board (CAB).

The ICC was the worst. It had been established in 1887 to protect the users of transportation services by regulating the transportation companies. But it had evolved into an agency that worked hardest to protect existing trucking lines and railroad lines from facing real competition. It regulated routes, applications for new service, and rates. All with the result of keeping true competition from emerging. For instance, if one carrier filed for rates to haul a certain product from one point to another, other carriers often complained that they would be driven out of business by such cutthroat prices. And that was more important to the ICC than cheaper immediate cost to the public.

One disgruntled trucking company highlighted this silliness by filing with the ICC a proposed rate to haul yak fat from Omaha to Chicago. The railroad immediately protested that the proposed rate was too low, that it could not possibly haul yak fat for such a pittance, and would thus be driven out of business by such unfair competition. The ICC agreed with the railroad and refused to allow the trucking company to post its proposed rate. Imagine the commission's chagrin when it learned that there never had been, probably never will be, any yak fat in Omaha for anyone to haul.

Being a born troublemaker, I dispatched a film crew to the Baltimore zoo to take pictures of the nearest yak (most of them are in the Himalayas) so that I could properly illustrate that story in my documentary.

The chairman of the ICC, George Stafford, was from the little town of Valley Falls, Kansas. Defending the need for ICC regulation, he insisted that if unrestrained competition were allowed, everyone would service the more profitable places and no one would haul goods to the small towns. We showed Stafford telling a congressional committee that if regulation was done away with, his hometown of Valley Falls and twenty thousand other communities like it "are going to be without truck service . . ."

The next shot was of me standing on a streetcorner. "This is Valley Falls, Kansas," I began, "Chairman Stafford's hometown. A community that does depend on trucks for its existence. But does it depend on ICC regulation?"

The answer, it turned out, proved to be no. We heard from Valley Falls merchants that the vast majority of goods, from groceries to fiber glass fishing boats, were hauled in on trucks that were exempt from ICC regulation. And the one ICC-regulated trucker who serviced Valley Falls told us he thought people gave him business because he was a local man who gave good service, not because he had an ICC certificate. Now, all of this had been carefully checked for accuracy by my hardworking associate producer, Ellen Samrock.

But when we put it on the air in February 1975, the regulated trucking industry went berserk. Now we were up against the popular *All in the Family* on CBS and just before the *NBC Saturday Night Movie*. Consequently our rating was so low it might have been worth importing yak fat to Omaha just to haul it for that amount. But the trucking industry screamed as if it had been mortally wounded and put out a booklet attacking our documentary. I spent days composing a response to be sent to all the ABC affiliates that had carried the program, showing them we had not been wrong or unfair.

Westin was the top producer at ABC News during this period, but he was not the boss. When Elmer Lower retired in 1974, his right-hand man, William Sheehan, stepped up to the presidency of the news division. Sheehan was a former correspondent who had gone into management ten years earlier. I shall forever be in his debt because he made me the network's White House correspondent in 1977. But Sheehan, nice guy that he is, found he was having no more luck than Elmer had in getting the company to commit the resources of money and air time that we needed. It was inevitable that he and Westin should come into conflict, particularly when it became clear that Westin was angling for Sheehan's job.

We held our breath over this power struggle. But not for long.

Westin has a great knack of getting favorable publicity for himself in the trade press, but to the top management of ABC, that wasn't a plus. He lost the struggle and was fired. And it seemed to many of us that the old ABC would just stumble along.

Enter Roone Arledge.

Chapter Four

THE ARLEDGE ERA

When Roone Arledge, the one-time boy wonder of television sports, took over the news department as president from Bill Sheehan, I didn't know him, had never met him. There were vague stories to be heard about a man who wore bush jackets and gold chains, often missed meetings and never returned phone calls, loved to be seen with celebrities—and to hire them—but above all was the most creative sports producer television had ever seen.

But could he do news?

Just before Arledge took over in June 1977, he held a series of weekend meetings at Montauk, Long Island, near his country house, so that we in the news staff and he could get to know one another. We all postured a lot, trying to impress him with our intelligence and knowledge. Late that evening, Arledge called me aside. He said he had heard I would tell him the truth. In those days, when Arledge called you aside, either in person or on the telephone, he meant to take some time. Not ten minutes or thirty minutes or an hour and a half, but I mean some time—three, maybe five hours.

One night shortly after he came to the news division, he called me at home about 12:30 A.M. and woke me up. He wanted to talk about things. I was scheduled to fill in the next morning on *Good Morning America* as the news anchor, meaning I had to get up at about 5:30. We talked on and on. Finally, at about 2:30, I said, "Roone, I don't know about you, but I've got to be awake in three hours and if I don't get some sleep now, I won't be."

Another time, when we still had our 6 P.M. start time for the evening news, he called me in the White House booth at 5:30. I had just that moment begun to write the piece that would lead our broadcast in thirty minutes. He seemed a little put out when in response to his cheery, "Hi there," I replied, "Roone, I can either talk to you now and we won't have a lead story on tonight's broadcast or I can call you back and we will. Let me call you back." He said okay, but when I called him back, his secretary said he was unavailable.

So when Arledge called me aside at that get-together meeting in Montauk, he meant to talk all night and we did. There were two people in particular I talked about; William Lord, who was then Sheehan's right-hand man and possibly headed for the door along with Sheehan, and Av Westin. I told Arledge that Lord could often be an SOB, but he was an excellent news producer and we ought to keep him. And I told him that Westin was the best in the business. He kept Lord and rehired Westin.

Roone Arledge is often described as a genius. I've seen why. Here's just one example. In November 1977, Egyptian president Anwar el-Sadat went to Jerusalem. It was a breakthrough in the search for peace and an overriding news story. All the networks carried Sadat's visit to the Knesset live.

That Sunday morning, as usual, President Carter went to the First Baptist Church on Sixteenth Street in Washington. Just as Sadat was preparing to enter the Knesset, Carter walked out the door to leave church. All the networks had their cameras there. But only Arledge was prepared to broadcast the scene live. And only Arledge, presiding as he sometimes does from a perch in the control room, switched from shot to shot as Carter talked on the steps of the church about the meaning of the Sadat visit even as Sadat was entering the Knesset.

"And you see the hand of God moving in all this, don't you," I asked Carter. ". . . yes, I do . . ." he replied. Cut to Sadat in the chamber receiving applause from Israel's leaders. It was gripping television.

The book on Arledge as far as how he treats people varies from one person to another. My own experience with him has been a good one. Shortly after he came, he hired the late Catherine Mackin from NBC. I had always admired Cassie's work and thought we were fortunate to get her. But soon the trade press began to spread the story that she had been given a one-hundred-thousand-dollar-a-year contract to make the jump. Think of it. A hundred thousand dollars is a lot of money today. But in 1977, before the really big salaries took over in television, that kind of money for a non-anchor correspondent was unheard of.

At the time, I was making sixty-two thousand dollars. I was upset. I wrote Arledge a brief note saying I was pleased he had hired Cassie and thought she was worth the money the trade press said he was paying her. Then I said, "But if your White House correspondent isn't worth that much also, you ought to replace him with someone who is." The next day, I got a call from Arledge. "I agree with you," he said. "Irwin Weiner [vice-president for finance] will be in touch to work out the details." That was the shortest and simplest negotiation with anyone I have ever had. I've gotten raises since, but none has been as sweet.

Now, my attorney Robert Barnett and I go through months'-long negotiations, during which the company lets me know I'm nothing more than ordinary help, lucky to still have a job, and we hint darkly that the competition is just panting to hire me at twice the salary (listen up there, competition).

I recommended Barnett to Chris Wallace. Wallace hired him to help negotiate his contract with NBC. When it was signed, the newspapers reported that he was making as much as I was. I let that pass—you know how newspapers exaggerate. But when one reported that Wallace was making *more* than I was, I called up Barnett to complain. "I told Chris you were good," I said, "but I don't want you to be that good." He just laughed.

Are television correspondents paid too much? Maybe. But the fact is, we work in a commercial business. Some television news people make lots of money because the management calculates they are worth it in dollars and cents to the network.

60 Minutes reportedly brings in $70 million a year to CBS. The program's producer, Don Hewitt, deserves much of the credit, but to the people watching, Mike and Morley and Harry and Ed and Diane are the draw. We can argue over how much they are worth, but it is clearly quite a lot.

Van Gordon Sauter, Roone's counterpart at CBS until he was ousted in the great CBS management shakeup of 1986, was once asked (on *60 Minutes*, by Mike Wallace) if paying Dan Rather something like two million dollars a year isn't obscene. "My attitude on the salaries, which are obviously a source of great speculation and discussion, of the anchor people, is, if they're successful, they're worth every cent," answered Sauter. "If they're unsuccessful, it's outrageous!"

I'm not going to apologize for what I make. If Arledge finds someone else who can do the job better for ABC, he'll surely let me know. I remind myself and my wife every once in a while that it could all end tomorrow. If it does, we'll get along.

The viewers may resent such big salaries, or they may be like that plant worker who stepped up to shake Edward Kennedy's hand early one morning as Kennedy was campaigning for a Senate seat in 1962. "Teddy," said the grimy workman, "I understand you never worked a day in your life." Kennedy, whose opponent was spreading that charge far and wide, braced himself, expecting the workman's pent-up resentment to come spilling out. "Let me tell you something, Teddy," said the fellow, still pumping Kennedy's hand warmly, "you haven't missed a thing."

When Arledge started the big push toward high salaries, he had a purpose in mind. By fighting hard to get them and pushing up their value, he made Dan Rather and Tom Brokaw wealthy men, but not because he was trying to do them a favor. He wanted to hire them and others because he felt he had to do something to beef up the ABC News staff. In particular, the anchor staff.

Arledge inherited the anchor team of Harry Reasoner and Barbara Walters and it wasn't working. When Walters had been hired the year before for a million dollars, most of us were uncertain about her. She didn't have a hard-news background in the traditional sense. But most of us were willing to give her a chance. My respect for Walters grew rapidly. She worked extremely hard and aggressively. And when she went on foreign trips with the traveling White House, she was always willing to carry her share of the load.

I used to say that Barbara Walters was someone who would come driving up to a story in a limousine, dressed expensively and fashionably, dive into the mud and swim to the story, grab it in her teeth, swim back to her limousine with it, and drive off to the studio with an exclusive—while the rest of us were still hopping from rock to rock trying to keep our trousers dry. I used to put it that way until one day one of the vampire bats of the press used my description in an article she wrote about me and made it sound like I was accusing Walters of slinging mud. Of course I meant it as a compliment, and I still do.

Once, on Carter's 1979 trip to Jerusalem, when we had finished transmitting our reports just in time for the evening news in the States, Walters pulled me aside to say Roone had called to tell her he was unhappy with Donaldson's anchoring of the Sunday night news. If I would come to her suite in a half hour, she'd tell me more. Well, now, I wasn't born yesterday. If Arledge wanted to replace me, he wouldn't call Walters to tell her about it. Of course I would come to her suite, but I just knew she must have something else in mind. I have always been struck by how handsome I am.

I went down to my room with David Garcia, then a fellow ABC White House correspondent, and Dorrance Smith, who was then the ABC White House producer. I shaved and put on some cologne. They egged me on. "She likes you," said Smith. "I've known it for a long time." I knocked on Walters's door. "Come in," she cooed. It turned out to be the classic surprise. It was my forty-fifth birthday and people came pouring out of the other rooms wishing me well. Walters, Smith, and John Weisman of *TV Guide* had planned the surprise party. They even had hired a belly dancer, a rather plump one as I recall. At least I could dance with her, if I wasn't going to cozy up to Walters. I didn't even get to do that. Walter Cronkite beat me to it.

But if most of us were willing to give Walters a chance, Harry

Reasoner was not. I can understand why he would be unhappy at being teamed with her on the anchor desk; she did not have a hard news background. It is less understandable that he refused to try to make it work. Moreover, Reasoner had grown increasingly unwilling to work hard himself. In those days, our operating studio in New York was across the street from our office building, in the basement of a building that houses the Café des Artistes restaurant and bar. Reasoner would stop off at the bar on the way to the studio. Consequently, he would often take to the air with more of that famous Reasoner mumble showing than usual. Bob Siegenthaler, the executive producer, assigned someone on our staff the primary duty of delaying Reasoner in the office building as long as possible so he wouldn't have much time for the bar.

Walters was not a terrific anchor. But she and we deserved better than Reasoner was willing to give us. He's a talented man, but he let us down and I was not sorry to see him return to CBS.

Arledge wanted to move Walters from the anchor spot, but her contract in those early days called for her to have no less a participation in the evening news than any other person. To get around that, Arledge devised a troika anchor system; Frank Reynolds in Washington, Peter Jennings in London, and Max Robinson in Chicago. Reynolds and Jennings were known quantities. Robinson was not, at least not to Arledge. He was to me. And I had big doubts about him.

When I worked at WTOP-TV in the sixties, I ran the weekends in a de facto sense. Management, and for that matter almost everyone else, would go home on Friday night. For two days I was the assignment editor, general supervisor, writer, and anchor for our early evening news broadcasts. From time to time, copy boys would be hired for the weekends and I would immediately show them how to use a sixteen-millimeter silent film camera and send them out to augment our news coverage. When Robinson was hired as a copy boy, he soon let me know he was having none of that film camera stuff. He knew from the start that he wanted to be a star, a principal anchorman. He was not interested in the menial work of learning the business.

I'll say this for him—Robinson was a born broadcaster. When the camera came on, he projected just the right amount of easy-going authority and concern that caused people to compare him favorably to Walter Cronkite. The problem was, he was just reading lines. Battalions of writers would follow him around to write his copy; a special TelePrompTer unit would go along with him so even standing on location, he could read his copy rather than memorize it. Without all this help, he was completely at sea. Those of us who worked in the field and had to answer his questions during live special broadcasts developed a certain adroitness in finding ways to tell the news even though Robinson didn't know what to ask.

When you're standing on the White House lawn and an anchorman asks you a nonsensical or totally irrelevant question, it is considered bad form to reply, "Really, your anchorship, that's a dumb question." After all, the management has gone to great lengths to try to sell the fellow to the public as the smartest, most authoritative being since Solomon, and for one of their lesser fry to puncture that image is considered treason.

I was once watching Walter Cronkite on the air during a space shot emergency. The astronauts, successfully launched, had run into trouble aloft. Cronkite had an exchange with Steve Rowan, the CBS correspondent stationed at the Johnson Space Center in Houston, which went something like this: "Steve, I see the lights are on throughout that building as they work to bring them back safely." When Steve replied, "Actually, Walter, that building has nothing to do with the rescue effort. The lights are on because the cleaning women are in there," I knew he was in trouble. He left the network a few months later.

No, what you have to do when the question is way off is to reply, "That's a very interesting question, but the main focus here is on . . ." or "I put that very question to Jody and he told me, 'Sam,' what you should be asking is . . .' "

The best anchors, of course, give the correspondents a chance to say what needs to be said by first asking general, all-purpose questions. Frank Reynolds was particularly good about that. Reynolds was able to demonstrate his authority and grasp of the story without trying to do it by asking the field correspondent some tortuous, arcane question.

Reynolds would say, "Sam, what struck you as important in that speech?" or "Sam, why do you think the president is so intent on pushing that proposal?" I am waiting for the day when an anchor turns to me and says, "Sam, tell us what's going on where you are that you think we should know." On that day, I will cause a star from the East to be fixed over that person's head.

After five years, Max Robinson left ABC, publicly denouncing ABC and its management as racist. The racism charge was an excuse and a bum rap. But it wasn't all Robinson's fault that Arledge's new troika-anchor concept didn't shoot to the top of the charts. There were built-in problems.

The troika was an unwieldy device per se. I thought it kept viewers a bit off balance, since they were never sure who would pop up next, and it also ate up time through what I called layering and smothering. Reynolds would introduce the broadcast each night. But if the lead story was in Jennings's or Robinson's court, they would appear next to introduce the story itself. Then, of course, along would come a correspondent with the actual story. One broadcast began this way:

REYNOLDS: Good evening. President Carter is now in Europe to begin a week of summitry and personal diplomacy. Before leaving Washington this morning, the president called on the Western alliance to sustain world opposition to Soviet aggression. Well, that will be one, but only one, of the problems Mr. Carter faces on this trip. We begin our report tonight with Peter Jennings in Rome. Peter.

JENNINGS: Frank, the president arrived here in Rome late this evening and from the very outset there was extremely stringent security. Italy has the most serious problem of terrorism on the European continent. The president's stay here will be divided into three parts, tonight and tomorrow with a state visit, on Saturday a visit to the pope in Vatican City, and then on to the much more important summit meeting in Venice with six of America's most significant allies. Our White House correspondent, Sam Donaldson, accompanied the president from Washington to Rome.

DONALDSON: All roads lead to Rome . . .

By the time I got on the air with the actual report showing Carter's visit, the competition was halfway into its next story.

Aside from such layering and smothering, this arrangement sometimes led to other difficulties. Jennings, sitting in London, had a penchant for referring to Carter, then Reagan, as "the American president," as if we were broadcasting to some other country. One night Jennings took his throw from Reynolds and said, "Overseas tonight in Nicaragua . . ." Overseas for him in London, maybe, but what about the people watching?

There was also a problem some nights about finding something for Robinson to do. How to get him into the show when nothing of any real importance had happened in or around Chicago, where he was based. Reynolds would sometimes have to say good evening from Washington, throw it to Robinson in Chicago, so that he could introduce a correspondent at a flood in Richmond. Richmond is one hundred miles from Washington, one thousand miles from Chicago.

The "field general" who presided over the *World News Tonight* during most of this period was Jeff Gralnick, the executive producer and the man responsible for making up the daily story lineup of what went into the show and how long each item would run. There sat Gralnick in New York, dealing on the phone with anchormen in Washington, Chicago, and London, trying to apportion the time so each thought he had gotten his fair share, trying to line up correspondent reports that made sense, and trying to arrange it all so that Jennings's segments could be on tape since London was, of course, six hours earlier than New York. Gralnick's nerves were temporarily shot at the end of his tenure but it's to his credit that he didn't go completely daft.

Despite all these difficulties, the broadcast did begin to prosper when Walter Cronkite stepped down at CBS. We actually slipped into first place for a week or two while Dan Rather tried to get his feet on the ground. And even after Rather steadied, we pushed him hard. Then in July 1983, Frank Reynolds died.

Reynolds had cancer, diagnosed in the summer of 1978, shortly after the troika anchor team was put in place. He concealed it from everyone at work right up to the end. His doctors had told him when they diagnosed his condition that they could not predict how long he would live, but based on similar cases, he might have three or five years or even longer. Perhaps he should have told the management of his illness. He was the principal anchor, which meant ABC and his colleagues in the news department had a lot riding on him. It's a tough call.

Reynolds's death at fifty-nine was a loss to all of us who knew him, a loss to ABC News, and a loss to the profession. He had his warts. He could be stubborn. He had an ego. He had great pride. But he cared about news, about the business, about getting it right for the viewer.

Reynolds and Arledge didn't really get along. There was fault on both sides. Arledge thought Reynolds would often resist doing something he wanted for no reason except stubbornness. Reynolds thought Arledge would often want him to do something for no reason except to demonstrate his authority. For instance, Arledge was always trying to get Reynolds to wear dark jackets on the air, not light ones. Arledge's point was that dark jackets look better on television and, small matter that it might be, audience preferences are often built on such things. Reynolds resented having to change his look and resisted it. Arledge got his way of course, but in the end Reynolds won.

After his death, we all went to the funeral home to pay our respects and one of the family members, gesturing toward the casket, told me, "Roone would have a fit if he knew. Frank's got his light suit on."

Peter Jennings was the logical person to replace Frank Reynolds as the network's principal anchor. His overseas experience puts him head and shoulders above the other anchors on such stories as the hijacking of TWA 847 and the Rome and Vienna airport massacres in 1985. He is particularly smooth and impressive in live special-events situations, such as the day the space shuttle *Challenger* blew up in January 1986. He cares about the news and about getting it right. Jennings is also his own man. He and Arledge have had some testy disagreements over news coverage, but neither of them has let it get in the way of their good relationship.

True, it's easy to get irritated at Arledge. For one thing, he often puts off decisions that need to be made. ABC announced in November 1978 that it would begin an early evening Sunday news broadcast the next year. We correspondents were all interested in who would anchor it. I really didn't think I was in the running. But one Monday in January, Av Westin called me to say Arledge had chosen me.

"When does it begin?" I asked. "Next Sunday," said Westin. "What's the format?" I inquired. "I don't know yet," said Westin. Now, that's not the right way to lurch onto the air with a new broadcast, but it seems Arledge simply couldn't be brought to focus on it until the last minute. When Arledge does focus, he frequently wants things done "right now."

One Sunday in the summer of 1979, he saw Hamilton Jordan, then Carter's chief of staff, on *Meet the Press*. Arledge decided the country had no idea who Jordan and the other key people around Carter were. So he called Westin and ordered up a seven-part series on the people around Carter. Westin called me.

"When does Roone want to start?" I asked. "He wanted to start tomorrow," said Westin, "but we got him to hold off until Thursday." *Thursday!* We needed a month. A small army pitched in to help me. David Kaplan and Mike Von Fremd served as principal producers, alternating days. A lot of people, ranging from James Wooten, the former *New York Times* reporter who had recently joined ABC, to Josh Mankiewicz, then an off-air reporter, did interviews for me. The White House cooperated and made events that week available for exclusive ABC taping. Then we began.

I would work all morning on shooting material for future pieces, all afternoon on writing and editing that night's report, all evening on screening videotape for the next night's report, and sleep a very few hours before starting again. That routine continued until the series, titled "Inside the White House: The Powerful Few," was done. Never in my television career have "so few" caused "so many" such misery.

That was exhausting work. But it only lasted a couple of weeks. The ABC around-the-clock effort on the Iranian hostage crisis, which came a few weeks later, lasted for months. That was the hardest, most sustained effort I've ever made.

The hostages were taken on Sunday, November 4, 1979. The next day, Arledge began 11:30 P.M. special reports on the story anchored by Frank Reynolds, which by Thursday of that week he had made permanent and given a name: *The Iran Crisis: America Held Hostage.*

I would show up at the White House every weekday at 7:30 or 8:00 A.M. and work all day through a live report at 11:30 P.M. On Sundays, I flew to New York to anchor the early evening Sunday news. We were all pretty much exhausted all the time. We kept thinking it would end any day. It didn't. It just kept on and the 11:30 P.M. broadcast turned into *Nightline,* on March 24, 1980. Frank did have a little respite after a while. On his birthday, November 29, Frank took the night off, and Arledge picked Ted Koppel to substitute for him. Later, Koppel began doing the broadcast twice a week. It is sometimes suggested that Ted's work the night of Frank's birthday earned him the anchorship of *Nightline* in one moment of blinding accomplishment.

Not true. People always say of a new star: "Where did he or she come from," as if the object of their sudden attention had sprung full grown from Jupiter's forehead. The truth is, most successful people usually work for ten or twenty years in comparative anonymity before they surface in the top ranks. Koppel is an example of someone who had prepared himself well, started at ABC at the bottom of the correspondents' ladder, worked extremely hard in the United States and abroad, and parlayed it all into a position of responsibility and prominence.

Aside from his keen intelligence, Koppel has another ability going for him. He is a master politician, the best at ABC. Shortly after Arledge took over, he replaced Koppel as the anchor of the early evening Saturday news broadcast. Angry and humiliated, Koppel handed in his resignation. But before it took effect, he calmed down and took it back. That was clearly the low point of Koppel's career. But to his credit, he set out to turn Arledge around. That is nearly impossible. We have a saying at ABC about some correspondents. "He or she has a 'Roone problem,' " we'll say, meaning no matter how good anyone else thinks they are, Arledge has some reservation about their work. And as a rule, there's no changing his mind.

There was once a correspondent who worked with me at the White House who most of us thought was good. The fellow worked hard, was intelligent, knew the story, and was a good broadcaster. But Arledge didn't like the way he looked on the air. We all went to bat for him. Grudgingly, Arledge stayed his hand for seven months. Then, one day, *zap!* Arledge transferred him to another post. And then promptly rewrote history. He told me a short time later, "Well, everyone said to me, 'He just isn't doing the job,' so I said to them, 'In that case, if you're not happy with him I guess we'll have to move him,' so we did."

Yes, Koppel had his work cut out for him to earn Arledge's regard. He was our diplomatic correspondent at the time, working at the State Department every day, so it was natural for him to jump at the chance to do a foreign policy series Av Westin suggested. Koppel proceeded to turn a proposed five-part series into ten episodes. He devised a first part that ran almost nine minutes.

Now, you don't run a nine-minute piece on a thirty-minute evening news broadcast unless it's the end of the world, certainly you don't as part of a routine foreign policy series. But Ted had jazzed up the piece with animation and special effects—for instance, he showed an atomic bomb dropping on the White House in Technicolor.

Koppel knew what he was doing. It was gripping television. Sure enough, Arledge loved it. And Koppel was on the road back.

Nightline is a perfect vehicle for Koppel's talents. It looks easy. It isn't. I have occasionally substituted for Koppel and can tell you that it is difficult to juggle three or four guests in the electronic window. You must listen to the conversation, decide when to follow up and when to introduce a new line of inquiry, apportion the time so that everyone has a say even though one of the guests is sure to be long-winded and virtually impossible to shut up, another willing to impart only name, rank, and serial number no matter what you ask, and do it all within the time restraints of the broadcast.

The problem becomes particularly acute when you have guests who are not articulate. And that problem is compounded when you have a subject about which you know very little. Once, substituting for Koppel under those circumstances, I hit rock bottom. The subject was the Us Festival, a rock music concert and computer fair in California organized by the Apple Computer whiz Steve Wozniak. He was one of our guests, along with others. One of the others was Sting, the lead singer for the rock group the Police.

Just before the program, I scanned a piece of wire copy that said that Wozniak's wife, Cindy, had given birth the day before. I made a mental note to congratulate Wozniak on the air. Sure enough, there was Wozniak in the TV monitor as I turned to talk to him. But he was not alone. He held a baby in his arms, and a woman was standing by his side. The producer yelled in my earpiece, "He's got his wife with him!" Thank goodness I was prepared.

The transcript of what happened next will speak for itself.

DONALDSON: Steve Wozniak, the man behind the Us Festival that got under way tonight in San Bernardino, is with us now live from the festival grounds; and standing with him is his wife, Cindy. Steve, first of all, congratulations on the birth of your first child—When? Last night?

STEVE WOZNIAK: Yeah, last night.

DONALDSON: Well, Cindy looks like she's—

MR. WOZNIAK: Actually, yesterday afternoon.

DONALDSON: Cindy's all right—

MR. WOZNIAK: Candy.

DONALDSON: —but I'm a little surprised to see her up.

MR. WOZNIAK: Yeah, Candy's doing fine.

So it was Candy, not Cindy as the wire copy had said, but I was the one who looked stupid on the air. Things hadn't gotten off to a great start; still, the major part of the show was still to come. Too bad for me, as it turned out.

I was not totally unfamiliar with Sting's work because my daughter, Jennifer, had given me a record by his group, the Police. I began asking Sting questions and it soon became obvious that Sting was not in a talkative mood. *Yep, nope*, and *sure* seemed to be the extent of his vocabulary.

Taciturn guests are always the most difficult. The record holder in this department is Mike Mansfield, former majority leader of the U.S. Senate, later U.S. ambassador to Japan. Mansfield used to come on the Sunday talk shows and field forty questions in twenty minutes. But at least when the subject is politics, I never run out of things to ask.

Sting was not in the Senate. I grew desperate trying to fill the time as he deflected my questions with *yeps, nopes*, and *sures*. Finally, for some reason that will never be clear to me, I found myself telling him that I really liked one of his records and, to prove it, began singing on the air.

"Da Da Da, Doo Doo Doo Doo," I warbled. In my panic I had, of course, gotten it wrong. It is, "De Do Do Do, De Da Da Da."

Sting, dumbfounded, as must have been the viewers, chose not to point out my error.

It's all yours, Ted; my hat's off to you.

The Arledge era has been a good period for ABC News. Roone's style and idiosyncrasies have been a subject of debate, but his instincts for what works in television news have generally been on the mark and ahead of the competition. He is a major force in broadcasting, and everyone knows him. Almost everyone. Once he persuaded President Reagan to address an ABC affiliate convention by satellite from the Oval Office. Reagan's mike was open before he went on (what else is new?) and I heard him say to an assistant, "Is it Roone or Roonee?"

"Roone," said a voice.

"Good morning, Roone," said the president a moment later. "It's good to be with you."

I feel the same.

Chapter Five

JIMMY CARTER

On the morning of January 20, 1976, I flew to New York to begin my coverage of Jimmy Carter. ABC had waited for the results of the Iowa caucuses held the day before to clarify the front-running positions before beginning man-to-man coverage of the presidential candidates. Iowa was important in those days but still not important enough for the networks to apply the overkill of later years. Carter himself had to fly to New York overnight in order to get on the morning network shows.

He walked into ABC alone at about 6:30 A.M. Where was the press assistant traveling with him, Betty Rainwater? In the car under a blanket, a little sick, he explained matter-of-factly. He was the most unpretentious politician I had ever encountered.

I had been assigned to Carter by a fluke, really. David Schoumacher was the correspondent at ABC who seemed headed for the best political assignment of the 1976 election year. But the previous fall, he had taken an anchoring job for more money at the ABC Washington affiliate, WJLA-TV. The way was clear for me to draw the top assignment. I was given two candidates: Jimmy Carter and Hubert Humphrey. I had covered Humphrey in previous years, particularly in his 1972 abortive drive for the presidential nomination. The theory was that if Carter slipped, Humphrey would come on strong and I would still have a good horse to ride.

In the weeks that followed, I traveled with Carter everywhere. I thought he was a little strange, but also quite appealing. He carried his own hanging bag. He slept in the homes of supporters instead of hotels. He was a Christian who kept yearning for a country "filled with love" but was quite capable of making very cold, calculating decisions.

I'll never forget Keene, New Hampshire. Carter finished his speech there late one Friday afternoon and we all went to the airport to board the two-engine charter airplane that had been booked to take us back to Boston for the night. Everyone was tired and looking forward to an evening off. But there was a problem. The chartered plane hadn't arrived.

We went into the lounge and stewed, particularly Carter. He couldn't stand inefficiency or failure, and he kept asking his staff to locate the plane. Finally, someone reported it was still on the ground in Albany, New York. There had been a snafu, but the plane would take off promptly and arrive in about an hour. Carter calculated the times involved and snapped, "Cancel the plane. And never do business with them again. I'm driving."

Well, I thought that was just great. I hate incompetence also. People who can't or won't do their job have no friend in me. I applauded until, as Carter was walking out to get in his car, it dawned on me that all the rest of us were going to be stranded. I caught up with Carter.

"Do you have an extra seat, Governor?" I asked.

"No," he said matter-of-factly, and drove away.

Now, I assure you, Hubert Humphrey would not have said no. He would have said to an aide, "Do we have a seat for Sam?" The aide might have shaken his head sadly, and Humphrey would have broken into tears as he explained to me how sorry he was he had run out of seats. But then, Humphrey, always late himself, would never have cancelled the plane. He would have spent the time looking for one more hand to shake in the airport and telling stories to reporters.

Carter just drove off, leaving me, a few other reporters, and all of his staff behind. I wound up renting a car and giving three members of his staff a ride. "Filled with love," indeed!

Carter was famous, notorious if you will, for his bluntness. I don't think he meant to hurt people; he just didn't see the need for coating his opinions with a lot of syrup. Once Judy Woodruff, then of NBC, asked him to defend the fairness of a policy that prevented poor women who depend on government medical help from obtaining abortions while wealthy women are able to get one if they choose.

"There are many things in life that are not fair, that wealthy people can afford and poor people can't . . ." began Carter, which, while certainly true, was perhaps not the most politic way of framing an argument on this particular subject.

He was also stubborn. In the summer of 1976, ABC's principal anchorman, Harry Reasoner, came down to Plains, Georgia, to do a piece on Carter. Reasoner was the first of the network anchors to do that after the primary season was over, and I was proud of him for coming. There was a fish fry that night at Miss Lillian's pond house and we all showed up. But Carter seemed to go out of his way to have nothing to do with Reasoner at first. He chatted with reporters, he chatted with radio engineers, he chatted with the children of press corps members. Reasoner kept his cool and didn't complain. Finally, at the end of the evening, Carter said a few words to Reasoner and left. He was trying to make a point, I guess, that to him everyone was equal and network anchors were no big deal, but I thought that was petty and the wrong approach.

Everyone who covered the 1976 Carter campaign will always remember that summer in Plains. My producer, Justin Friedland, and I took up residence at the Best Western motel in nearby Americus along with the rest of the press corps. It had been a Holiday Inn until Jimmy Murray bought it a few months earlier and signed on with Best Western. I lived in Room 141. The big event at the Best Western was the semi-continuous pool party. Throwing each other in the swimming pool was a favorite way of passing the time. I often entertained my colleagues by allowing myself to be thrown into the pool. Let's face it, I was given no choice. Once, in an effort to get even, I tried my hand at throwing in Eleanor Randolph, a *Washington Post* reporter who was then with the *Chicago Tribune*, but alas—poor Eleanor—I missed and bounced her on the concrete coping instead. She managed to roll in of her own accord, one of her ribs cracked. Eleanor has forgiven me that moment of physical weakness (a stronger man would have hurled her in clean) but says she is still put out that she had to make her own way to the hospital.

We ate steaks at Faye's Barbeque Villa, which was actually a double-wide mobile home. Faye Wells served. Her husband, David, who was a Georgia highway patrol lieutenant in the daytime, cooked. Except to go through a little piece of the Florida panhandle once to see the Gulf of Mexico, Faye had never been out of Georgia. When Carter went to New York one day that summer, we took Faye along on the plane. Several of us took her on her first subway ride and bought her lunch at "21." It was hard to tell which of us (we or she) had more fun.

On Sundays, we all went to the Plains Baptist Church. Bruce Edwards, the pastor, preached a sermon, and the choir, led by cousin Hugh Carter Sr., sang hymns. Then, in the afternoon, we would play softball. Carter always got the Secret Service to play on his team. They were in somewhat better shape than the press corps and would usually beat us.

Rick Kaplan, then the CBS Carter producer, now the ABC *Nightline* executive producer and a good player, got frustrated and tried to sell the idea that we should field the very best team instead of letting everyone play. I knew I had to be against that proposal.

I wasn't very good, and Carter would often strike me out. Once he did so in front of my son Tom, nine years old at the time. I got my revenge in that game, however. I have a picture of myself playing catcher, yelling for the ball while Carter was running home from third base. The picture doesn't show it, but my recollection is I caught the ball and smacked him a good one with it as he streaked by. Another time we were playing a game when Billy Carter's gas station caught fire. We threw down our gloves and ran over to cover the story. When the fire was out, we came back and finished the game.

In between such recreational events as playing softball and draining water ponds on the Carter farms, we worked hard chasing Carter up and down the Georgia roads, dogging him on his early morning visits to his peanut warehouse. I've got a lot of pictures and keepsakes from the Carter era, but the only one I display is a blown-up reprint from the *Washington Post* of November 12, 1976, quoting Billy Carter:

> Sam Donaldson is the only one worth a [damn] because the rest of them send the cameraman out to get a story and then they fill in the words. He hasn't been fair to Jimmy, but at least when the crew's up at six in the morning, Sam's out with 'em.

That probably wasn't fair to the other reporters, most of whom were out there with their crews also. But I did stick as close to Carter as I could.

I went into that campaign convinced that the way to cover a candidate was to be with him every moment you possibly could. Get to know him, watch him, learn his mannerisms, learn how to anticipate his actions, his thoughts. The reporter learns as much about the candidate as possible and the candidate comes to expect that he must deal with someone who knows his habits. Also, from the standpoint of competitive advantage and personal recognition, the reporter who practices this around-the-clock coverage comes out on top.

As Carter was leaving office, he said to me that because I had dogged him so indefatigably he had never been sure who I represented in covering him, myself or the entire press corps. The answer is that I represented both, depending on the circumstances.

I was then and am now ambivalent about Jimmy Carter. He is a man of truly admirable qualities, but also some glaring shortcomings. I liked his family, especially his brother, Billy, his sister Gloria and his mother, Miss Lillian.

Miss Lillian would come knocking on the door of our ABC editing trailer underneath the Plains water tower almost every morning. The ritual went as follows:

"Just came by to see how you were," Miss Lillian would say.

"Won't you have a little something to perk you up?" I would volunteer.

"Well, just a little something," she would respond.

And with that, we'd pour a small shot of Jack Daniel's sourmash bourbon into a glass. She'd sip it as we talked. Then she'd be off.

One of Miss Lillian's most admirable traits in my opinion was her sometimes brutal outspokenness. Jody Powell tells the story of the woman reporter who, gaining an interview with her, was pushing Miss Lillian hard on the subject of whether her famous son had ever told a lie. During the campaign he frequently told his audiences, "I'll never lie to you, I'll never mislead you, I'll never dodge a controversial issue." Miss Lillian, pinned down, replied, "Well, maybe a little white lie." The reporter, sensing a journalistic breakthrough, asked her to define a little white lie. "Well," said Miss Lillian, "do you remember when you came in and I told you how pretty you looked and how glad I was to see you . . ."

I know Miss Lillian had a fierce ambition for her son Jimmy, and I know she had her faults. But none of that bothered me. She reminded me a lot of my own mother. They were about the same age, although my mother has to the best of my knowledge never tasted a drop of alcohol.

One day, when I was about sixteen, my mother found a bottle of scotch hidden in the garage after I had been using the car. I tried a little white lie of my own by telling her one of the Mexican farm workers must have hidden it there to keep the others from finding it. She took the bottle, and as Alvaro Ramos, our foreman, and I watched, she poured the scotch on the ground. Miss Lillian would never have done that.

When Miss Lillian died, I went to her funeral. There was a family viewing at her famous pond house, where she was laid out—in the back room. When Jimmy Carter's sister Gloria Spann asked me if I wouldn't like to see Mama for the last time, I knew you couldn't say, "My, doesn't she look great," but I had forgotten you are supposed to say, "My, doesn't she look just like herself," so I simply shook my head and said, "That's her, all right." Gloria didn't seem to take offense.

David Hartman, the longtime *Good Morning America* host,

showed up at her funeral also, which I thought showed class when you consider that a lot of people in this business fawn over political celebrities who are in power in order to get interviews and special treatment, then drop them hard when they lose their important positions.

It's always bothered me that some people accused the Carters of a lack of class, of being hayseeds, of bringing Dogpatch to Washington. Maybe that's because I'm from farm country myself, but then, so are a lot of those who looked down their noses at the Carters. I think something happens to people when they stay around Washington too long and rub elbows with the powerful. They forget the way ordinary Americans live and think. To be sure, such highly publicized incidents as Hamilton Jordan's "I've just seen the Pyramids of the Nile" remark (while inspecting the bodice of the wife of the Egyptian ambassador) didn't help the image. Nor did the time when Carter was greeting the cherry blossom princesses in the Rose Garden and his press secretary, Jody Powell, brought out a big live Georgia bullfrog and let it loose on the grass. The frog began to hop, the princesses began to squeal, Carter began to grin, and the photographers began to trample one another manuevering for a better shot. The shots they got were not the most dignified. But if every administration had to rise or fall on whether its members occasionally make fools of themselves, the Republic could not survive.

Then, too, not all members of Carter's official family carried on that way. Rosalynn Carter in particular helped project a good image, in my opinion. Nancy Reagan has the reputation of performing good works because of her anti-drug crusade, but Rosalynn Carter was intensely involved in serious projects that helped both her husband and the country. Some people have criticized her for attempting to interfere in affairs of state—yes, she often sat in on White House meetings, taking notes and later discussing issues with her husband. But I'm convinced Carter always kept the reins in his hands, and I see no reason why the president's spouse should be relegated to the social pages only. Don't forget, someday the president's spouse will be a man.

If some of his people were getting stuck with the Dogpatch label, however, Carter himself was getting stuck with the tag of wimp, even though he was often "tougher" on the Soviets than Reagan (who was it who imposed the grain embargo, anyway?) and even though his policy of putting the lives of American hostages first in the Iranian situation was the same policy of restraint Reagan later adopted in the case of the 1985 TWA 847 hijacking. Still, there was a perception of lack of leadership—ironic, surely, since he tried so hard compared to Reagan's casual approach. Reagan sees the forests; Carter saw every tree and tried to deal with each one. Moreover, he thought that if he worked hard and did a good job, he didn't have to waste a lot of time on media events designed strictly to build his image. He was warned early in his term by his pollster, Pat Caddell, that politicians get defeated if they concentrate on substance at the expense of style, a mistake Reagan has never made.

Carter did not organize his presidency well. At first he tried to do too much on too many issues rather than concentrate his initial clout and energy on one or two. Moreover, he and his Georgia aides often acted as if they thought they could do it all by themselves, without enlisting the old established power brokers on Capitol Hill or elsewhere. Also, in some cases, he did not choose the best people to serve him. Unlike Reagan, who is surrounded by true-blue loyalists, many of Carter's cabinet choices, for all their ability, were not devoted to him or his causes. When, in desperation, he finally got around to firing people like HEW Secretary Joseph Califano, who had been regularly undercutting him, it made him look even weaker.

Historians, however, will concentrate on the record dispassionately, and history, I am sure, will treat Carter better than did the voters in 1980. His record, particularly in foreign affairs, is quite good.

Within fifteen months of taking office, he pushed the Panama Canal treaty through the Senate. If we'd tried to hang on to the canal much longer as Reagan counseled, I'm convinced it would have led to a nasty jungle war in Central America with the Panamanians. Carter also completed the normalization of relations with China. Finishing his television address on this action, and believing his microphone closed, he quipped, "That sound you hear is the applause of a grateful nation." What is this with presidents and supposedly dead microphones?

Carter completed the SALT II arms-control treaty with the Soviets. True, Secretary of State Henry Kissinger had negotiated 90 percent of the treaty during the Nixon and Ford administrations, but contrary to Reagan's opinion, I think it was a step forward in imposing limits on the arms race.

The biggest Carter success was his work for peace in the Middle East. His trip there in March 1979, in an effort to bring about a peace treaty between Israel and Egypt, was, to me, his finest hour. Yes, the Camp David accords that he, Egyptian President Anwar el-Sadat, and Israeli Prime Minister Menachem Begin hammered out the previous September represented the essential breakthrough toward a peace agreement between Israel and Egypt. But the accords merely set the framework; they were not the actual treaty. And as the months dragged on, it began to look like there would never be a treaty.

Carter decided to go to the region personally, with no guarantees. Almost all his advisers told him he was risking his prestige, with the odds against him. He went anyway, first to Egypt to see his friend Sadat, then to Israel to see the irascible, maddeningly stubborn Begin.

When Carter got to Israel, he found Begin seemingly intransigent. On the night before Carter was scheduled to leave for home, it looked like he would fail. Jody Powell briefed reporters on the lack of progress, as did other U.S. officials. I thought Powell was careful and honest. He said it looked grim, that the Israelis weren't budging on some key points. But he said Secretary of State Cyrus Vance and Israeli Foreign Minister Moshe Dayan were meeting that night and Carter and Begin would be having breakfast together the next morning. It seemed clear to me Powell was saying there was still a chance. But none of us could wait. Our deadlines were now.

A lot of reporters got caught in Jerusalem that night. Some people wrote flatly that the mission had failed. They filed their stories, and their reputations, and went to bed.

I came up with a fence-straddling close to my report that night that I don't think I've matched since, and believe me, many nights I've tried. So often, deadlines arrive at the most inconvenient moments, when you're still not sure how things will turn out. But the Roone Arledges of this world do not pay us to stand on the White House lawn night after night and say, "Gee, I haven't a clue as to what's going to happen here. Beats hell out of me how things will work out."

After showing the pictures of officials coming and going all day, I arrived at the moment of truth and said the following: "Is there any hope left that this could still work out? Yes. Mr. Carter is seeing Begin for breakfast in the morning and seeing Sadat at the Cairo airport. Is there much hope? No . . ."

How's that for having it both ways?

The next morning, after Carter and Begin had breakfasted together, we all went to the airport for the departure ceremony thinking he had failed. In fact, when Begin, during his speech, said the two of them had accomplished a great deal, I inadvertently laughed out loud.

Yitzhak Rabin, the former Israeli prime minister, standing in the line of officials, looked around angrily. Begin paused and looked a little startled. Secretary Vance squinted against the sun, trying to determine where the laugh had come from. But Carter just shook his head with a look that said he knew exactly who it was, and please, wouldn't I give them a break.

From Israel, Carter flew to the Cairo airport, to see Sadat. The two of them conferred for about an hour, then came out to the microphones, where Carter delivered a tortuous speech. He said the main ingredients of a peace treaty between Egypt and Israel had now been defined. What did that mean? It sounded suspiciously like something politicians say to paper over a failure. But no one could be sure. As Carter and Sadat walked side by side down a red carpet to review troops, I shouted, "Does this mean peace? Mr. President, is it peace?"

Carter stopped and replied, "I think I'd better stick to the statement because it's been approved by President Sadat and Prime Minister Begin."

I persisted. "But it sounds like peace—if the Israeli cabinet agrees?"

"Right," Carter said.

At that moment, every reporter around dashed for the phones and the radio circuits to file the story that Carter had done it. I had any number of reporters tell me later that they had understood perfectly well what Carter was saying in his speech. Maybe so; I never want to doubt my colleagues' word. But the fact is, many of them hadn't run to file until I asked Jimmy Carter, "Is it peace?"

That night, I concluded my report on our news special over a shot of *Air Force One* lifting off the Cairo runway for home with the words, "For Jimmy Carter, what a gamble. What odds. What a victory!"

I remember a lot of reports I did on Carter that were positive, some, like that one, even glowing. It's not true that I spent my time savaging him or spend it now beating up on Ronald Reagan. I suppose ultimately, though, a good many of my reports about Carter were negative because that was more and more the day-to-day story of his presidency.

And it is true, I used to go through the press room and press offices of the White House exclaiming in mock ferocity, "We've got him now, he can't survive," as I waved my script reporting the latest fiasco or setback. You'll have to take my word for it; I was only jesting.

"You know," Jody Powell once said to me, "it's not the fact that you trash us so much that I mind. What I mind is you seem to get such a kick out of it." But I didn't get a kick out of seeing Carter go down the drain. It is simply not true that reporters want to tear down a president. You cannot cover someone for a great length of time, particularly a president, without feeling an emotional tie to him and a sympathy for him.

This was particularly true during Carter's long hostage crisis ordeal. Here was a man who had not thought it wise to admit the exiled Shah of Iran into the United States for medical treatment in 1979. "And what will you advise me to do when they seize our embassy in Teheran?" Carter asked his aides one day while wrestling with the decision on whether to admit him. But the U.S. foreign policy establishment view prevailed. The Shah was admitted and the embassy seized. I watched Carter wriggle and squirm for 444 days. It sapped his spirit and cost him his job.

As he walked out to the west front of the Capitol to watch Ronald Reagan be sworn in as his successor, I asked him on television, "Are the hostages free, yet?" "I can't say that," he replied grimly as he walked by. The moment Reagan took the oath, the plane carrying the hostages lifted off from Teheran.

Carter's hopes had been dashed by the Iranian refusal to deal with him after the failed rescue mission the previous April. That spectacular failure, however, produced a splendid moment in the modern annals of public service. Cyrus Vance, Carter's secretary of state, argued against the raid, just as Secretary of State Shultz argued against Reagan's decision to sell arms to Iran. Whereas Shultz felt able to continue even though he had been overruled, Vance felt so strongly that he could not defend Carter's raid to other countries that he turned in his resignation *in advance*—to be made public after the raid took place, success *or* failure. Now that's acting on principle.

As for selling arms to the Ayatollah's Iran, Carter discovered that Israel was doing it even while the hostages were being held. On April 15, 1980, he confronted Prime Minister Begin in the Oval Office. At first Begin denied it, but when Carter described for him in some detail the type of aircraft at that moment being loaded at an airfield in Israel, Begin said he would stop the shipment if Carter made a personal request to him. Carter did, but of course other shipments went forward from Israel later.

After I watched Carter debate Reagan during the 1980 campaign, I thought the election was all over. Carter, so uptight, Reagan, so much in command of the evening, if not the facts. I asked Carter a day or two later about the polls, which showed him behind. "I'm not going to give up," he replied with that determined set of his jaw. I had to restrain myself from saying, "Hang in there."

And the morning after his smashing defeat, when he held an Oval Office news conference to prove to us he was taking it in manly fashion, my heart went out to him as he tried to make us believe he didn't feel rejected. I was particularly sympathetic when, with a catch in his voice, he told us that his wife had seen one of the Reverend Jerry Falwell's Moral Majority preachers on television that morning declaring that the American electorate had put "a true Christian in the Oval Office." A few years later, I was interviewing Reverend Falwell and asked him about that. Falwell said if one of his associates had said that, he shouldn't have. I'll say he shouldn't have.

Jimmy Carter is a religious man. He practices it, he lives it, it is clearly an important part of his life. Ronald Reagan has certainly given us no public evidence of a commitment more intense. No one can look into someone else's heart, but to suggest that Reagan is a true Christian and Carter is not is ridiculous. Worse. It is a malicious evaluation motivated by political judgments, not religious ones. The religious right has always been a bedrock of Ronald Reagan's political support. So be it. But defining a person's religious sincerity by what you think of his or her political opinions is the worst kind of anti-Christian behavior.

When Carter left the White House, I did a long piece about his presidency. Nothing profound. Nostalgia, really, including Carter from the past once again trying to explain to us why he took that oar and whacked away at a rabbit that had invaded his pond and was trying to climb into his boat. "Rabbits can swim, you know," he said earnestly as I asked him one day about the incident that came to be known far and wide, to his great embarrassment, as the affair of the Killer Rabbit.

But as I say, I remain ambivalent about him. Every time you get to thinking he really was a swell fellow after all, something comes up to remind you about his other side.

Jody Powell organized a Labor Day reunion in Plains in September 1985. I went down for a day and got a kick out of seeing everyone again. And, of course, we played softball.

Carter was the pitcher, as usual. I played on the other team, as usual. And we all had a good time until I tried to steal third base.

"You can't steal in softball," said Carter. "You're out."

"Let's let him just go back to second," said Frank Moore, Carter's old chief of congressional liaison, who was the umpire. "He doesn't know the rules."

Carter was unmoved. Things like that are very important to him.

"No," said the former president, jaw jutting forward, sweat running down his face. "The rules say he's out, and I'm not going to pitch another ball until he leaves the field."

I left.

Chapter Six

RONALD REAGAN

On November 1, 1986, Ronald Reagan's lucky streak snapped. More precisely, the flaws in this likable man and in the way he had been operating his popular presidency caught up with him. On that day, a small Beirut magazine named *Al Shiraa* published a story about secret U.S. arms sales to Iran in exchange for the release of U.S. hostages held in Lebanon. Three weeks later, it came to light that funds from those sales had been diverted to aid the Nicaraguan contras. Reporters were just as startled as everyone else when these events came to light, but to those of us who cover Ronald Reagan regularly, it was not surprising that they could happen. An understanding of the man who was elected fortieth president of the United States and how he has operated his presidency helps explain them.

Clark Clifford, the Washington lawyer who has served Democratic presidents beginning with Truman and was Lyndon Johnson's last secretary of defense, described Ronald Reagan in 1981 as "an amiable dunce." That may be a bit harsh, but it captures the contradiction of the man. He is certainly amiable.

Reagan can turn on a big "aw, shucks" smile, incline his head in that self-deprecating fashion, and charm the pants off a lady wrestler. Unlike Jimmy Carter, whose smile more resembled a rictus than an expression of affability, Reagan probably means it. For instance, Carter hated to make small talk. Reagan loves it. Carter gave visitors the impression that he couldn't wait for them to leave so that he might get back to work. Reagan makes visitors feel he has all the time in the world and would like nothing more than to spend it with them. Reagan likes people.

I think if you somehow got into the Oval Office, past the Secret Service, and told him you were down on your luck and needed some help, he would literally give you the shirt off his back. But there is another side to the man that is cold and calculating. While you are gratefully putting on his shirt, he will sit down at his desk in his undershirt and happily sign legislation that would take your elderly parents off social security, throw your worthless relatives off welfare, and remove your children from the school lunch program—all in the name of his political ideology.

Unlike Jimmy Carter, who tried to solve each problem on its own merits as it came along, Reagan has a unified philosophy into which he can fit any problem. This ideological foundation is both a strength and weakness; a strength because there is rarely doubt as to where he stands. Everyone is looking for the person who gives off the confident air of knowing what he or she is doing. "I am the way, the truth and the life . . . follow me" is one of history's most persuasive rallying cries. And if someone protests, "But the path we're asked to follow leads over a cliff," someone else is quick to answer, "Yes, but at least he knows where he's going."

Ideological commitment can be a weakness, however, when it results in thoughtless and false certainty. Which brings us to the dunce part of Clark Clifford's description. Reagan is not a dunce in the dictionary definition of the word. He has a good mind when he wants to use it. Unfortunately, he doesn't seem to take the trouble to use it very often. Lou Cannon, the *Washington Post* reporter and resident press room Reagan expert, has called him intellectually lazy. Cannon jokes that he titled his biography of the president *Reagan* because he wanted a title so simple that even the president could understand it.

Reagan's lack of knowledge about the modern world doesn't stem from any intellectual failings but from his disinclination to take the trouble to find out what's going on. Consider that until the fall of 1983, he was, by his own admission, not aware that the Soviets have most of their strategic atomic warheads on land-based missiles. That information is not just something to store away for a game of Trivial Pursuit when it comes to presidents. After all, a U.S. arms reduction proposal had been tabled at Geneva in Reagan's name almost two years earlier that, in effect, would have required the Soviets to dismantle a significant portion of their land-based missile system while we kept almost all of our submarine-based missiles. Most of *our* strategic warheads are on submarines. What a deal.

When he finally discovered the facts, I wonder if Reagan said to himself in a flash of understanding, "So that's why they haven't agreed to our proposal. And here I thought all the time they were just being the 'focus of evil' in the modern world."

Somewhere back in the good old days of Norman Rockwell, *The Reader's Digest*, and Hollywood, Ronald Reagan stopped revising his store of knowledge. In 1981, he could reminisce to a session of the Canadian parliament about a young lady from Toronto named Gladys Smith who came to Hollywood and "was embraced by our entire nation." Many of the Canadian legislators had no idea who he was talking about. Reagan explained, "Gladys Smith . . . embraced by our entire nation . . . became Mary Pickford . . . known the world over as America's sweetheart." The same legislators, being young men in their forties and uneducated as to the stars of the silent film era, remained unenlightened.

I once argued with him (gently) over his insistence that the size of the Social Security trust fund does not affect the size of the deficit. It's true, as Reagan says, that Social Security monies are not part of the general treasury funds. It's true that a payroll tax, not general revenues, funds the system. But beginning in fiscal year 1969, the federal government switched to a unified budget that includes all the trust funds. Social Security's balance sheet, therefore, affects the overall deficit figure in that unified budget. But the president refuses to know it. He doesn't deliberately try to tell an untruth on the subject. It's just that when Ronald Reagan gets something fixed in his mind, it stays there regardless of efforts to pry it loose.

Of a far more troublesome nature, though, is the fact that often Reagan does not seem to know the details of what is going on around him, even though he is a participant.

In December 1982, the lame duck session of Congress killed the MX missile, or so it appeared. Reagan called key senators of both parties down to his office to see if something could be worked out. It turned out it could. Reporters were notified that in fifteen minutes the president would come to the press room to announce a compromise that would keep the MX program alive.

Sure enough, the president appeared, flanked by senators of both parties, to say he was pleased to announce that a compromise on continued funding for the MX had been reached. He praised the senators for putting the country's interest, as he saw it, before partisanship and working with him to hammer out the compromise.

Helen Thomas of UPI asked the key question: "What is the compromise?"

"Well, the compromise is going to involve . . ." At this point Reagan stopped, clearly at sea. There was an embarrassed pause as the president groped for words. He looked around him at the senators.

"Would you like to explain what the compromise is, John Tower . . ." said Reagan. And up hurried Senator Tower to do just that. Reagan clearly could not.

Now, what does that tell us? Ronald Reagan could not explain the compromise just worked out in his office to save a program that was important to him. Jimmy Carter could have explained that compromise backward and forward. The trouble is, Carter might not have been able to reach it. Reagan won agreement on it, whether he knew anything about the details or not. And we pay our presidents to get results.

We want those results, however, to be *informed* results. As the Iranian arms sale story began to unfold, the press room joke was that the old Watergate question "What did the president know and when did he know it?" should be rephrased in Reagan's case to "What did the president forget and when did he forget it?"

Despite the many instances when Reagan does not seem to know the details of what's going on around him, I have never subscribed to the notion that he is a man being led around by his handlers, a puppet manipulated by others. Early in my coverage of Reagan, when he was still president-elect, I got a strong, direct sense that wasn't so.

One evening, as he was getting into his limousine outside Blair House to go to a reception at a nearby hotel, I asked him when his cabinet choices would be announced. "I don't know," he replied genially. "They haven't told me yet." I was flabbergasted. I shot back, I must admit, with a trace of sarcasm, "Well, Governor, you ought to see if you can't get them to start telling you what's going on."

Michael Deaver, the aide riding with Reagan, said later that his boss tried to back out of the car at that point to confront me, but momentum carried him forward and they were off. We all went over to the hotel to cover the reception. As he was leaving, Reagan sought me out. He stopped and looked me squarely in the face. "Sam," he said sternly. "They don't tell me, I tell them." You could tell this was no blusterer trying to save face but the guy in charge—when he chooses.

Of course, sometimes Reagan purposely gives the impression that he's not master of his own destiny, as a technique for protecting his nice guy image, as when he tells an audience that he'd just love to stay and answer some more questions, but "they won't let me, they tell me I've got to go." He says that right after some assistant, such as Jim Kuhn, his thirty-four-year-old personal aide, has just sung out, "We've got time for only one more question, Mr. President." But he doesn't use that "dodge" with the press much anymore since the day I shot back at him,"But, sir, remember *they* don't tell you what to do, *you* tell them." Not only does he tell them, he clearly sets the agenda, direction, and tone for his administration. And if he doesn't want to do something, he doesn't do it.

Reagan makes no bones about his leisurely work habits. He cracked once that he had been hard at work at the office burning the *mid-day* oil, and another time that after he's gone they'll put a plaque on his chair in the cabinet room: "Ronald Reagan slept here." He will never collapse from heavy labor. On the campaign trail in 1980, he said, "Show me an executive who works long overtime hours and I'll show you a bad executive." He works relatively short hours and he vacations frequently at his California ranch. When the Soviets shot down KAL 007, on September 1, 1983, Reagan was at his ranch. He saw no need to interrupt his vacation.

At 10:20 A.M., California time, White House spokesman Larry Speakes held a briefing in the Santa Barbara press room dressed in his usual vacation attire of open shirt, no tie, casual slacks. He read a relatively mild statement criticizing the Soviets and insisted under questioning that the president had no plans to return to Washington. Speakes even went through the usual explanation about how modern communications allow presidents to stay on top of things no matter where they are.

That's true. It's also irrelevant when public leadership is the issue. I told Speakes as he was leaving that I'd bet he'd be back soon, dressed in a coat and tie, to announce the president would cut short his vacation and return to Washington. In a few hours he was back in a coat and tie—to say just that. I was told later that before the president agreed to return, his staff had to make the case to him in the strongest term that it was important for him to be visibly involved.

Reagan's first instincts on such occasions are often off the mark. When the space shuttle *Challenger* blew up in January 1986, Reagan wanted to go ahead with his State of the Union message, scheduled for delivery on Capitol Hill that evening. He saw a group of reporters, briefly, to express his sorrow about the space shuttle. He said the speech would go on, however.

He and I had the following exchange.

DONALDSON: But how does that affect your State of the Union speech tonight? I mean, we were told you were going to give an upbeat "the state of the union is good," you know, optimistic speech. This has got to cast a pall on it, doesn't it?

REAGAN: Yes, I'm sure it does. And certainly there could be no speech without mentioning this. But you can't stop governing the nation because of a tragedy of this kind. So, yes, we'll continue.

Only later after checking with the congressional leadership, who all said he couldn't possibly want to make the speech that night, did he postpone it.

The truth is, Reagan depends on his staff to do the work and the thinking for him more than any other modern president. When his advisers don't have their thinking caps on straight, neither does he, making it appear that he is a captive of the system, not its captain.

Remember Bitburg? Going to the cemetery in Bitburg, Germany, in April 1985 where Nazi SS graves were located was a mistake. Never mind that Reagan had promised Chancellor Kohl he would visit a cemetery, or that Deputy Chief of Staff Michael Deaver had, in a moment of oversight, approved that cemetery (they said it was the snow on the ground that obscured the SS graves). Once the outcry began, the losses should have been cut. The visit should have been canceled. But the staff was in transition. Deaver was leaving the White House; Chief of Staff James Baker III and Treasury Secretary Donald Regan were switching jobs; and the folly just kept compounding. Elie Wiesel, the Nobel Prize winner who has devoted his life to keeping the story of the Nazi Holocaust alive (he lived through the Auschwitz concentration camp although his parents did not), pleaded with Reagan at a public White House ceremony to cancel the visit. "I implore you to do something else to find a way, to find another way, another site. That place, Mr. President, is not your place. Your place is with the victims," said Wiesel.

Reagan, who can stubbornly dig in his heels, remained unmoved. He made the visit. That mistake put him on the defensive and contributed to the bad spring he had with Congress on other issues.

It is not just broad policy advice Reagan asks of his staff. He assigns his aides almost total control of day-to-day operations. Finding out who exactly is responsible for what is sometimes difficult.

I once asked Reagan, "Mr. President, on January eighth the Justice Department announced the decision concerning tax-exempt status for certain schools that clearly gave aid and comfort to racial discrimination. My question is: What happened? Are you responsible for the original decision, or did your staff put something over on you?"

Reagan replied, "Sam, no one put anything over on me. No, Sam, the buck stops at my desk. I'm the originator of the whole thing . . ."

My question about the staff putting one over on him was not just a flippant, gratuitous insult on my part. Many of us had been told by one of his aides that it was somebody else, not Reagan, who had authorized the decision. Indeed, one of the frequent excuses reporters hear around the White House these days when embarrassing decisions are uncovered is that the president had nothing to do with it, that it was somebody else's doing and the president shouldn't be blamed.

Once I asked Reagan about a directive he had signed authorizing lie detector tests for government officials that had prompted Secretary of State Shultz to threaten to resign. After Shultz's outbursts, the directive was modified. I told the president ". . . and one of your aides said to reporters that you really hadn't understood what was in it when you signed it. My question is, did you understand it when you signed it originally, and if so, why did you change your mind?"

Now, presidents will sometimes admit they are responsible for things. But they never, never admit they don't know what they're doing. So Reagan first tried humor.

"If there was an aide that said anything of that kind, he wasn't an aide." Then, when the laughter subsided, the president went to his second line of defense, which was that there had been no change in the order whatsoever. Tell it to Shultz.

Another case in point about Reagan's dependence on his staff. Almost three months after the Treasury Department had published the first draft of a tax reform plan, he was asked in an interview by the *Wall Street Journal* about the plan's feature of increasing the tax revenue from American business.

The president was nonplussed. He said he didn't think that was right, that the plan actually reduced business tax rates and he wouldn't be for something that levied more taxes on business.

A few days later, four of us were having a background session with a senior White House official. We asked him about the president's answer. "He's for it [the plan]," said the official. "The problem is he just doesn't understand it. He'll be for it when I explain to him how we're closing loopholes at the same time we're lowering rates."

Sure enough, at his very next press conference the president was asked about his *Wall Street Journal* answer and he said he had misunderstood the question, then proceeded to outline his support for the business provisions, using the very words the senior official who briefed reporters had said *he* would use in explaining it to the president.

On another occasion, the same senior official told a group of reporters that Reagan had been "very interested" in the story in the morning paper that James Fletcher would be appointed NASA administrator. The official explained that no one had taken "the short list" of candidates to the president for his decision before Reagan had read in the paper what he was going to do. The official sounded properly sheepish about the bad timing. Later in the day, the president's appointment of Fletcher was announced, however.

The president and his staff often confer on what to say about critical matters. That's only sensible. A problem sometimes arises, however, when Reagan is asked a second question on which he has not had the benefit of staff advice. He can get in horrendous trouble—as he did one morning in the fall of 1985 in Chicago over the *Achille Lauro* cruise ship hijacking.

The hijacking had ended. The hijackers were off the ship, and no one knew where they were. Egyptian president Mubarak had said publicly that they had left Egypt. The United States wanted desperately for them to be tried as the murderers of Leon Klinghoffer, an American citizen.

The president was flying to Chicago that day on other business, and aboard *Air Force One*, he and his advisers worked out a statement to make about the hijacking situation. When *Air Force One* landed in Chicago, the president walked over to the press pool, gathered near the plane's wing. He told us it appeared that the hijackers had departed from Egypt for "parts unknown," but it was the U.S. view that no responsible nation would harbor them and should, in fact, turn them over to "whichever country has the proper jurisdiction for prosecution." That said, the president took a few questions and promptly got in big trouble.

In the give and take, I asked him how the hijackers would be brought to justice if they had already gotten back to the home base of the Palestine Liberation Organization (PLO), headed by Yasser Arafat, as was widely suspected. The president said we would make a demand of Arafat that he turn them over to another country. So far, so good.

Then Chris Wallace of NBC asked, "Arafat says that he'll punish them. Is that good enough for you?"

"Well," said the president, "I would think that if he believes that their organization has enough of a—sort of a kind of a national court set up, like a nation that they can bring them to justice and—carry that out, all right; but just so they are brought to justice."

Question: "But you'd let the PLO punish them, then?"

Answer: "What? Yes, I said if they were determined to do that."

Alarm bells went off in several quarters. Some of the president's aides, straining against the noise to hear the dialogue, looked stricken. Several of us reporters looked at each other with open mouths. Here the president had just not only contradicted himself on the point he had set out to make about turning the hijackers over to "whichever country has the proper jurisdiction for prosecution," he had turned long-standing U.S. policy toward Israel and the PLO on its ear. We did not recognize the PLO as anything but a gang of terrorists.

And what did I do? I tried to save him.

Now, some press critics like to say that reporters try to get presidents to make mistakes. Jimmy Carter once told an interviewer that the only reason reporters came along was to be there in case he choked on a fish bone or said something ridiculous. That's not true. There are other reasons.

I tried to steer Reagan back to firm ground, because I felt certain that what he had said was not what he had meant, or at least ought to have meant.

"But, sir," I asked, "if you would let the PLO punish them, wouldn't that be, in effect, recognizing the PLO as a governing nation, which we don't do?"

The president's eyes narrowed. Something was telling him that I was trying to send him a message, which, I admit, I had not worded very well. Reagan's aides looked hopeful. The president thought for an instant about whether letting the PLO punish the hijackers would be recognizing it "as a governing nation," but he did not think long enough. "I don't think that would necessarily follow," he said. And the last escape hatch slammed shut.

A few minutes later I found then national security adviser Robert McFarlane. "Is that U.S. policy?" I asked McFarlane.

"Of course it isn't," he replied.

"Then you'd better get him out again to correct it," I said, "because it is until he does."

Sure enough, later that day, Reagan met the press again to take it back.

"I shouldn't have made a statement of that kind," he explained honestly. But the damage was done. The next day's headlines were sure to blare "President Tries to Rewrite Mideast Policy; Jerusalem and Capitol Hill up in Arms."

But that headline never appeared. The staff (and Reagan luck) came through with flying colors. His aides brought a plan of action to him that afternoon in Chicago to intercept an Egyptian plane carrying the hijackers. He approved it, and it worked. The next day's headlines read something more to the effect, "U.S. Intercepts Hijackers of *Achille Lauro*, President Wins One against Terrorism at Last."

Representative Patricia Schroeder (D-Colo.) coined the term *Teflon presidency* to describe Reagan's ability to deflect "bad news," but I like George Will's description better. Will used to say Reagan is the only person he knew who can "walk into a room, have the ceiling fall in on him, and walk out without a fleck of plaster in his hair."

And usually it's his staff there with the blow dryer.

Think of it this way. The Reagan staff is like the engineering and production departments at a successful motor company. The president of the motor company says he likes cars with big fins that are painted black. The staff designs, produces, test markets, and distributes cars with big fins that are painted black. The boss has no idea how the car works or how it's made. But the boss, in this case Reagan, then goes out and sells them. And he sells them better than anyone else.

Reagan is called the Great Communicator, and indeed, he has a sense of theater (I should hope so) that makes him quite effective in putting across his message. "There you go again" is the well-known line Reagan used to demolish Jimmy Carter in their presidential debate, but my favorite is the one he hurled at the New Hampshire newspaper editor who was trying to force him into a two-man debate up there in February 1980. "I paid for this microphone, Mr. Green," said Reagan, carrying the day with that display of righteous anger. That line was first uttered by Spencer Tracy in the movie *State of the Union*, and it fit perfectly except for the fact the newspaper editor's name was Breen, not Green.

Effective as such movie ripostes may be, Reagan is really only at his best when he has a script. At other times, he can mangle a thought out of all recognition. There was a minor flap in the presidential campaign of 1984 over whether Reagan *knew* that you couldn't recall submarine-launched missiles. In a May 1982 press conference during an answer to a question about arms control negotiations, he began by observing that land-based nuclear missiles could not be recalled once the button was pushed. Then he attempted to contrast the danger from such missiles with the danger from missiles launched elsewhere.

Here is what he said: "Those that are carried in bombers, those that are carried in ships of one kind or another, or submersibles, you are dealing there with a conventional type of weapon or instrument, and those instruments can be intercepted. They can be recalled if there has been a miscalculation."

Now, if you diagram that sentence, the word *instruments* refers to the word *those*, meaning missiles, and he has plainly said he thinks submarine missiles can be recalled, which they cannot. But when I heard him that night, I didn't even make a note. It wasn't that I was trying to protect him, it's just that eventually you get on to Reagan-speak. He was clearly trying to say that the submarines could be recalled and were therefore more stable weapons. As the Goldwater supporter once admonished us, "Write what he means, not what he says."

Deciphering Reagan-speak is a constant job in the White House press room—and elsewhere. When Reagan returned from his Iceland mini-summit of October 1986 with Soviet leader Gorbachev, there was a fearful row as people tried to figure out what it was that Reagan had tentatively agreed to in the field of strategic arms reductions. Some members of Congress said the president had told them he had agreed to a ten-year phase out of *all* nuclear weapons. At times the president talked publicly of a tentative agreement to phase out all *ballistic* missiles; at other times he dropped the word "ballistic" to make it all missiles. Many people suggested this was another case of the president "not knowing the details of what is going on around him, even though he is a participant." I don't think so. I believe it was another case of Reagan's knowing what he had done or at least meant to do but not putting it into precise language. Mind you, I do not fault anyone, including Gorbachev, for being confused.

But give Reagan a TelePromTer rolling smoothly in front of the camera lens, and he can communicate without ambiguity and, in the process, sell you a defense budget that will reduce you to rags or a Nicaraguan policy that will curl more than your hair.

When Reagan went on television to soothe the nation after the *Challenger* space shuttle disaster (the speech he gave instead of the State of the Union), a top news executive who is normally no slouch in the sophistication department called me to sing Reagan's praises for having said just the right thing, hit just the right themes, used just the right words. I thought about calling White House speech writer Peggy Noonan, who wrote the little gem Reagan read, to tell her of the call, but what the heck. As Reagan likes to say, "There is no limit to what a man can do or where he can go if he doesn't mind who gets the credit." Noonan has since left the White House and Reagan's speeches are the worse for it.

Today, the homeliest man or woman can still be elected to high office but only if they understand how to communicate their thoughts engagingly and persuasively on television. The good news is they don't have to write those thoughts themselves. Moreover, those thoughts do not have to be profound. In fact, for the best communication, they probably ought *not* to be. Reagan, who was once fond of saying "There are no easy answers, just simple ones," has never been worried about people finding him less than profound.

For instance, the president loves numbers and he loves to use them, never mind former budget director David Stockman's complaint that he doesn't understand them. Right after he took office, in an effort to bring home just how much money a trillion dollars of national debt really is, he said in a speech that if you stacked thousand-dollar bills one on top of another in order to make a trillion dollars, you'd have a stack sixty-seven miles high. Some columnists immediately accused him of exaggeration, claiming the stack would only be sixty-three miles high.

The next day, when I questioned him about this, Reagan rose to the bait joyfully. He said he had computed it out himself that "at four inches per million dollars' worth of thousand-dollar bills, 63.3 miles would be the height of the trillion dollars . . ." but that the Treasury Department had pointed out that that was using tightly packed bands of brand new bills and ". . . if you just make a stack of (used) one thousand-dollar bills, it comes out to 67."

"I thought we ought to get that settled . . ." said the president with an air of great satisfaction. If it seems strange that the president of the United States would spend all that time and energy on working out the math on a sky-high stack of money, you must understand that the oddest things capture Reagan's interest. Take the matter of the not so new suit.

In the fall of 1984, as he was leaving the Rose Garden and after he had effectively ducked all the questions we shouted at him, I sounded the give-up signal by saying, "Well, at least congratulations on your new suit." He was wearing a suit I thought I hadn't seen before.

"This isn't a new suit," replied the president, suddenly interested. "I've had this one for four years."

"Okay," I said. "I withdraw the congratulations." And with that he entered the Oval Office.

A few minutes later, I was sitting in the ABC booth at the White House when the phone rang. "Mr. Donaldson, the president is calling," said the operator. "One moment please." What could it be? I wondered.

"Sam," said Ronald Reagan when he came on the line, "I left you with a piece of misinformation and I don't want to be responsible for your making an error . . . I told you my suit was four years old. But I was wrong . . . I checked the label and I remember I bought it five years ago. It's five years old, not four."

Now, reporters don't get calls from a president very often. And when they do, they usually try to keep him on the line as long as possible and learn as much as possible. There's nothing like beating the competition with an exclusive story straight from the horse's mouth. But I was struck dumb. I appreciated that the president wanted to spare me a mistake he had authored. But really! What were the chances that I was going to rush on the air with a bulletin that Ronald Reagan was wearing a four-year-old suit? I thanked the president, made a sentence or two of small talk, and hung up, shaking my head.

Yes, Reagan sometimes comes across as a very simple person. Yet this very *Reader's Digest* approach to life that these anecdotes illustrate is also one of Reagan's strengths. He may not quite be the guy next door, but he is the guy you'd like to have next door. Once, when saying goodbye to a foreign visitor, he backed into the soldier standing behind him at stiff attention holding the American flag. The poor youngster swayed on his heels, plainly scared to death to find that his commander-in-chief had barreled into his chest. But it was Reagan who reacted the most. He stood there apologizing to the soldier profusely while his foreign visitor drove off unattended.

I think it's this good-natured hometown America part of Reagan's personality more than anything else that set him apart in the minds of the public for so long from others in his administration who carry out his policies. We could complain that Secretary of State Shultz was giving away the store to the Soviets, that Secretary of Defense Weinberger was spending us into the poor house, that Attorney General Meese was assaulting our liberties, and that CIA Director Casey was performing unspeakable acts in the world's dark alleys but, as the saying goes, "Not our Ronnie."

The Iranian arms sale story crashed through this cellophanelike partition. The usual ploy of distancing the president from the actions of his administration wasn't available. The facts got in the way. Reagan authorized the sale of arms to Iran because he wanted to free the U.S. hostages in Lebanon. The public was horrified.

The public didn't believe the cover story of efforts to contact "Iranian moderates," a story they had heard from Reagan's own lips. Three weeks later came the news that some of the money had been diverted to the contras and a substantial portion of the public didn't believe Reagan's insistence that he had known nothing about that. The only defense for the White House was to portray the president as being totally in the dark, a ploy that exposed Reagan's style of nonmanagement so glaringly that like vile medicine for a tapeworm it was a cure almost worse than the disease. The public began to focus on Reagan flaws, which it had chosen to ignore before the roof fell in and the plaster stuck.

In the summer of 1985, when Robert C. McFarlane, then Reagan's national security adviser, brought him the idea of secretly enlisting Iran's help in the hostage situation, Reagan began thinking with his heart, not his head. That year Reagan met twice with relatives of the hostages. They pleaded with him to do something to bring their loved ones home. At the same time, the CIA was desperately casting about for a way to free its station chief in Lebanon, William Buckley, who was among the hostages. Reagan responded in a personal way typical of him. If the cloak and dagger aspects of the plan might have put off another man, they probably attracted Reagan, who loves the military, the covert operation, the derring-do—just like in the movies.

The thought of McFarlane and Lt. Col. Oliver North of the National Security Council staff flying into Iran on crates of military equipment did not raise a warning flag in his mind. It probably thrilled him. It is true that some influential advisers tried to dissuade the president, among them Shultz and Weinberger. But Reagan's belief in his own rightness and in his own luck were clearly at work.

The fact that Reagan went ahead notwithstanding the objections of such senior cabinet officers also provides telling commentary on the way he and, to some extent, all recent presidents lean on those who have the greatest access, not necessarily those who have the most experience. The people with the office down the hall tend to be listened to more than those who hang their hats across town. McFarlane saw the president almost every day, as did his successor,

Vice Admiral John Poindexter; Shultz and Weinberger saw him perhaps once a week.

And how could Reagan square in his own mind his frequent rhetoric about never making concessions to kidnappers with his decision to try to get the hostages out by selling arms to Iran? Reagan has always operated on two levels, like most politicians, the one of public rhetoric, the other of practical policy. Reagan the public figure projects an image of macho toughness on such matters as concessions to terrorists. But when other, stronger considerations weigh on him, he is capable of bending his public position in order to satisfy them.

For instance, in the name of his fierce anti-communism, he urged U.S. allies in 1982 not to give subsidized help to the Soviets in building a natural gas pipeline to western Europe even though the allies wanted the gas. But when it seemed helpful to American farmers in advance of Election Day in 1986 to offer the sale of subsidized grain to the Soviets, why Reagan had no problem in doing that. So, once embarked on a course to free the hostages, he had no problem in fudging his own arms embargo or his stated policy of not making deals for hostages.

The way Reagan reacted when the bottom fell out of the scheme is also typical of him. His first response was to deny everything. When asked at a photo opportunity about the matter, he complained about the speculation concerning "a story from the Middle East which to us has no foundation. . . ." No foundation? His second response was to blame the American press for picking up, pursuing, and publishing the story. Harmful, hurtful, unwarranted speculation was his cry, putting forward, as so many of his predecessors had on other occasions, the illogical and insupportable contention that one should blame the messenger rather than the message and seemingly unaware that "truth will out." You simply can't keep the lid on something once it is published. Finally, having been forced by the mounting clamor to admit that he had, indeed, authorized shipments of arms to Iran, he responded by attempting to deny the obvious link with the hostages' release and other aspects of the story. In the exchange of American reporter Nicholas Daniloff for Soviet spy Gennadi Zakharov, Reagan insisted that a trade was not a trade. In revising judgment on his Iceland summit, he insisted that a failure was not a failure. So, in this case, after acknowledging that one of the side benefits of shipping arms to Iran was the release of U.S. hostages, the president insisted that a ransom was not a ransom. What's more, he probably believed it! Whereas many presidents try to rewrite the facts in an effort to convince the public, when Reagan tries it he seems to have the ability to convince himself. That's how he reconciles ideological rhetoric with more pragmatic action. Some wag once observed that Reagan could probably pass a lie detector test on any subject because he always believes what he says. Words to him do not seem to have a fixed meaning as defined by a good English dictionary; rather, they seem to be flexible "tools" that he uses to do the job of the moment.

Reagan's Hollywood career was built on using words to project a fictional scene, an emotion, a feeling as defined by the script's author. Like any good actor, he puts himself into the story line, he believes it, and he says it. Thus, new taxes proposed in 1982 are not called taxes but "revenue enhancers," U.S. servicemen killed in a barracks bombing in Lebanon as they slept are not called victims but "heroes." In the press conference Reagan held on November 19, 1986, when he was asked repeatedly about a third country's involvement in his sale of arms to Iran, he repeatedly denied any knowledge. Told that his chief of staff Donald Regan had confirmed the fact on the record, he replied, "No, I've, I never heard Mr. Regan say that and I'll ask him about that . . ." Regan and the president's other principal advisers, watching on television, knew that wouldn't fly. A few minutes after the press conference ended, a White House statement was issued in the president's name acknowledging that a third country had indeed been involved. Why had Reagan misstated the facts? Because he didn't want to identify the third country as Israel and to him, the use of words to deflect the questions was not telling a lie; it was simply playing out the scene that he—the scriptwriter in this case—wanted to project.

But of course, the Iranian arms sale story isn't fiction. The administration officials knocked down by the exploding land mines in this drama won't get up when the day's shooting is over. It's too bad the crises happened because in the first six years of his presidency Reagan had written a new chapter in the art of political leadership; if you like his ideology and policies you couldn't have asked for a better captain to lead the charge. Reagan used Teddy Roosevelt's "bully pulpit" brilliantly to restore confidence and pride, not bad things for a person or a country to have. He told us it was "morning in America" and in believing him, we came a long way toward making it so. Furthermore, no matter what one thinks of Reagan's policies, after six years of his presidency the country as a whole wasn't doing badly on the surface. There had been a strong economic recovery, the longest period of prosperity since World War II, which may or may not have come from "voodoo" magic, but so what? World oil prices plunged. The stock market went up. Inflation went down. The Soviets were still troublesome but manageable; Reagan's fans argue *more* manageable because of his defense buildup.

There is a temptation to attribute all the good things that have happened under Reagan to outside forces and to luck. Reagan is lucky. And there is a temptation to point to the dry rot of budget deficits and a continuing arms race as looming tidal waves about to engulf us quite apart from the impact of the Iranian arms sale scandal. The problems are there and the "morning after" may be awful. But to try to deny Reagan the credit for the good things that came about after he took office is to deny logic and fairness. Unhappily for Reagan, the mishaps in late 1986 have drained much of the joyful feeling from his presidency as it draws to a close. In Reagan's Hollywood, almost all stories had a happy ending. In Washington, as Reagan is discovering, reality can be harsher.

Chapter Seven

COVERING THE PRESIDENT

How often have you watched this scene on television? The president of the United States comes out of the diplomatic entrance of the White House and heads toward a helicopter waiting on the South Lawn. Above the roar of the engines, reporters can be heard shouting such things as, "Do you still believe there will be another summit?" and "What do you think about the budget committee proposals to cut defense spending?"

Ronald Reagan, smiling jovially, cups his hand to his ear indicating that he can't hear the questions. He points to his watch as if late to an appointment. But if he gets a question he wants to answer, his hearing improves dramatically and he finds time, after all, to shout back a reply.

"Yes," he answers, he still believes there will be another summit.

"I don't like them," he says of the latest proposals to cut defense spending.

Then, saluting the marine aide at the foot of the helicopter steps, he waves expansively as if to a crowd (a crowd composed mainly of television cameras, of course) and is gone. Reagan's picture is always on television and sometimes, as in the above scene, you can even sense the presence of reporters. Consequently, it's easy to get the idea that reporters see and question the president frequently, that we watch him conduct the business of his office every day. That was the case in the Carter presidency, but if you think that's the case in the Reagan presidency, you are mistaken. We used to complain about access to Jimmy Carter but compared to access to Ronald Reagan, I was practically one of the Carter family.

Covering Reagan directly is a big problem for reporters. There are news conferences, but very few. In his four years as president, Jimmy Carter held fifty-nine formal, televised news conferences. In his first four years, Ronald Reagan held twenty-six. Sometimes four and five months will go by without one. Reagan and his advisers simply don't like them. And believe it or not, some segments of the press don't like them, either.

Hugh Sidey, *Time* magazine's veteran president watcher, has advocated the abolition of the televised presidential press conference. Sidey said it no longer serves a serious purpose because both sides have come to view it as a gladiator's contest rather than a format for putting important information on the public record.

Sidey is dead wrong. I'll agree, we often don't get a lot of information from Ronald Reagan. But it's the only format we have that allows the public to see presidents for themselves in something other than a precooked White House presentation. Print interviews are valuable, but it isn't the same. And as for considering press conferences a contest, that's nonsense. Reporters are not in competition with presidents. Our job is to ask the questions; his to give the answers. Sidey's complaints aside, the White House staff doesn't like press conferences for another reason. They don't like any situation that they cannot control absolutely. Jimmy Carter was willing to take his chances on fielding questions frequently. Ronald Reagan isn't.

On news conference days, Reagan's staff runs through a dress rehearsal with him, bringing up the obvious questions prompted by the news of the day, suggesting answers that properly describe administration policy. But Reagan is perfectly capable of getting things mixed up when the time comes to deliver those answers. He is forever calling up figures that are wrong, asserting facts that aren't, and rewriting history with wild abandon. During one thirty-minute session in June 1986, Reagan outdid himself in making mistakes. He was asked about a Supreme Court ruling on abortion and delivered an answer on a completely different Supreme Court decision that had nothing to do with abortion. He was asked about a Warsaw Pact proposal to reduce troop strength in Europe and responded by talking about cutting missile strength instead. He was asked about building another space shuttle and replied he thought one should be built, only to have his spokesman assure reporters immediately after the news conference that no decision on that had been made. He assured his listeners that he had not made the decision yet on whether to install cruise missiles in the 131st B-52 (which would put the United States over the SALT II missile limits), only to have his spokesman assure reporters the next day that the decision to do so had in fact been made. "[The president] made it, he signed it," said Larry Speakes, referring to the new SALT II policy announced two weeks before.

It was, perhaps, Reagan's worst press conference to date. Later, some officials tried to blame Reagan's misinformed answers on the SALT II questions on national security adviser John Poindexter. They said he hadn't adequately prepared the president on what to say about it. Imagine, Poindexter gets blamed because Ronald Reagan cannot remember what it was he authorized and signed two weeks before.

On top of the hazard of giving mixed-up answers, even when Reagan can anticipate the questions, there is the hazard of the unanticipated question for which he has not prepared. An unanticipated question can be deadlier than a silver bullet. Consider the one Mary McGrory, the *Washington Post* columnist, asked Reagan at the beginning of 1982. After recalling that he had recently called upon the rich to help the poor in the present economic difficulty, McGrory asked him if he planned to increase his own contributions to charity to set the example.

I have never seen Reagan so uncomfortable. He knew he had a problem. He had begun making public his income tax returns two years previously and he knew that in 1979, on an income of $465,710, he had given exactly $4,108 to charity. In 1980, on an income of $227,968, he had given exactly $3,085 to charity.

Reagan said he realized "that some have noticed what seemed

to be a small percentage of deductions for worthwhile causes" and he said it was going to be true again for his '81 tax return. He said he was one who believed in "tithing—the giving of a tenth," but he had been doing it for a number of years in ways that were not tax deductible. He did not explain how or to whom, although on other occasions he said a minister had once told him if he helped support his big brother Neil, that was charitable in the eyes of the Lord, if not the IRS.

McGrory hasn't been called on since.

Because of the stakes involved in putting Reagan in a situation where he stumbles frequently on live television, the White House tries to exercise tight control over press conferences. Carter held most of his in the afternoon. Reagan holds most of his in the evening. Why? Well, he does have a larger immediate television audience. But the main reason is to prevent the television networks from making their own news judgments on what he has said and how he has said it and putting it on in concentrated and analyzed form on their early evening newscasts. Reagan's advisers know that their boss's genial, father-figure manner can almost always get him through a thirty-minute give and take with a passing grade from his television audience. But if most of the people who see the result of his news conference are getting it on the evening news, they are likely to be treated to a stiff dose, not of Reagan's geniality, but of the substance of his most newsworthy answers. And an attempt at substance can often be Reagan's downfall, so his advisers don't want that.

I sit in the front row at press conferences, along with the reporters from the three wire services (AP, UPI, and Reuters), the other three networks, and selected other major news organizations. Why? Because the White House staff thinks it is to the president's advantage to put the representatives of the news organizations with the largest circulations there, not because we are personally liked. I'm well aware that when the president calls on me, he is not calling on his "old buddy, Sam" without whose question no evening would be complete. He is calling on the reporter from ABC News.

Before he comes out, Reagan looks at a television monitor and inspects the lay of the room. His staff suggests to him reporters who are attending their first press conference or who, for some other reason, the president might wish to call on in addition to the regulars. That can sometimes lead to embarrassing incidents.

Once, Reagan swung around after answering a question, pointed in the general direction of a second-row seat, and said, "Bob. Bob Thompson." There was a problem. Bob Thompson of Hearst News Service had decided at the last minute not to attend. He was watching the press conference at home and said later that he stood up in his living room immediately and waved, saying, "Here I am, Mr. President," but to no avail. Fortunately for all concerned, the reporter sitting in for Bob had enough presence to rise and, without making a fuss over what his name was, ask a question. Later that evening, Reagan called on a second reporter who wasn't there.

Another time, Reagan followed his staff's suggestion and called on the new White House correspondent for *Time* magazine, Barrett Seaman. Unfortunately, Seaman did not have his hand up, in fact he had his head down and was scribbling notes on Reagan's last answer. To make matters worse, the president forgot his name.

"No, right there," said Reagan, waving off an interloper and pointing vigorously at the top of Seaman's head. "Wake up," hissed a nearby reporter, punching the miscreant lightly in the side. "Put your pen down," pleaded Reagan. Seaman's head came up. "I thought you had your hand up," explained the president.

To his credit Seaman, nervous first-timer though he was, got up and asked a pretty good question.

Of course, reporters don't always ask brilliant questions. Disappointing Reagan news conferences are not all the president's fault. Sometimes reporters "worry" one subject past the point of profitable answers at the expense of other important subjects; at other times we fail to follow up key points that need elaboration or clarification. And sometimes we simply waste our questions. Once, someone asked Reagan if he would impart to the American people why they should be thankful for their blessings as Thanksgiving Day approached. I'm not against Thanksgiving, but what a waste of a valuable opportunity. And I once asked Jimmy Carter if he had any plans to sell M-1 battle tanks to Zaire. There had been a suggestion to that effect from a minor administration official, but I could have gotten the answer from the press office on that farfetched idea rather than spend precious time at a presidential news conference on it.

Still, with all the fumbling and stumbling on both sides, news conferences are extremely valuable. But they don't happen every day. And every day there are new questions for the president; which is why, as I said at the beginning of this book, we seize any available moment to shout a question. Why do we shout at that nice man, you ask. The answer is to make ourselves heard, since we are kept such a great distance away.

It wasn't that way with Jimmy Carter. Do you remember us shouting often at Carter? No, you don't, because shouting was unnecessary. When Carter came out of the White House to go to his helicopter, the reporters were lined up along the walkway just a foot or two from his side. Now, we are lined up behind a rope fifty feet away or farther. Why? It is not physical security for the president, of course. The press has never physically attacked a president. It is political security the White House staff wants. And in this pursuit, they misuse the Secret Service.

In the old days, Secret Service agents used to tell reporters and photographers they were glad we were around the president when he moved down an airport fence line or up a sidewalk lined with people. The agents made no secret of the fact they thought we were helping to act as a shield against attack.

We would walk down the streets of Plains, Georgia, surrounding Jimmy Carter, peppering him with questions. Once my son Robert, then eight years old, took it into his head to shake hands with Carter. Robert just darted through the Secret Service ranks and thrust out his paw. Carter shook it without breaking stride. Today, Robert would run the risk of having his hand cut off by an agent's karate chop.

Now, the press has always understood that the agents have a vital job to do. We have tried not to interfere with it. We even understand that the Secret Service must protect a president against harm even when no harm is meant. Once, Mark Knoller of AP radio accidentally hit Jimmy Carter on the nose with his fish pole microphone as he was trying to swing it in closer in order to pick up better quality sound of Carter's answers. After that, when agents insisted we keep the fish poles back a little, we did.

But with the general tightening up of security in the aftermath of John Hinckley, Jr.'s, attempt on Reagan's life, the White House staff has seized the opportunity to use the Secret Service to keep the press back, when physical security is not the issue. Except, of course, when it suits the president's purpose.

In the fall of 1984, Ronald Reagan walked at least a hundred and fifty yards outdoors from his helicopter right past the press area to the door of a high school gymnasium in which he was to speak. That may not strike you as out of the ordinary. But you have to understand that since the assassination attempt, Reagan has almost never walked anywhere in public. If he goes across the street, he is driven in his armored limousine from one curb to the other. When he arrives at a building, his automobile is driven into an underground garage if one is available, and if one isn't, the Secret Service puts up a tent into which it is driven so that when he alights to go inside, no one can see him.

Believe me, walking that distance that day in 1984 was *highly* unusual. But it was not hard to figure out why he did it. A few days before, in his first presidential campaign debate with Walter Mondale in Louisville, Kentucky, Reagan had looked tired and unsteady. Suddenly, the age and health issues were on the front burner. So he decided to walk to show his fitness. And the Secret Service safeguards, tent and all, were momentarily put aside. I couldn't resist asking the presidential party as it walked by why it was suddenly safe for the president to walk outdoors, when it had not been before. But of course all I got for my trouble was dirty looks.

Yes, it is the Secret Service that keeps the press away but on orders from the president and his White House staff. We are permitted to be close enough to see—they want the pictures shown—but not close enough to ask questions in any civilized way. The White House Rose Garden is small enough so that when a ceremony is held that the staff wants covered, we must necessarily be positioned well within hailing distance of Reagan as he enters and exits. Recently, the staff has tried assembling scores of junior White

House employees to stand between reporters and the steps Reagan must use. The theory was if we couldn't see him, we couldn't question him. Wrong.

As he was leaving the Rose Garden in November 1986 after congratulating the world baseball champion New York Mets, I watched the body motion of all these employees as they responded enthusiastically to his passage, sort of like watching the rippling wheat stalks to locate a fleeing deer. As he pulled even I sang out, "Mr. President, are you going to give Congress the facts about Iran, or are you gonna stonewall like the Democrats charge?"

Rising into view as he mounted the steps he borrowed baseball terminology to reply he would "never talk about a no-hitter till it's over," which wasn't much of a reply. But that very afternoon he called the bipartisan congressional leadership to the White House to tell them for the first time he had indeed been selling arms to Iran. When we listened to the videotape we noted something else that I had not heard at the time. Just as the president started to leave the Rose Garden, Vice President Bush, surveying all those loyal employees acting as a barrier, said to him with a chuckle, "You're in luck. I don't see Donaldson anywhere."

A moment later I spoke up. Ah ha, Mr. Vice President, "He who laughs last, laughs best." But, of course, in the public's eye, we don't win. Shouting makes us look bad. I know that. The staff knows that, also, and doesn't mind one bit. But we aren't going to stop trying to do our job just because they make it difficult. We often get answers, even if they are shouted back. Some information is better than no information. But as someone once said, "That's a hell of a way to run a railroad."

There is another way we get access to the president directly. We see and talk to the president of the United States at photo opportunities. And the tug-of-war over this type of access has taken up a considerable amount of energy over the lifespan of the Reagan administration. In fact, it has come to be known as the great photo-op war.

A photo opportunity is just that—a quick ninety seconds or less at the beginning of a meeting or some other occasion involving the president to let photographers take pictures of him in action. Reporters go along to see what the photographers are shooting and to hear what the president may say to his visitors. Since these photo opportunities are not formal occasions—the business of the moment has not begun—we also seize the opportunity to ask the president questions about the day's news. We did this consistently throughout the four years of the Carter administration. We kept on doing it the same way in the early part of the Reagan administration. But a problem soon arose. Reagan's staff moved to limit the practice.

Reagan often makes mistakes in such impromptu sessions, often demonstrates that he doesn't know things. His staff worried that it might reflect badly on him. Once, early on during a photo opportunity, I asked him if it was true that he wanted to cut money from Social Security. He said he didn't know what I was talking about. And when I told him that was on the front page of that morning's *Washington Post*, he replied that he hadn't read the papers yet. Perfectly sensible reply, perhaps, but it was ten o'clock in the morning and his staff worried that people would wonder why he hadn't.

Once, introducing the press to a prize fighter who had just retained his title in a hard fought match and had come along to the White House with his wife to be photographed in the Oval Office, the president said, "I'd like to introduce you to my guests today, Sugar Ray and Mrs. Ray."

"Leonard, sir," I told him.

Another time, he introduced a foreign visitor as Chairman Moe. *He* turned out to be Samuel K. Doe, the president of Liberia.

Mr. Reagan does that sort of thing often. He greeted Singapore Prime Minister Lee Kuan Yew during a White House South Lawn ceremony by saying, "Well, it gives me great pleasure to welcome Prime Minister Lee Kuan Yew and Mrs. Yew [sic] to Singapore." And who can forget that memorable toast during a glittering White House dinner in 1985 to those royal Britannic visitors "Prince Charles and Princess David."

Jimmy Carter was not immune to the same kind of "foot in mouth" disease. He welcomed Golda Meir, then retired as prime minister of Israel, to the Oval Office by inquiring whether she got back home often—to Chicago. "Milwaukee," she murmured, correctly naming the Midwest town where she had once lived and taught school. Carter pressed ahead by telling her she was the same age as his mother.

Now, folks, I don't care how realistic a woman may be about her age, she really doesn't want to hear that. No wonder Carter didn't get along all that well with the Israelis.

And once during a photo opportunity with Michael Blumenthal, his treasury secretary, Carter told him with the press in attendance how badly French officials had treated him when he went to France while governor of Georgia. No wonder Carter didn't get along all that well with the French.

These gaffes are not important, perhaps. Let's face it, every one of us does the same thing on occasion. But a president's staff is never satisfied to have the president's image projected in any way short of perfection. The staff worries about the image when the president makes mistakes, and it also worries when the president is too open with reporters, sharing his innermost and perhaps undiplomatic thoughts with the press.

When Italy's Red Brigade terrorist group kidnapped U.S. Brigadier General James Dozier in 1981 and I asked Reagan about it during a photo opportunity, he replied in his best John Wayne style (*Rambo* had not yet been filmed), "They are cowardly bums . . . they wouldn't have the guts to stand up to anyone individually in any kind of a fair contest . . ." True, perhaps. But how would you like to have been General Dozier, chained to a cot and gagged in the initial hours of your kidnapping, surrounded by desperate criminals, and hear that the president was calling your captors names in public.

When after a few months in office, his off-the-cuff remarks began to be a problem, Reagan's staff suggested that he simply reply to a question by saying, "This is a photo opportunity and I'm not taking any questions." But Reagan bridles at using such a tactic since, like most self-assured individuals, he thinks he can handle himself and it bothers him that he is being asked to hide. Also, he often *wants* to answer the question. So the transcripts of photo opportunities are studded with the president saying, "No questions," only to have him follow up when the next question is asked by saying, "Now, I'll answer just this one," or "I'll answer that."

Once, I said to him, "You can say 'no answers,' sir, but you can't say 'no questions.' "

"No answers," shot back Reagan with a twinkle in his eye. He is a quick study.

Reagan sometimes comes to the press room to read a statement, then almost always begs off questioning by bringing along an expert to answer the questions or simply by saying he doesn't have time to stay. We start asking him questions anyway. He sidesteps off the platform, hands out in supplication, answering some, dodging some, until he reaches the safety of the door. And when he does answer questions in the press room, his staff is ever alert to cut them off if he gets in trouble.

One morning in February 1983, the president found himself in heavy seas as he took questions in the press room. He was mixing apples and oranges in a failing attempt to demonstrate that his proposed military spending wasn't as much as that projected in the final days of the Carter administration. He was digging himself in deeper and deeper when suddenly Nancy Reagan came through the door carrying a birthday cake. Actually, she was all but pushed through the door by then communications director David Gergen, who was determined to save the president from drowning in a sea of funny military spending figures.

Well, you should have seen what happened next. Perhaps you did, since all the networks had been carrying the mini-news conference live and were trapped into staying on the air. The candles were blown out. The cake was cut. Mrs. Reagan offered me the first piece. "Now, now," I said, laughing. "I won't sell out for a piece of cake."

"You've sold out for a lot less," shot back the president, neatly ending any lingering thought that we might get back to serious business.

When there's no birthday cake around, the president has other ways to ward off questions, or at least answers, beginning with his patented ability to deliver humorous one-liners.

He'll turn aside a serious question with a joke. His one-liners are usually funny and reporters, naturally, laugh. Funny or not, it's difficult to say, "Now, hold on, Mr. President, this is important, stop clowning around." Even I haven't been able to bring myself to do that.

In 1984, I told him, "[Walter Mondale] says you're intellectually lazy and you're forgetful. He says you're providing 'leadership by amnesia.' "

Reagan rose to the moment. "I'm surprised he knew what the word meant," he replied with a grin, effectively undercutting the substance of the charge.

My favorite Reagan one-liner also involved Mondale. It occurred in the fall of '84, as he was leaving the Rose Garden after some ceremony, dodging and weaving away from questions about the campaign, when Andrea Mitchell of NBC yelled, "What about Mondale's charges?"

"He ought to pay them," said the president, ducking out of range.

When he went to Grenada, where he was hailed as "a national hero," Reagan gracefully turned aside the title when I offered it. "How does it feel to be here and be hailed as the hero of Grenada?" I asked him as he stood with nine leaders from friendly Caribbean nations on the steps of Governor's House.

"Sam, don't embarrass me," he replied.

"But this is the scene of your greatest military triumph, sir," I persisted.

"I didn't fire a shot," quipped Reagan.

Those snappy one-liners don't always make it, however. Told that Nicaraguan leader Daniel Ortega had accused him of having taken leave of his senses, Reagan responded, "It takes one to know one." Tilt! The next time someone accuses you of being an idiot, do not reply, "It takes one to know one."

Another way Reagan turns aside sticky questions about a controversial policy or difficult issue is by implying he is not really involved in it. I call this the "who, me?" tactic.

A perfect example of the "who, me?" tactic came up during that same photo opportunity on the steps of Grenada's Governor's House. Sugar is an important export crop in many Caribbean nations, and restrictive new quotas on sugar imports to protect U.S. domestic sugar growers do not sit well with these nations. I asked Reagan, as the other leaders looked on, if the new U.S. sugar allowances weren't upsetting to the other leaders.

"The farm bill did that," said Reagan with the tone of a man who is confidently reporting to the sheriff that it was a lightning bolt from the heavens that burned down his neighbor's barn, the smell of gasoline on his clothes notwithstanding.

"You signed it, sir," I told him. The audio tape has some muffled words on it at this point that sound like one of the other leaders whispering, "He's got you now," but I can't be sure.

What Reagan did next was to bring up his ultimate defense in twisting away from a hard question; that is, to launch a reply so totally confused or irrelevant as to render the listener transfixed, as if from a lobotomy. It's the political equivalent of laying smoke and escaping through the haze.

So when reminded that *he* had signed the farm bill, Reagan replied, "We're dealing with all these problems," leaving unclear whether he meant the problem of getting Congress to revise the sugar quotas or, perhaps, the problem of his signing things. In any event, absolutely nothing could be made of it and if, in fact, one of the Caribbean leaders had mumbled, "He's got you now," he had spoken way too soon.

Once at a news conference, however, I put it to the president that he personally might have been responsible for something bad, and he admitted it straight out. "Mr. President," said I in the fall of 1982. "In talking about the continuing recession tonight, you have blamed the mistakes of the past and you've blamed the Congress. Does any of the blame belong to you?"

"Yes," said he. "Because for many years I was a Democrat." Exit Ronald Reagan, soft shoe, stage left, to gales of laughter, including my own.

Another time, when Reagan came under heavy fire at a photo opportunity he was saved by British prime minister Margaret Thatcher, who demonstrated to me why her nickname of Iron Lady is well deserved. It was at the economic summit at Versailles in 1982. The press was ushered in to the palace dining room, where the summit leaders were lunching. Naturally, I seized the occasion to ask some questions.

The night before at the United Nations, the Security Council had voted on a resolution asking Britain to negotiate the sovereignty of the Falkland Islands with Argentina. Britain and Argentina were at that moment at war over the islands and Britain expected the United States to vote no. Instead, we abstained and the British were reported to be furious.

I asked the president why we had abstained. You always take a chance that he won't know what you're talking about when you ask Reagan something of an immediate nature. And sure enough he replied that he didn't have all that information, but if we had abstained, he wanted to point out that it was not the same thing as voting against Britain.

I followed up by telling him the British were reported to be furious that we had abstained instead of joining them in a veto of the resolution. Reagan just shook his head and made a "what more can I say" gesture with his hands.

I then turned to Mrs. Thatcher, who had been watching all this with a frozen smile. "You're not angry with the president, you're not angry, ma'am?" I asked.

She cut me off with a stiletto. "I don't give interviews at lunchtime," she replied.

The most disastrous questioning of Reagan from the standpoint of his image came in the summer of 1984. It wasn't that Reagan said something wrong or crazy—on the contrary. What he said was perfectly reasonable. The trouble was, his wife was caught coaching him, and while that is not a federal crime, it gave ammunition to those who believe that Reagan can't go out without a keeper.

The two of them stood in front of their California ranch house. Charles Bierbauer of Cable News Network pressed the president as to how he was going to get the Russians back to the negotiating table in Geneva. As Reagan thought about it, the First Lady, standing by his side, dropped her head so her lips could not be seen and murmured, "Doing everything we can."

In a flash, Reagan found his voice. "We're doing everything we can," he said triumphantly. This blatant plagiarism might have gone unnoticed were it not for the fact the CNN microphone was close enough to pick up the First Lady's murmur.

For the record, Mrs. Reagan denies she meant to coach her

husband. "You know what I was doing, I was talking to myself," she explained to me a few days later.

I've told a lot of stories here about Reagan fumbles during photo opportunities and how his staff has wanted to curtail the questioning to minimize their impact. But there is another and perhaps more important reason the staff has wanted to discourage questions at photo opportunities. It is their desire to manage the news that comes out of the White House. They want to maintain tight control of the information reporters have to work with.

On October 12, 1982, the White House's principal deputy press secretary coined a slogan that has become the hallmark of press operations in the Reagan administration. Said Speakes, "You don't tell us how to stage the news, and we won't tell you how to cover it."

Staging the news is of great importance to the Reagan White House, some would argue, of great importance to Reagan's success. The staff meets every morning to decide what they want to be "the story of the day" from the White House. Then they let the press in at presidential appointments or gatherings that lend themselves to that "story" and keep the press away from those that don't. This forces television into a choice of airing the pictures and words they let us see and hear or not having any White House pictures that day. We can always put on a story without them, but pictures are our main commodity—and the staff knows it.

Now, you can understand that if the press is allowed to see the president with his foreign policy advisers because that is the approved "story of the day" and some reporter gets him to answer questions about the stock market collapse, the "story of the day" is blown. And if the president fumbles around in his answers on the stock market, why, those underhanded jackals of the press have got themselves a "two-fer."

In the first term of the Reagan administration, the keeper of the presidential image was deputy chief of staff Michael K. Deaver, the California public relations man who had helped fashion the president's media campaigns for years. Actually, Deaver had two responsibilities. One was to devise ways to use and reinforce the president's positive image and communications skills so as to further his interests; the other was to be the conduit through which Nancy Reagan's wishes for her husband were carried out.

It was Deaver who surveyed and approved the setting for the president's moving speech at Pointe du Hoc on the fortieth anniversary of D day. Deaver selected the spot where the president was to stand, looking over the steep cliff that the rangers had climbed back on June 6, 1944, a spot just right for the camera angles. It was Deaver who placed veterans of that day in the audience so the president could say so movingly: "These are the boys of Pointe du Hoc. These are the men who took the cliffs. These are the champions who helped free a continent. These are the heroes who helped end a war."

The scene brought tears to your eyes, as written by speech writer Peggy Noonan, directed by Michael K. Deaver, and delivered by Ronald Reagan.

It was Deaver who checked the spot where red tape marked the president's place on the observation deck of the advance post in Korea's demilitarized zone, enabling Reagan to look into North Korea with the cameras catching him just right. This scene made Reagan look strong and tough.

It was Deaver who blocked the shots and stage-managed the programs for the Reagan 1980 and '84 election campaigns. By his own admission, he knew little about the issues. But he knew a lot about how to project and protect the president's image. And he took care of Mrs. Reagan's wishes for her husband, also.

If Mrs. Reagan, looking out an upstairs White House window one day, was horrified to see those scruffy-looking news technicians sunning themselves on the lawn outside the press room, it was Deaver who caused a black chain and ivy bed to be set in place, barring the way and thus cleaning up the neighborhood. And after the first 1984 presidential campaign debate in Louisville, at which Reagan had stumbled so, it was Deaver who got the angry call from the First Lady, demanding, "What have you done to Ronnie?"

It was natural therefore that Deaver and not James Baker, the chief of staff, or Edwin Meese, the counselor and third member of the original big three advisers, should shield the president from reporters by cutting off the questioning at photo opportunities.

Naturally, he didn't say it was to protect the president's image or to protect the White House designated "story of the day." He complained that the questioning was undignified and obtrusive, particularly when a foreign visitor was present.

First, he tried sending the message that reporters who persisted in asking questions would be barred from the room. We television correspondents sent back word that if we were barred, we wouldn't send our cameras to cover the event. "No reporters, no cameras," was our rallying cry. Deaver of course wanted the cameras, so we stayed in.

Next, he had Larry Speakes begin a drumbeat of criticism, both publicly and privately, complaining that we were destroying the decorum of important state occasions, if not Western civilization in its entirety. After a February 1982 photo opportunity in the Oval Office with Reagan and Egyptian president Hosni Mubarak, Speakes accused me of creating an international incident. What had I done? As the two men sat there saying nothing while the cameras recorded the scene, I had simply asked Reagan, "Is Cuba getting dangerous again?" The morning papers had carried front page stories about then Secretary of State Haig's disclosure that Cuba had received a second shipment of Soviet MIG-23 war planes. Haig said it was part of a Cuban design to project its military power. Speakes said my question was embarrassing to both presidents and had created an international incident.

"White House Threatens to Ban Press in Oval Office," screamed the banner headline in the final edition of the *Los Angeles Times*, with a sub headline, "Question for President Stirs Flap." An old picture of me at a political convention with an antenna sticking out of my headgear assaulted the reader's frightened eyes.

Now, really. If I had chosen the moment of Mubarak's visit to ask of Reagan why there are so many pictures of him campaigning with a yarmulke on his head but never a fez, I could see Speakes's point. But Cuba?

Finally, in an effort to cut down photo-op questioning Deaver had a brainstorm. He had Speakes and communications director David Gergen summarily inform the network bureau chiefs that the rules had changed, and henceforth, only one broadcast correspondent, rotating daily by organization, would be allowed to attend the photo ops. Naturally, all cameras would still be welcome. The bureau chiefs took it to their bosses. Roone Arledge backed me in the "no Sam, no ABC camera" stand. CBS also stood firm. But NBC collapsed immediately. One of its top executives at the time was reported to have said flatly, "We need the pictures." NBC sent in its camera without its correspondent. In a few days, CBS followed suit. ABC held out for two weeks and then, on my recommendation, we surrendered. Deaver had us.

So now, a small pool of reporters covers these photo opportunities. The broadcast-reporter slot in this pool rotates, not just among the major news networks, but among all the multistation television and radio organizations that cover the White House, eleven of them at this writing. Many days, there is no tough questioning, just as Deaver planned it. On other days, we try to get through all the defenses but get shut out.

The most effective shut-out in the Oval Office came one day, not from Reagan, but from his visitor, Andrei Gromyko, then the Soviet foreign minister. I would have given a lot to have been the pool reporter for the Oval Office that day in September 1984. But it was Jeff Kamen, a reporter from Independent Network News.

Gromyko was a sourpuss. They called him the Great Stone Face. He never answered questions from the press. He would always say, "Next time I will answer a thousand questions." He would always say that, but next time never arrived.

Kamen gave it his best shot, asking Gromyko if he thought progress could be made at the meeting. "Too early to tell," said Gromyko in guttural English. "I'm sure president would agree, too early to tell, too early to say, conversations have not yet begun."

"Are you hopeful?" Kamen pressed.

Gromyko replied forcefully, "I am hopeful . . ." and at this point he gestured stiffly toward Kamen, dropped his voice, and muttered a word or two more that couldn't be clearly made out. The press was excused. Kamen was a hero. Gromyko had actually answered a question, however innocuous the answer. The Associated Press ran a story on its wire, slugged "urgent," to the effect that Gromyko was "hopeful" at the outset of his talks with Reagan.

Then we all listened more carefully to the tape. The press had lost again. What Gromyko had actually said to Kamen at the end of his sentence was: "I am hopeful *that you stop*!"

That, of course, is the hope that Reagan's aides always have when reporters begin asking questions. And when we don't stop, the staff has been known to step in forcefully.

In the summer of 1984, as part of his election year strategy, Reagan's aides devised a campaign to cast him as a great friend of the environment and conservation, a status not supported by the record. But as usual, the PR-minded Deaver apparatus had no intention of arguing the record. They intended to sell Reagan as the greatest conservationist since Teddy Roosevelt by staging a series of photo opportunities (yes, one of them was at the base of Teddy's statue on Roosevelt Island in the Potomac River). The Reagan White House has truly taken that old adage "one picture is worth a thousand words" and converted it to its own saying, "One picture is worth a thousand *facts*."

They might have gotten away with it, too, if it hadn't been for an extraordinary lapse in timing. A couple of days before the Mr. Conservationist campaign got under way, the White House announced that Anne Burford had been appointed to head the National Advisory Committee on Oceans and Atmosphere, a little-known and largely ceremonial presidential committee on the environment.

Anne Burford, who had been forced to resign in 1983 as director of the Environmental Protection Agency under heavy fire from environmentalists, conservationists, the Congress, the courts, holy rollers, and right-thinking Americans everywhere, was the last person in the world you wanted to be associated with if you were selling yourself as Reagan the environmentalist.

But there it was—the press office had slipped up in not withholding that routine announcement for a few days. And as we all know, timing is everything. So when Reagan went to the Blackwater National Wildlife Refuge, on Maryland's eastern shore, reporters were ready with the embarrassing questions. The president watched a presentation about eagles and other birds, then got up to leave.

"Sir, do you think this will limit the damage done by the Burford appointment?" I sang out.

Larry Speakes yelled, "Lights," a signal, indeed an order, to the lighting technician to cut the candlepower so the video cameras couldn't make a picture. The technician didn't move fast enough.

I asked the president for an answer. Speakes stepped in front of the president and thrust his hand, fingers splayed wide, into the ABC camera lens. "My guardian says I can't talk," explained the president of the United States.

A chorus of protests came from reporters; my own contribution was to admonish Speakes that the president was a grown man and could take care of himself. Reagan, observing this melee with a growing lack of enthusiasm, decided the better part of valor was to answer the question. "Frankly, I don't think there should be any thought of damage"—at that instant, the lighting technician managed to get his hands on the cord and plunged the room into near darkness—"about the Burford appointment," the president concluded from the gloom.

That night, on the evening news broadcast I ran the whole sequence, from question to stiff arm to darkness. It was beautiful.

Every time I tell this story of how difficult it has become for reporters to cover the president of the United States directly, Jody Powell replies with a touch of bitterness, "Jimmy Carter answered your questions every day, and look what happened to him." Yes, Carter got hit by a train, but Powell is wrong if he thinks the press corps was driving the engine. Carter's own mistakes and bad luck as perceived by the public did him in, not the messengers. Reagan and his aides are always preaching the gospel "Trust the American people," but when it comes right down to it, what they practice suggests they don't trust the public to see Ronald Reagan in action unless he's on the same carefully prepared sound stage that he worked on for so long in Hollywood.

Chapter Eight

PRESS ROOM WARS

The White House day for me usually begins at about 9:00 A.M. In the Carter years, I'd get there an hour or so earlier. You could usually scratch around Jody Powell's office and pick up a little news. But news is much more rigidly controlled now, and coming in early doesn't often pay off.

The press room is built over President Franklin Roosevelt's old indoor swimming pool. When Richard Nixon took office, he didn't like the fact that reporters sitting in the lobby of the West Wing could spot and talk to every visitor who came in. So he had the swimming pool covered over and built a press room there. It may have been large enough for Nixon's day, but it's terribly cramped now. At busy times, reporters pick their way over video cameras and sound gear, trying to find a seat in the briefing room. Still photographers climb all over everyone trying to get a clear shot.

The network booths in the back of the room were built to house two people. We all now have at least four people there. In the fall of 1986, you would have found the three ABC White House correspondents—Sheilah Kast, Kenneth Walker, and me—sitting practically hip to hip in front of a narrow countertop on which were a typewriter, two word processors, a computer printer, newspapers, press releases, letters, half-empty coffee cups, and assorted junk. In the shelves just above could be found the digests of presidential papers, books, office supplies, makeup kits, a television set, a radio, press releases, letters, empty coffee cups, and assorted junk. In a small glassed-in closet, you would have found a radio engineer huddled over his gear ready to pipe back reports. None of the networks has ever assigned a fat person to the White House beat and now you know why they never will.

In this situation, of course, it is hard to work and there is certainly no privacy. Every reporter I've ever known loves to gossip—it's the nature of our business to seek and trade information—but I've told all the correspondents who have worked with me that we must not discuss each other's private business, which we can't help but overhear. When the bill collector, the ex-wife, the distraught child, or the angry boss calls, we hold each other hostage in not repeating the gossip. So far, all of my colleagues have respected this need. I reserve final judgment, of course, until I read *their* books.

At 9:15 A.M., the morning press briefing is held in the press room. A second daily briefing is held there at noon. During most of the first six years of the Reagan administration, these briefings were presided over by Larry Speakes, the principal deputy press secretary, who took over the top press job if not the title when his immediate boss, Jim Brady, was wounded in the 1981 assassination attempt on Ronald Reagan. Speakes, like all press secretaries, saw his job first and foremost as one of advancing the president's interests. To the extent that that meant passing on information to the press and answering reporter's questions, he did it. To the extent that it meant withholding information and not answering reporters' questions, he tried to do that. And we reporters, of course, tried to get him to tell it all. Or if not tell it all, at least make it clear that he wasn't.

Speakes had certain techniques he used in trying to duck questions. He belittled the questioner. He attempted to set print reporters against broadcast reporters. He debated the need to even ask questions on a particularly sore subject. He pretended any fool "with two grains of sense," as he put it, knew the answer without his having to deliver it. He was very adroit, the admiring view would be "good," at imparting only that information he wanted to impart but no more.

If you asked him who the president had in mind when he said enemies of freedom must be strongly opposed—was it the Democrats on Capitol Hill?—Speakes would reply sagely, "They know who they are." Ask him to explain what the president meant by declaring he couldn't exactly say how he would react to an oil import fee, Speakes would reply earnestly, "He meant exactly what he said." And once when pressed as to how Reagan knew he was making progress on something, Speakes lifted his eyes toward the heavens and answered with a grin, "The moon."

Jody Powell could also dodge and weave with the best of them. My favorite example involving Powell came one day when we were trying to check a published report that President Carter in a meeting with the late Senator James Eastland had made certain promises about judgeships. Eastland was then the chairman of the judiciary committee, which had the first congressional say about judgeships. Powell first said he was certain that in the meeting with Eastland the president had not made any promises. But, asked Jody cautiously, what was Senator Eastland's recollection? We told him that Eastland denied there had been a meeting at all. That, said Powell with obvious relish and relief, was, upon reflection, the president's recollection also.

Powell, of course, was more than a press secretary. He was a principal adviser of Carter's. His access was without parallel, and you have to go back to the days when James Hagerty served President Eisenhower to find a press secretary who felt so confident in speaking for his boss.

Once I went up to Powell's office to find out what Carter was going to do about something or other. "I don't know," said Powell. "Just a minute, I'll ask him." Whereupon he got up, went down to the president's study off the Oval Office, asked him, came back, and told me. Now, that's service.

Mind you, Powell didn't always tell me what I wanted to know. But he was pretty good about not stone-walling as a matter of routine practice.

There is no requirement that a press secretary volunteer information out of the blue about things. Ask Powell or Speakes or any other press secretary the question "What's new today?" and he is under no obligation to tell you, even though there may be fifty things new. Ask him a specific question about a specific subject, and the transaction gets more complicated.

When the Chinese leader Deng Xiaoping made his visit to the United States in 1979, everyone speculated that he would stop off in San Clemente to see Richard Nixon. Every day, as the visit grew nearer, we'd ask Powell about that possibility. Every day he would say he knew of no plans for Deng to make such a stop.

One night shortly before our air time, the light bulb went off in my head. If Deng wasn't going to go to Nixon, might Nixon be planning to come to Deng? I found Powell. "Jody," I said, "is Richard Nixon invited to the state dinner here at the White House for Deng?" Powell could have said, "No comment," but I guess he figured I was smart enough to know that any answer he gave except no meant yes. "Yes," said Powell, and I ran off to deliver my little scoop.

What a press secretary must not do is lie. He can evade if necessary. We won't like that, but we will all fight again another day. Lie, and you're through.

Larry Speakes almost got in trouble on this vital point in the Grenada invasion. The night before U.S. troops landed on Grenada, Bill Plante of CBS got a tip from someone in the intelligence community who told him an invasion of Grenada was going to take place the next morning. It turns out a Barbados newspaper was suggesting the same thing on its front page that day, but who in the White House press room knew what they were printing in Barbardos?

As Plante tells the story, he went to Speakes with his tip and asked him, "Are we going to invade Grenada tomorrow morning?" Speakes laughed at what he thought was a silly question but at Plante's urging took the inquiry to Rear Admiral John Poindexter, then the number two man on the staff of the national security council, later a vice admiral and Reagan's national security adviser. Poindexter told Speakes to "knock it down hard," to say it was "preposterous." Speakes reported that to Plante, who so advised his office. The next morning, the U.S. invaded Grenada.

Most of us were convinced that Speakes was honestly passing on what he believed to be the truth. I can't say the same for Admiral Poindexter. Poindexter knows what he's saying when he twists the truth. Consider what happened during the first days of the Iranian arms story. On November 4, 1986, coming back from California to Washington aboard *Air Force One*, those of us in the press pool were pressing Speakes to respond to initial reports that the United States had sold arms to Iran. Speakes would not comment. When we asked him if the U.S. arms embargo against Iran was still in effect, he still would not comment. I told him his "no comment" would surely be taken as a strong signal that the policy had changed, which would, in turn, be seen as an indirect confirmation of the story of an arms shipment. He said he understood and disappeared forward on the airplane. Three hours later, Speakes was back to read a statement he told us had been written not by him, but by national security adviser Poindexter. The statement read in its operative part: "As long as Iran advocates the use of terrorism, the U.S. arms embargo will remain in effect. . . ."

Wouldn't you take that to mean that the United States had not been shipping arms to Iran? Just to make sure, I asked Speakes if the arms embargo was in effect at the moment. "Yes," he replied. And has our view concerning Iran's advocacy of the use of terrorism changed? "No," he replied. All right, that seemed to square the circle. But, of course, it had not. Poindexter clearly had meant to mislead. He clearly had wanted that statement to be taken as a denial of the arms shipment story without actually denying it. It is typical of Poindexter's belief that the end justifies the means and when the means has to be an untruth, so be it. It was Poindexter's shadow that fell across the infamous "disinformation" campaign the administration launched in the summer of 1986 against Libya's Muammar Qaddafi. If the issue was simply one of deceiving Qaddafi by spreading false information, that would be one thing. But in knowingly disseminating untruths through the public press in the name of fooling Qaddafi, the American public was deceived as well. Now, as the old saying goes, "Truth is the first casualty of war."

But some of the Reagan crowd don't wait for war to dispense with the truth, apparently in the belief that a policy decision by Reagan justifies the use of any means to carry it out. That attitude is not only wrong, it is dangerous, particularly when it comes to the use of U.S. military force.

After Secretary of State Shultz complained during Reagan's first term that reporters always seem to be "against us" and "try to screw things up," I asked the president whether he agreed with Shultz's view. He replied that at sometime beginning with the Korean conflict and certainly in the Vietnam conflict it did seem to him there was more criticism leveled at our own forces and what we were trying to do than at the enemy. I followed up by suggesting that the problem in accusing reporters of being "against us" may lie in defining the word "us."

"Is 'us' the administration in power, or is there a higher duty that the press has?" I asked him. Reagan, looking genuinely puzzled, replied, "I thought the 'us' [Shultz] was talking about was our side militarily. In other words, all of America."

It is easy to understand how presidents can get it in their heads that to question their policies is to question "all of America." But they are wrong. It was Lyndon Johnson who escalated U.S. involvement in the Vietnam War, not Uncle Sam, and it was not un-American for the press to report the bad results that that policy produced. It is Ronald Reagan who pursued a vigorous policy aimed at overthrowing the Sandinista government of Nicaragua, or aimed at bringing down Qaddafi, not "all of America."

When U.S. forces invaded Grenada, the press was kept out until the action was over. Why? Government officials gave two reasons: 1) to keep the operation secret so as not to endanger the lives of service personnel, and 2) to keep the press from getting hurt. Both those stated reasons were artful dodges. No reporter suggested the press should have been told in advance of the invasion so that the word could be spread publicly. The press wanted to go along to see the operation unfold, not to talk about it in advance. And as for the danger, the press has always been willing to take its chances in covering wars and we would have done so again on Grenada.

The fact is, "our forces," as Secretary Shultz put it, didn't want the press there to see the mistakes that invariably occur in combat and didn't want television there to show the bloody side of war as it had in Vietnam. The military fervently believes that the American public must be spared the gruesome details of what happens when people set out to kill each other. Out of regard for the public's sensibilities? Oh, no. Out of fear that the public will intervene in the policy directing the war. I have heard sophisticated men in government service complain about how the sights of war brought into the living room make it so difficult for presidents to promulgate and carry on a war policy (as if somehow the American people are a bothersome interloper when it comes to the smart guys being able to do what they think best). Most reporters profoundly disagree. That is why when government officials attempt to carry out a policy that involves disinformation to the American public, no matter how well intentioned that policy may be, they will find they are "walking on the fighting side" of me. And of former Assistant Secretary of State for Public Affairs Bernard Kalb. Kalb, who had spent years as a CBS and NBC diplomatic correspondent, had taken the job of department spokesman in November of 1984. When the Libyan disinformation story broke, he read about it in the newspapers; he had not been part of the scheme nor had his boss, Secretary Shultz. But he felt so deeply that it was wrong that he resigned in protest. "Anything that hurts America's credibility hurts America," he said. Right on, Bernie.

An official can say, "No comment," "I have nothing for you on that," or dozens of other things that do not confirm a story but do not tell a falsehood, either. Reporters may guess all they want when they get a "No comment," but we do not report guesses.

When people ask me how to get a favorable story, I tell them that you can't bribe me, you can't intimidate me, you may be able to bamboozle me (but when I find out about it, I'll be mad as hell), but you can get the best story possible by taking me seriously and leveling with me. And usually, it is far better to tell the press what you can if you want to avoid a bad story. A perfect example of this came in the summer of 1985 and had to do with Reagan's colon cancer operation.

One Friday afternoon, Reagan checked into the hospital for a routine surgical procedure to remove a small benign intestinal polyp. During the course of an examination, another, larger polyp was found and doctors scheduled major surgery for the next morning.

It was a tense time. The next morning at a briefing carried live by all the networks, watched by millions, Speakes announced that Reagan's surgery had begun. Then he said, as if in passing, that press office aides were going to hand out copies of a letter to the vice president from the president having to do with a transfer of duties.

This was important. Had the president turned over power to the vice president, as provided for in the Twenty-fifth Amendment to the Constitution? Had the president resigned? What was in the letter? Speakes refused to say. Read it yourself and make of it what you will, he told us and the millions of television viewers tuned in at that moment.

It's not unusual for the press office to hand out statements and other pieces of paper at a briefing to be read later. But at this briefing there was no later. The television networks were all live.

I appealed to Speakes to read the letter, reminding him that millions of people who had no idea what it was all about were watching. He refused, insisting that the briefing proceed. So, remaining seated, I turned to the ABC camera and read the pertinent portion of the letter aloud, explaining that it appeared to be a turning over of power under the Twenty-fifth Amendment. In another moment, Bill Plante of CBS and Chris Wallace of NBC read the letter aloud to their audiences.

While we were doing this, Speakes started complaining that he couldn't carry on a briefing if the television reporters insisted on interrupting it by reading the letter. He said this all reminded him of an Amal news conference, referring to the Shiite Muslim group that had held the passengers from the hijacked TWA 847 airliner a few weeks earlier.

Egged on by Speakes, print reporters started booing us and demanding that we shut up. It was an awful scene. And totally unnecessary. Why didn't Speakes read the letter for the television audience? I'm not sure I'll ever really understand that. It's been explained to me that the staff, sensitive about the president's relinquishing of power, with all the real and public relations ramifications involved, wanted to minimize the transfer. It's like saying, "We've done this, but we don't want you to make too much of it."

The way not to make too much of something is to explain it, not throw it over the transom and run for cover. That incident set the stage for the worst fight I ever had with Speakes. It came a few weeks later over the matter of the president's skin cancer and the attempt to conceal it.

One day, shortly after Reagan returned to work following his intestinal surgery, reporters noticed a small bandage on his nose. What was it, we asked. We were told that a small patch of skin had been scraped for testing. Had a biopsy been performed to check for cancer? Speakes dodged and weaved. He refused to say yes or no. Uncertainty reigned. Then, late that Thursday afternoon, the following notice was distributed, which Speakes said would be the last word on the subject.

THE WHITE HOUSE
Office of the Press Secretary

For Immediate Release August 1, 1985

On Tuesday, July 30, a small area of irritated skin on the right side of the President's nose was removed. The irritation had recently been aggravated by the adhesive tape used while the President was in the hospital. It was submitted for routine studies for infection, and it was determined no further treatment is necessary.

How would you read that notice? Was a biopsy performed? *Time*, *Newsweek*, *U.S. News & World Report*, the *New York Times*, ABC, CBS, NBC, and everyone else all said a biopsy had *not* been performed. We were all wrong. There had been a biopsy, and it had shown that the president had skin cancer.

It seems that Mrs. Reagan had ordered that the news not be disclosed. Speakes, looking into his professional grave no matter which way he jumped, had attempted to serve both masters, the First Lady and the truth, by allowing a misleading statement to be put out from the press office.

On Monday, after a full top-level discussion of whether to continue this cover-up, the president himself revealed the truth to reporters.

The next day, at his morning briefing, I told Speakes he had lost some of his credibility with me over the episode. He grew furious, demanding to know if I was calling him a liar. I carefully did not call him a liar but continued to say he had lost some credibility. I told him that regardless of who had asked him to conceal the facts, it was his reputation on the line. He was the one who had to answer the public questions. Helen Thomas of UPI joined me in arguing the matter with Speakes, getting him to admit that he had rung down an iron curtain on the truth, even if he hadn't lied.

Speakes more or less cut me off after that from the type of helpful private guidance press secretaries can give from time to time, as he had cut off many other reporters before me with whom he had had disputes. But he was extra careful after that in what he allowed to go out from his office in his name. And when the Iranian arms sale matter surfaced and stories began to beat against the White House from every side, he made sure to establish that he was speaking for others when he issued denials or argued against the obvious. The example of Ronald Ziegler, Nixon's spokesman, who knowingly told lies from the press room podium during Watergate to his everlasting shame, must have been uppermost in Speakes's mind. After all, press secretaries' reputations live on forever.

Jody Powell and I also used to have knock-down drag-out fights. Once on a press plane flying between El Paso and Cleveland, we stood toe to toe and almost came to blows. Neither of us can now remember what the problem was. Another time, as Powell recalls in his book, he threw a glass of red wine on me on a press plane while we were coming back from an overseas trip. He says he was glad I didn't make a public stink over it. We were all unwinding after the trip, and it never occurred to me that anyone on that plane had the right to complain about anyone else's conduct. I'm just glad he didn't have a full bottle handy.

I like both Powell and Speakes and respect the fact that the job of press secretary is a very tough one. You have to go out there every day and walk a tightrope, sometimes with inadequate information; you have to answer the phone at all hours of the night and on weekends; you have to fight to hold on to your turf and your office's integrity in the shark tank of the White House bureaucracy; you have to support decisions loyally even though you may not fully agree with them (and if you can't, like Jerry terHorst, who could not support President Gerald Ford's pardon of Nixon, you have to resign). And you have to put up with reporters like me, who don't seem to give a damn that you're trying your best and who, in your view, are always looking for one tiny mistake to complain about.

The best press secretaries understand that while they must serve their boss's interest, it is self-defeating to do this to the point of unreasonableness or meanness. The fighting will go on. But it should not be allowed to get personal. Only the amateurs in this town get angry. When Speakes announced his resignation from the White House in December 1986, one reporter spoke up on the record following his announcement to wish him well and good luck in his new job—me.

Not all of the information reporters pass on to the public from White House officials comes from these daily on-the-record briefings. Much of it comes from background briefings, either in groups or individually, at which the official speaking requires as a condition for speaking that he not be identified by name in the story.

In a way, that's cheating the public out of being able to make up its own mind about the importance of information, based on whom it comes from. It also allows officials to hide under a cloak of anonymity so that if they change their minds or things don't work out as they predict, they don't have to face the music. It tends to be the press that gets blamed when the story turns bad. So why not refuse to accept background information? Why not always identify sources by name? Sounds like a good idea, but in the real world it wouldn't work. Reporters wouldn't learn a lot of things the public needs to know that officials won't say on the record.

A spokesman will say on the record that the president has made no decision on the nuclear agreement with China. But on background, the same spokesman may tell reporters that the President is being advised by the appropriate officials to allow the agreement to be signed. Knowing that, people who oppose the agreement can mount an appeal in hopes of heading it off.

The official line is that the president welcomes a new Soviet arms proposal and promises to study it carefully. But on background, officials say the Soviet proposal appears to be nothing more than propaganda and is about as welcome as a hailstorm on the cotton crop.

The president says he is willing to meet with the Congressional Black Caucus if a time can be worked out. But on background, officials confirm that the black caucus shouldn't hold its breath waiting for the right time to come around.

Sometimes officials can be brutally frank when they know they won't be quoted by name. Once, at the end of Reagan's first term, a senior White House official told four reporters during a background session that he thought the MX missile was a "turkey" system whose only value might be to pressure the Soviets to the arms-control table. The official said the MX certainly wasn't worth its price for anything else. Its price at that point was already $12.7 billion. Warming to his thesis, the official then told us that in his view, most of the money spent during years of defense build-up under the Reagan administration had been wasted. Here was a man who, when he spoke on the record, was among the most ardent defenders of the Reagan build-up and, for that matter, of the MX. I reported his true feelings on the air, but of course, without being able to reveal the official's name, it didn't make much of an impact.

Ronald Reagan once said he was up to his "keister" in leaks and wanted them stopped. The truth is, most leaks from the White House come from the highest officials around the president, who tell reporters things on a background basis because those officials believe it serves their purpose. Reagan seems either not to know this or deliberately chooses to try to fool the public into thinking it is otherwise.

One of the most glaring examples of this came when Reagan was flying to Geneva with his top staff aboard *Air Force One* to hold the November 1985 summit meeting with Soviet leader Mikhail Gorbachev. A letter Defense Secretary Caspar Weinberger had written to the president about arms control and the need to beware the Soviets had been leaked. A senior official aboard Reagan's plane came back to talk to the press pool and was asked if he thought the letter had been deliberately leaked by someone hoping to wreck the summit. "Of course," replied the official. That comment was widely reported, although under the rules, the official's name could not be used. When Reagan saw the resulting stories, he told reporters he doubted any such comment had been made, implying the press had simply made it up. When we told him it had come from someone on his own airplane, he just shook his head. Reporters use leaks to find out what's really going on, but it's very clear that high officials do the leaking because they want the public to hear their version of the truth as well.

There's another way the White House tries to get out its version of truth: through the "spin" patrol. Every time the president gives a major speech or holds a news conference or does anything subject to various interpretations, shadings, or weights, White House officials fan out looking for reporters in order to impart the "correct" spin. They almost always do this on a background basis so their names cannot be attached to their handiwork. And no wonder. Did the president suggest there had been fraud on both sides in the Philippine elections? He didn't really mean it that way, says the "spin" patrol of officials. Does the opening statement accusing Congress of shirking its responsibility on the budget apply to everyone? Only to the Democrats, says the "spin" patrol. Did the president say he favored building a new space shuttle? Well, yes, but while that is his *inclination*, no decision has been made and in fact senior White House officials may advise against it, says the "spin" patrol.

Often, when you want to ask a question of White House officials you can't get your telephone call returned, but when White House officials want to make certain you put their interpretation on breaking events or presidential statements, they track you down. Larry Speakes would come back to the wire service and television network booths, stick his head in the door, and ask ever so sweetly,

"Do you need anything?" and then proceed to explain how the president really didn't mean "such and so" the way it sounded.

The best "spinner" in modern times is Robert Sims, who was on Speakes's staff at the White House before becoming assistant secretary of defense for public affairs (the Pentagon spokesman). Just as we would be about to take the president at his word and report he had pulled a verbal boner, Sims would come back to try to explain, argue, wheedle, and jolly us into softening the edges of the presidential goof, all in the name of fairness and good sportsmanship. Sims never gets angry or insults reporters. He knows that the quickest way to lose an argument over the "spin" is to inform the reporter that he's a dim-witted jerk for not seeing it the administration's way.

One of the spin patrol's greatest challenges came in October 1986, when the Iceland mini-summit between President Reagan and Soviet leader Gorbachev broke up in complete collapse. Going into Iceland, U.S. officials had tried to keep expectations low. After all, the outcome of an event is often judged by the yardstick of advance expectations. But at the end of the first day, after the Soviets had put on the table such breathtaking proposals for deep reductions in nuclear weapons, some U.S. officials lost their heads. Selected reporters were briefed under the deepest of background rules and told that progress was indeed being made. Progress not just on medium-range missiles, as had been widely anticipated, but also on long-range missiles as well. Expectations shot sky high. The television networks and two major newspapers were all saying that this Iceland summit, which was called under such modest circumstances, might well produce a historic breakthrough in the search for arms control. It didn't, the two sides parting in bitter dispute over President Reagan's Strategic Defense Initiative ("Star Wars" missile defense shield). And how did we reporters covering the summit learn of its collapse—we weren't in the meeting room to judge for ourselves. Why, top U.S. officials told us. Secretary of State Shultz came to the briefing room in Iceland looking like his dog had just been run over by a truck and said he was "deeply disappointed" by the outcome. White House Chief of Staff Donald Regan angrily lashed out at the Soviets as having been "[shown up] for what they are," people who "are not really interested in [an agreement]." There was no talk of "progress," only of missed opportunity. The great expectations were dashed on the rocks and reporters fell to with a will to spread the news. After all, those who live by the spin, die by the spin.

But the spin patrol had one final, powerful kick in it. Coming back from Iceland, U.S. officials simply decided to rewrite the summit's outcome. No facts had changed, mind you, only the decision to reinterpret what had happened. In the next few days, the patrol captained by the Red Baron of the spin squadron, Larry Speakes, and his wing man Deputy Press Secretary Peter Roussel put forward maximum firepower. Every senior official in the White House and State Department (for all I know assistant secretaries of agriculture were pressed in to service to take the word to Omaha and Des Moines) came forward to search out reporters and television cameras and describe the great success that had been achieved in Iceland. The line was that great progress had been made and if no final breakthrough had been achieved, well, the ball had been moved to the one-yard line. Shultz explained away his initial assessment by saying he had been tired; Regan explained away his tongue-lashing of the Soviets by saying he gets angry when he loses. It was something else. And, in the three weeks remaining before the November elections, it worked. The problem of course in "spinning" is that eventually the facts control. If real progress was made at the Iceland summit, why, we'll know it down the line when the two leaders sign that "historic" arms control agreement. If, on the other hand, it was really the collapse that U.S. officials first reported, then we'll know that, too, when no agreement based on the Iceland discussions is forthcoming. The spin patrol cannot control the facts, only their short-term interpretation. But, then, the spin patrol never plays for history, only for the next election.

And the Reagan White House has never worried about the "facts" when setting about to mold public opinion. In reviewing the awful setbacks the White House experienced toward the end of 1986—the Daniloff/Zakharov swap with the Soviets, the Iceland summit, the loss of the U.S. Senate to the Democrats and the initial unraveling of the Iranian connection—Chief of Staff Regan made it clear the spin patrol's efforts had nothing to do with the facts. Regan told Bernard Weinraub of the *New York Times,* "Some of us are like a shovel brigade following a parade down main street cleaning up!" Unfortunately for Regan, he was cleaning up after himself as much as after others. He had helped guide the White House strategy onto all those "rocks" and could hardly claim a place above the muck.

Although much of what we report comes from public briefings and private sessions with officials, there is another source: a reporter's own seasoned knowledge about the story. Such assessments must be carefully and judiciously delivered. No one runs out to the White House lawn to pass on a "hunch." But we all try to tell what we know even if we don't have the time in ninety seconds to cite all the sources and reasons why we believe something to be the case.

In the last fifteen or twenty seconds of my reports, in that part known as the "stand up close," I often try to round out the story and answer the question What's really going on here? When Carter announced his energy conservation proposals in 1977, there wasn't much time to get reaction. One of the proposals called for a gasoline tax that could go as high as fifty cents a gallon. Having covered the House Ways and Means Committee for so many years on Capitol Hill and knowing its makeup so well, I was able to tell my viewers that based on the committee's past record, that particular proposal would have very rough sledding.

I've been away from Capitol Hill for ten years now, so I rely on ABC's ace reporters there, Brit Hume, who covers the Senate, and Charles Gibson, who covers the House, to give me a quick read on how something from the White House will play. They often have a better grasp of the congressional mood than Reagan's own legislative strategists.

If using your own judgment in explaining a story sounds like a departure from straight reporting, think about how you, yourself, report to others on things that go on in your life.

Consider: You go to work one day to find that the hot topic in your office is whether Whipple, the branch manager, is getting ready to hang it up and retire. You talk to three different people who say Whipple has been grumbling a lot lately about how his back is hurting and how nice it would be if he could take off for Florida and do some fishing. You remember that last month the company changed its retirement rules slightly in order to make it easier for blue-eyed, white-haired men who have held the job of branch manager in three separate locations to retire early on full pension. You can think of no one that change might apply to except Whipple. Furthermore, someone tells you that personnel has just placed an ad in the financial pages of the local newspaper looking for qualified branch managers with experience in your company's field. And when you go in to see Whipple on a piece of business, he appears distracted and disinterested. Despite all this, however, a notice is tacked up on the bulletin board that reads: "Suggestions that I am about to retire are without foundation and should be ignored. Signed, Whipple."

So you go home and your husband asks you, "What's this I hear about Whipple retiring?" You reply, "He denies it," and then you add, "But even so, there are a lot of signs that it may happen."

You have just tried to answer the question about what's really going on at the office concerning Whipple. In my book, you've been a good reporter.

You can't always be right in your evaluation of what's really going on. You must be very careful about going out on a limb. You live or die by your track record on these things, since the viewers soon get on to whether you generally know what you're talking about or not.

Once, I knew what I was talking about, but I didn't get to pass it on to the audience.

One Monday in April 1980, Jimmy Carter gave Walter Cronkite an interview in which he had used new and threatening language in talking about the Iranian hostage situation. It seemed clear to me that whether intentionally or not, Carter was signaling a change in policy. That night I prepared and taped the following report for *Nightline*.

SAM ON CAMERA: In an interview with CBS News, the president expressed new worry about the hostages safety . . . and, for the first time, hinted he may be considering a military rescue effort to free them.

VOICE OVER PICTURES: Mr. Carter said of the hostages, "I consider them in jeopardy now. There is a volatile political situation in Iran. I think the structure of the government, the societal structure and the economic structure lately is deteriorating fairly rapidly . . . I don't know how much longer we can sit here and see them kept captive while the situation around does deteriorate . . ."

SAM ON CAMERA: The president did not elaborate on those words about not knowing "how much longer we can sit here and see them kept captive," but the hint of action was certainly there.

I went out to dinner when the report was finished. When I came back, I discovered that Ted Koppel and executive producer Bill Lord had cut out my assessment that Carter seemed to be hinting at a military rescue effort. They told me that my conclusion was way off base, that everyone knew the president had ruled out military action. That was on Monday. You remember, of course, what happened the next Thursday. A military rescue mission was attempted and ended in failure.

Later, Lord called me and said, "You were right, we shouldn't have cut it." I appreciated his apology. But he has not mended his ways. Six years later, I did a stand up close from Grenada on the day Reagan went there to celebrate his 1983 victory over communist forces on the island. In a speech to the local inhabitants, Reagan reminded his audience that we had helped liberate Grenada from the communist yoke and coupled that reminder with a warning that we could not allow Nicaragua to become a Soviet base in the Western hemisphere, either.

I concluded my report that night by observing, "The president's trip was meant to send a message—Grenada today, Nicaragua tomorrow." Lord, by this time the executive producer of the evening news broadcast, cut out the line! Stand by the phone, Bill. You may need to call me again if U.S. policy toward Nicaragua continues to progress in the direction it's been going.

You get a feel for stories that repeat themselves and for situations that keep coming around. On November 2, 1986, one of our guests on ABC's Sunday broadcast *This Week with David Brinkley* was

White House chief of staff Donald Regan. That morning David Jacobsen had been freed from his captivity in Lebanon. I had the following exchange with Regan.

MR. DONALDSON: Our policy has been firmly one of not ever giving up something in the way of a demand for someone who's being detained. And is that still the policy?

MR. REGAN: Yes, that's still our policy.

. . .

MR. DONALDSON: Well, Mr. Regan, if I may—it's like the Daniloff-Zakharov affair, you all claimed there wasn't a deal, there wasn't a direct swap.

MR. REGAN: And there wasn't.

MR. DONALDSON: A lot of people saw it differently. When the record is finally revealed of what's been going on with Jacobsen, and we hope some others, will a lot of people still say, "Well, they may say there's no deal, but there it is"?

MR. REGAN: I don't know what people will say in the future, Sam. I mean that would be silly of me to try to say in advance until we can—

MR. DONALDSON: But are we meeting demands? That's what I'm suggesting. Are we meeting demands?

MR. REGAN: No, we're not meeting demands. Absolutely not.

I knew nothing about the Reagan sale of arms to Iran for hostages story at that moment, although the first word was only hours away. So, why press Regan about a "deal"? Because the release of the third hostage (Benjamin Weir, Lawrence Jenco, now Jacobsen) without any apparent reason, seemed strange. You could feel that something was up. It was like what Senator Howard Baker said during the 1975 Senate investigation of the CIA, "There are animals crashing around in the forest. I can hear them but I can't see them." Reporters depend on their instincts. Once you have some seasoning, if you follow your instincts you seldom go wrong.

Not all my energy in the press room these days is devoted to boring in on White House officials. I'm also after some of my friends in the press corps, and it's fair to say some of them are after me. The issue is smoking; I've declared war on smoking in the White House press room. It is a war we non-smokers cannot lose. Numbers and the surgeon general are on our side. But our opponents, those misguided souls among us who still puff the weed, are giving ground grudgingly, and ever so slowly.

In late December 1985, I wrote a letter to the buildings manager superintendent at the White House, Jeter Morris. The General Services Administration oversees the White House, and Morris was at that time the top GSA man on duty there. I asked him to set aside a designated smoking area in the press room for smokers, so situated or partitioned that the smoke could not encroach on other areas. I asked him to designate all the other space, including the common space that everyone has to use, like the briefing room itself, non-smoking. I sent an informational letter along the same lines to Larry Speakes. I sent another informational letter to Fred Fielding, the White House counsel. It's always good to get the lawyers stirred up on something like this.

The hue and cry of tyranny(!) went up from the smokers, led by that excellent reporter Jeremiah O'Leary. O'Leary, like his father before him, worked for the *Washington Star*, until the paper folded in 1981; now he works for the *Washington Times*. He was in the marine corps in World War II and Korea, later rising to the rank of colonel in the marine reserves, and is not to be trifled with. He once asked Reagan at a news conference why the marines, then stationed in Lebanon, were being forced to violate the sound military principle of seeking the high ground by being quartered at the Beirut airport. Reagan, missing the point, explained to him that airports are just naturally flat.

I knew that Colonel O'Leary's battalion of smokers would be formidable opponents. And to tell you the truth, I had some sympathy for them. I understand what it's like to want a cigarette. I smoked one pack a day for twenty-three years. I began in my sophomore year of high school, when I was sent to New Mexico Military Institute. The old cadets smoked, so naturally I wanted

COURTESY OF SAM DONALDSON

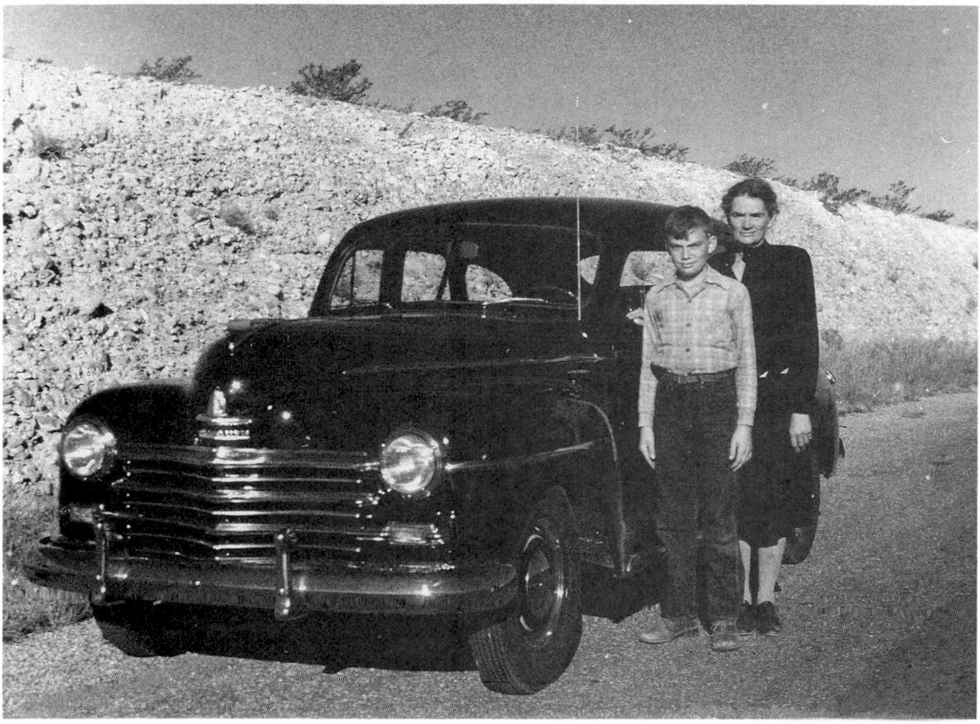

My mother and me on the way to school in El Paso, Texas, 1941.

COURTESY OF SAM DONALDSON

COURTESY OF SAM DONALDSON

Left: With my brother, Tom, a pilot in the U.S. Army Air Corps, 1942.

Right: My mother, Chloe Hampson Donaldson, and me on the family farm, Chamberino, New Mexico, on her ninetieth birthday, November 1984.

COURTESY OF SAM DONALDSON

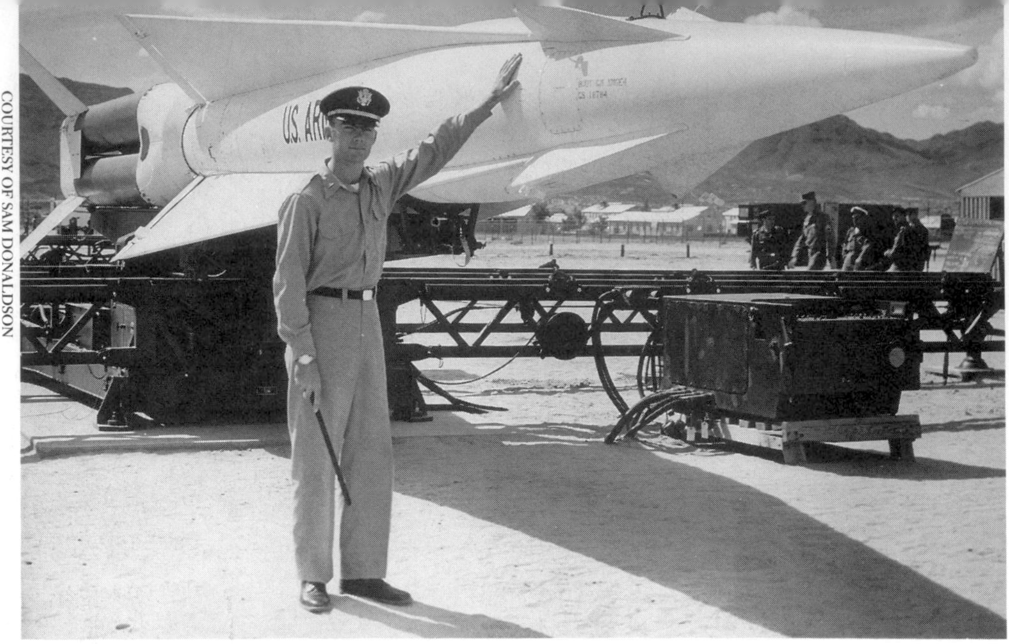

On active duty with Nike Hercules missile at Ft. Bliss, Texas, 1957.

COURTESY OF SAM DONALDSON

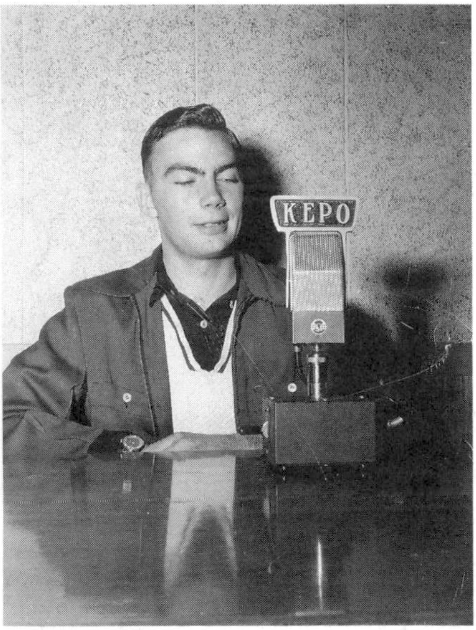

Broadcasting "Sam's Show" on KEPO, El Paso, Texas, 1952.

Aboard *Air Force One* with Lyndon Johnson, March 1968.

COURTESY OF SAM DONALDSON

In Vietnam, April 1971, interviewing General Creighton Abrams (Westmoreland's successor) as U.S. Ambassador Ellsworth Bunker looks on.

COURTESY OF SAM DONALDSON

Interviewing President Nixon on the final night of the Republican National Convention, Miami Beach, 1972.

COURTESY OF SAM DONALDSON

With Frank Reynolds in the House Judiciary Committee hearing room on July 27, 1974, covering the vote on Article One, recommending impeachment of Richard Nixon.

COURTESY OF SAM DONALDSON

JOE McNALLY/ABC NEWS

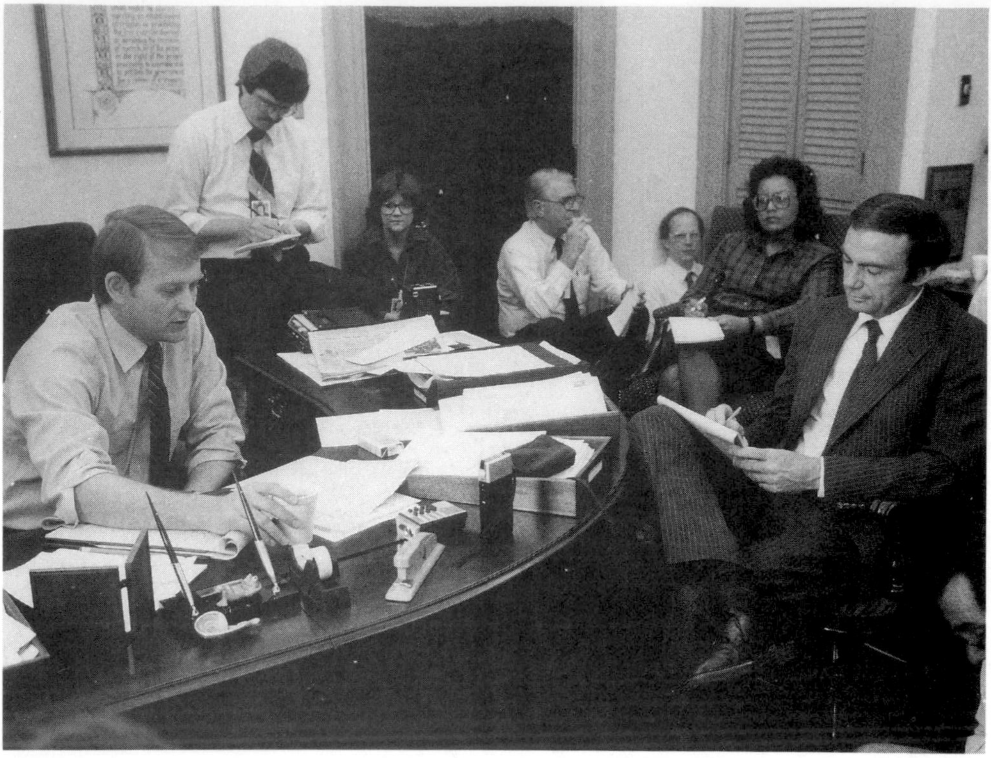

Jody Powell behind the press secretary's desk, White House, 1978.

DENNIS R. WARREN

COURTESY OF SAM DONALDSON

Left: Playing baseball with Jimmy Carter in Plains, Georgia, 1976.

Right: Slogging through the mud at a pond draining, Plains, Georgia, 1976.

Left: With Jimmy Carter at Carterpuri, India, on the banks of a manure pit, January 1978.

Right: In the rain at some airport, 1976.

KARL H. SCHUMACHER, THE WHITE HOUSE

COURTESY OF SAM DONALDSON

Best Wishes
to Sam
Jimmy Carter

JACK KICHTLINGER, THE WHITE HOUSE

The Carters and Sadats with the press corps before the Great Pyramid at Giza, Egypt, March 1979.

COURTESY OF SAM DONALDSON

Left: Taking advantage of the podium on which the presidential seal had been left to engage in a fantasy of role reversal.

Right: Interviewing Nancy Reagan at the Republican National Convention, Dallas, 1984.

JACK KIGHTLINGER, THE WHITE HOUSE

To Sam Donaldson
With best wishes, — and of course I'll take your questions!
Warm Regards
Ronald Reagan

With Judy Woodruff, Lesley Stahl and Reagan after being briefed by Reagan before his first television speech as president, February 1981.

GEORGE TAMES

On *This Week with David Brinkley* with Brinkley, George Will and George Shultz, October 5, 1986.

OFFICIAL PHOTOGRAPH, THE WHITE HOUSE

Reagan entertaining the press in the Blue Room, fall 1984.

COURTESY OF SAM DONALDSON

Jan and me on our honeymoon, Athens, 1983.

MRS. DONALDSON... YOU'VE GOT TO DO SOMETHING ABOUT SAM.

DOONESBURY

By G.B. Trudeau

to, also. At first I tried all the brands, even Kool menthols (ugh!), but in a few years settled down to Lucky Strikes, a brand my girl friend's mother introduced me to. I can still remember sitting in Kathy Roberts's kitchen, her mother and me puffing away on cigarettes, while Kathy, who never took up the habit, coughed away by the window.

Like most ex-smokers of my generation, it was the late Dr. Luther Terry, the U.S. surgeon general, who got me to stop. In 1964, Terry issued his famous report from that office linking cigarettes to death. I thought about it. It was clear that smoking could, probably would, kill you if something else didn't get you first, and it made sense to stop. Easier to say than do, I know full well.

I gave up smoking for the first time in August 1967—just stopped, cold turkey. It was hell. I was nervous, upset, a terror to live with. I ate Popsicles by the boxful as a substitute. I gained weight. But after eighteen months, I thought I had it made. Then, on New Year's Eve, 1968, my ABC colleague Stephen Geer came over for the evening and brought cigars. One cigar wouldn't hurt, I thought. Bang. I was hooked again, this time on cigars, which I inhaled lustily. But on assignment in India the next summer, the humidity there ruined all my cigars and I went back to Lucky Strikes.

I kicked the habit for the second and, I trust, last time in the early morning hours of September 2, 1971. I woke up with an imagined combination heart and cancer attack ravaging my chest. I was coughing and wheezing and finally did the thing most people do under such circumstances. I fell to my knees and blurted out a frantic promise. If I could only make it to morning, I would never smoke again. I did, and I haven't. But for years afterward I wanted a cigarette in the worst way.

I know what it is to smoke and not smoke. Not smoking is better. But I believe the choice ought to be a free one. I'm not for prohibition of tobacco—we tried that with alcohol and it doesn't work. That's why in my letter to the estimable Jeter Morris I did not ask that smoking be banned entirely. But I was clearly asking that it be banned anywhere that non-smokers had to go.

Here's my position exactly. When the right of smokers to smoke and the right of non-smokers not to have to inhale somebody else's smoke collide, the non-smokers' rights are supreme. There is an old legal dictum that says "Your liberty to swing your arms ends where my nose begins." How can it be argued that just a little "passive" or "side-stream" smoke forced on the non-smoker is permissible in the name of evenhandedness? How about just a "little cancer," friends? The important exception to me is that non-smokers do not have the right to seek out the smokers in their private lairs in order to force on them abstinence. If you invite me to your house for the evening and I accept, knowing you smoke, I don't have the right to charge in with a fire extinguisher and cover you and yours with foam. I can stay away if I like. But that's the point. When non-smokers can't "stay away," such as in the common areas of the press room, our right to be left alone seems to me to be absolute.

That's not the way Larry Speakes saw it. Treating my request more or less like a joke, Speakes turned it over to the White House Correspondents' Association for its consideration. The association is not very active, except for the purpose of putting on a yearly black tie dinner, and he thought my request would be buried. Speakes had used the association before as a means of disposing of a troublesome matter. When Gary Schuster and Bill Plante of CBS and I hopped a ride in a press pool van in a Reagan motorcade one day when we weren't members of that day's pool, one of Speakes's aides, Denny Brisley, came storming up to his office with fire in her eye. Brisley had not yet learned the old maxim "live and let live" and was demanding that something awful be done about these transgressors, whom she seemed to regard as only slightly less harmful to the country than the Walker spy family.

Speakes couldn't get excited about our sin, but he felt he had to back up his aide, so he told her to deliver a strong verbal protest to the president of the White House Correspondents' Association. Brisley marched right back to the press room and delivered her strong protest to the president of the association, who was, as Speakes well knew, Gary Schuster. Schuster immediately turned the matter over to the association's vice-president, who happened to be Bill Plante. Plante appointed me to the committee to study the protest, and at last word, we transgressors still have the matter under review. This time, in trying to use the Correspondents' Association to bury my no-smoking request, however, Speakes miscalculated.

The association's board was about to meet to plan the annual black tie dinner. My letter was put on the agenda. I was invited to testify and did so eloquently, although not altogether persuasively in the opinion of board member Col. Jeremiah O'Leary. Still, the colonel knows when to give ground. He agreed to the following recommendations: That we ask Speakes to designate the lavatories off-limits to smoking and to ask that there be no smoking in the briefing room during briefings. The colonel insisted that the briefing room ban be voluntary. Furthermore, we would ask the man who runs the White House buildings, Jeter Morris, to install a smoke filtration device in the work areas. I said that was all acceptable to me as a start, that we could try it and see how it works. It wasn't enough, of course, but I attained the rank of captain in the army reserve and know how to give a bit of ground myself.

Speakes accepted these recommendations. Morris put up the smoke filtration device. Someone immediately pasted my picture on its face. One NO SMOKING sign was posted in the briefing room—about the size of a postcard, but it's there.

The colonel and his friends tacked up letters of outrage they had received from citizens protesting my priggish and Hitler-like demands. I tacked up letters of commendation I had received from citizens praising my courageous and forthright stand in the name of health and happiness. The few letters we received from people complaining about the expenditure of eight hundred dollars of taxpayers' money for the filter we turned over to former budget director David Stockman's publisher for inclusion in his book about waste in the budget.

Shortly after I started my no-smoking campaign, I attempted to enlist a powerful ally. Going through a receiving line, I said to Ronald Reagan, "Tell me, when you go into the cabinet room for a meeting, does anyone blow smoke in your face?"

"No," said Reagan, looking a little shocked at the idea that anyone would think his official family might try to asphyxiate him.

"Well then," I shot back triumphantly, "I'm sure you'll help me stop people from blowing smoke in my face in the briefing room." Now, there was a Hobson's choice for the president. But he was up to it.

"You can always carry around one of those little portable fans to blow it away, like Larry Hagman," he replied.

Despite the lack of top level support, I'm not giving up, although many days in the press room, I have felt like General Custer with Speakes in front of me and Col. O'Leary and his gang behind me.

My day in the press room normally ends by 7 P.M. I phone my office at the bureau for one last check for messages. More often than not, my efficient assistant Mari Hope has waited to hear from me. Hope keeps my schedule and handles invitations and speaking requests for me. Without her I wouldn't know whether I was coming or going outside of work. Then I go home with either a victory or a defeat under my belt, however small. I go home with the feeling that I was on top of the story that day or I wasn't. Some people work all their lives for the equivalent of a single gold watch. I'm luckier. In my business, every day brings you home a winner or a loser.

When I win, I'm in a great mood. Everybody around me benefits from my smiles. When I lose, watch out. Jimmy Carter wrote in his book *Why Not the Best?*, "You show me a good loser and I will show you a loser." I'm tempted to agree. But if I go home in a bad mood because things didn't go my way that day, I don't have long to feel the pain of failure.

Tomorrow, in the press room it all starts even again.

Chapter Nine

NEWS FOR TELEVISION

There I was in Tokyo waiting for Secretary of State George Shultz to hold a news conference and explain what had happened at the 1986 economic summit. Shultz was due to begin an hour before air time. But he was running desperately late—it was now six minutes to air—and I was running desperately short of nerves. I had prepared the first third of my taped report, the part where I set the stage and led the viewer to the start of the Shultz news conference. One third of a report won't do, of course, and there is no way in television to stop the clock.

At that moment, just as strong men began to weep, weaker ones contemplated suicide, and the squawk box from New York was demanding that my report, any report, be put on the satellite immediately, Shultz walked in. I seized on practically the first thing out of his mouth and declared it news, and while my White House producer, David Kaplan, and tape editor, Steve Cain, added that particular "sound bite" to the previously prepared set up portion, I ran out to the hotel balcony and taped a stand up close that tried to make sense of what we had learned. I ad-libbed it, since what we had learned had come only an instant before. We put the finished product on the satellite, and New York cued up the tape for replay on the air even as I was being introduced.

"Whew," said Kaplan.

"Boy, oh boy," said Cain.

"Piece of cake," said I nonchalantly, wiping the sweat from my brow. It was close, but we made it.

As you can see, I work on deadline. I can't do it any other way. Daily news reporting, whether from the White House or any other beat, does not lend itself to considered, studied, letter-perfect work.

I am fortunate to have worked for six years now with David Kaplan. He's the best all-around field producer I've worked with in the White House. He understands the story and knows the players. Moreover, he has an encyclopedic mind for pictures, the thing television is all about. Do I need a shot of Nancy Reagan in conversation with Michael Deaver? When was it Reagan almost fell to his knees while boarding *Air Force One*? Kaplan remembers exactly where such pictures can be found. And he is able to swing with the deadline pressure and my own idiosyncrasies without getting flustered or ruffled.

Most of my reports for ABC are short. They may run anywhere from ninety seconds to three minutes, perhaps a little longer in extreme circumstances. But long or short, they are *my* reports. People ask, Do your bosses at ABC tell you what to say? The answer is no. Several times a day I discuss the White House news with the *World News Tonight* senior Washington producer, John Arrowsmith. He makes recommendations to the program's top producers in New York, and they decide whether I will do a report or not. Through Arrowsmith I lay out for them the general theme and outline of my report, but most of the time they don't know exactly what I'm going to say until it goes on the air, and they and you find out together.

That's not because I don't need an editor—everyone does—or think I'm above having to work under the same supervision as my colleagues—I don't think that. But it's the nature of my beat that the news often breaks near air time, that filing my reports as the president moves around the nation and the world requires me to work down to the wire, and I'm therefore mainly on my own.

There is a certain satisfaction that comes from this pressure. When I'm working in an edit room, putting together a long lead report on the president's activities, there's a lot riding on the outcome. The network has spent a great deal of money to cover those activities and is engaged in a highly competitive race with the other networks to demonstrate that our coverage is the best. And there is a great thrill in knowing that it finally all comes down to what I think, how I decide to put it together, what I say, and whether I make air on time. Call me a braggart, call me arrogant. People at ABC (and elsewhere) have called me worse. But when you need the job done on deadline, you'll call me.

The ideal way to produce a television spot-news report is to write the entire script, select the sound bite and pictures to go with it, time everything, then, with all elements firmly in mind and hand, begin the editing process. But when it's forty-five minutes to deadline, you don't have time to do that. You must begin, not quite sure what you'll include, what you'll leave out, what precisely you're going to say, not even sure of the pictures you have to cover your words since there may not have been time to screen all the videotape.

Furthermore, there is no time to form a committee to determine what the story is. The debate over what's important to tell in a limited time can fill hours in the classroom or the seminar hall, but at forty-five minutes to deadline, there can be no debate. Deadline television reports must be constructed by a dictator who says, "Right or wrong, this is the way it will go." If you find it impossible to make up your mind about things, for goodness' sake, don't get into the daily news business.

Consider that when the hour of 6:30 P.M. strikes and the announcer in New York says, "From ABC, this is *World News Tonight* with Peter Jennings," and Peter says, "Good evening. Today in Tokyo, President Reagan won a victory in convincing his summit partners to name Libya as a sponsor of terrorism. Here's Sam Donaldson with details . . ." I cannot say, "Hold everything, Peter, I'm not quite ready. Give me five minutes more, please."

Sometimes, things don't work out no matter how hard you try. Once, in Rome in June 1980, Terry Ray, who was then the White

House producer, David Harten, one of our best tape editors, and I finished editing my report moments before air time and rushed the tape into the transmission room for relay to New York on the satellite. A technician, new to the job and perhaps a little nervous, pressed the record button instead of the playback button and managed to erase the first twenty seconds of my three-and-a-half-minute report. There was no time to repair it, so when the anchorman introduced my taped report, I came up talking in the middle of a sentence. I had to be restrained from punching that technician (fortunately for me, since he was bigger than I was).

The most unusual deadline problem I've ever heard of happened not to me, but to Lesley Stahl of CBS. One day during the 1980 campaign, the principal NBC and CBS correspondents dropped off in Lexington, Kentucky, to prepare their reports on President Carter's campaigning there, while Carter went on to Dallas. I went on with him. As the press plane began to roll, Al Bargamian, the CBS cameraman, came running down the aisle swinging a bag containing all the CBS videotape that had been shot in Lexington, shouting, "Stop the plane, stop the plane."

No one had told Bargamian that Stahl was dropping off. Much as I would like to have been helpful, we were late and there was nothing I could do to stop the plane. So off we went, leaving Stahl behind with absolutely no material from which to fashion a television report.

She put something on the air, though, begging shots from the Lexington CBS affiliate, voicing-over some shots fed up the line from Dallas. Stahl even managed to say she was in Dallas in her sign-off. Now *that's* a good trick.

I believe it's important to stay with the president when he's on the road and not drop off early, even though it means a tight squeeze at the final destination in putting together your report. Arriving at Ogden, Utah, with Reagan one afternoon, we were so late that I couldn't wait for the press plane stairs. When they opened the 727 aircraft door, I swung down from the edge and dropped to the tarmac. I raced over to a camera position and got an answer I wanted from the president as he descended the steps of *Air Force One*. The competition had dropped off back in Kansas.

I'm sure their reports looked more polished than mine, but I was where the news was at air time.

Don't get me wrong. I can't produce my television reports alone. The news production desk must dispatch crews and couriers at the right time to the right places. Producers, directors, graphic artists, control-room technicians, tape editors, and many others must do their job right if I am to get on the air with a competitive news report. Above all, perhaps, the camera crews must provide the raw material that we use in television news.

The people who haul a camera around on their shoulder are not only indispensable to this business, they are the ones who do the heaviest lifting and often the ones who must take the most risks. Reporters who miss an event can get a fill-in from someone who was there. The people who shoot the pictures have to be there. Reporters can watch out for trouble and jump. Those who are loaded down with heavy equipment and are looking through their lens cannot.

My favorite story about the camera person's vulnerability concerns Carl Larsen of ABC News, one of the all-time great "shooters." In 1976, Larsen covered Carter's general election campaign with me. Carter's second stop on his opening day was Darlington, South Carolina, where he went to the motor speedway to be seen by the crowd before the running of the Darlington 500.

The Carter advance team had arranged for a pickup truck to carry the camera crews around the track with Carter. I got on the truck also. For safety's sake, a light wooden railing had been constructed around the truck bed. But it wasn't much. Larsen positioned himself near the tailgate. We waited along the side of the track for Carter's convertible to drive by. When it did, the truck driver started off with a lurch, throwing us back against the wooden railing, which promptly broke. Larsen pitched over the tailgate backward but managed to grip the tailgate top with the back of his knees. His head was hanging just inches above the tarmac as the truck gathered speed. We grabbed him and hauled him back up. Now, all during this wild ride, Larsen had held on to his camera, and when we looked at the tape later in the editing room, we found that while there were a few seconds of swirl and sky, he had never stopped shooting. Moreover, when we pulled him up, he had brought his camera down to focus exactly on Carter's car. That night I put the entire sequence on the air and gave Carl Larsen a name credit. He deserved a medal.

Reporters and camera "shooters" work together to produce the best reports. Once, in Tokyo, when Jimmy Carter met Emperor Hirohito, I began a report with a picture and word sequence that will always stick in my mind. It wouldn't have been possible without Vincent Gaito, who's been an ABC cameraman for twenty-five years.

Dorrance Smith, then my White House producer, and Pat Roddy, then a videotape editor who has since become senior producer of *World News This Morning* and *Good Morning America* news, and I were looking through the material when Gaito's shot of the high-level greeting leaped out at us. Any camera person can point the camera in a specific direction and give you a picture. But the great video "shooters" know what the story is, have a feeling for composition and a sense of the flow of the action.

When Carter and Hirohito met, Gaito had followed Carter up the stairs with his camera lens, holding him in a fairly tight shot until he stepped onto the palace doorway landing. Then Gaito widened out and panned the picture to the left just perfectly to capture Hirohito, stooped and trembling, walking out through the palace door to shake hands with the president. The picture suggested to me the opening words for my report that night. "When this man was one year old," I said, following the picture as it unfolded, "this man was crowned emperor of Japan." Reveal Hirohito on cue.

Was that earth-shaking information? No. Brilliant writing? No. It was a combination of words and picture that got across a mood and a sense of historic proportion for the story.

Another time, as we all waited on the tarmac at the Aswan landing strip in Egypt for Carter to arrive to see Egyptian President Sadat, Doug Allmond, another of ABC's great "shooters," had his camera trained on Sadat. The two presidents had never met in person. Sadat was hoping that in Carter he would find a friend. Through his lens, Allmond saw Sadat look up toward the sky. Allmond panned up smoothly in the direction in which Sadat was looking and focused on *Air Force One*, circling in. That night we were able to open my report with that shot, which, without having to cut from one picture to the other, accurately set the mood for the story that followed.

Bob Schieffer of CBS is another reporter who tries to use the work of good camera people to communicate mood. Once, Carter was walking back toward the Oval Office after saying good-bye to Menachem Begin. It had been a particularly contentious visit by the prime minister of Israel. We all suggested in our stories that there had been tension and frustration. But Schieffer, who was then the CBS White House correspondent, said it best using the camera work of CBS's Cal Marlin showing a picture of Carter absentmindedly plucking a dead leaf off the Rose Garden hedge as he walked by. The gesture gave a visual sense to Carter's frustration. The combination of words and picture fixed the mood vividly and accurately in the viewer's mind.

Consider the day in October 1986, when President Reagan went to Oklahoma to campaign for Republican Senator Don Nickles and, in a moment of passionate oratory, urged the voters to send his good friend Don *Rickles* back to Washington for another term. That slip was funny enough, but what really brought it home to my television audience was the camera work of ABC's Terry De Witt, another fine camera person who thinks. When De Witt heard Reagan make that verbal slip he panned over to the line of White House officials accompanying Reagan and caught Chief of Staff Donald Regan shaking his head in sympathetic amusement. I ran the Reagan line, then cut to Regan. His expression told the story better than any words of mine could have.

On rare occasions, the pictures do not tell an accurate story, however. That's why reporters should be present when they're shot. If I had only seen the pictures of Jimmy Carter's motorcade through the streets of Oak Ridge, Tennessee, in 1978, I would surely have used them to show how popular he was with the workers who lined his route. I mean the pictures showed men smiling, waving and shouting as the motorcade went by. But I was there and saw that it was not Carter's limousine that caused the wild cheering. It was the ABC camera wagon driving by a few cars behind it with our ace "shooter" Ginny Vicario, standing upright on the tailgate, her ample figure clad in a skintight tank top, swaying from side to side as she leveled her camera on the crowd. It would have been grossly unfair to credit Carter with Ginny's popularity.

One of the most powerful political reports I've done from Washington was one in which I had the sense to shut up and let the film do all the work. It was back in the days when the late John W. McCormack of Massachussetts was speaker of the House of Representatives. A group of Democratic young turks was waging a campaign to replace him. One of their complaints was that McCormack had grown too old and frail to conduct a vigorous leadership of the party and the House. I asked McCormack's assistant, John Monahan, for an interview with the speaker. Monahan said no, but he'd let me take some pictures of McCormack working in his office instead. From McCormack's standpoint, that proved to be a mistake.

We went into the speaker's office and set up the camera. I thought we'd just get some film of McCormack signing papers or something. Instead, Monahan and the speaker, all on their own, decided they really wanted to show that McCormack was up to his job. So when the camera began to roll, Monahan thrust a piece of paper into the speaker's hand. McCormack, frail-looking and hard of hearing, took it with trembling fingers.

"Mr. Speaker, this came up yesterday," said Monahan in a loud, firm voice. "You were up to Mr. Brooks about Flag Day." McCormack looked puzzled. "The second of January," Monahan prompted, trying to get McCormack to remember when he had previously focused on the matter.

"Um, what's that?" demanded the speaker, unable to grasp the message. Monahan was trying to get the speaker to make a routine appointment of Congressman Jack Brooks to chair a Flag Day committee.

"You appoint the chairman and the members," Monahan coached as the speaker continued to read the paper in his hands.

"Have I appointed them this year?" asked the speaker, clearly not following his aide's lead.

"Not yet, no, sir," said Monahan slowly, and distinctly.

"Don't you think I'd better appoint them?" said the speaker querulously. "I think Brooks was the chairman." At this point Monahan registered clear delight that the speaker had finally come on board. "Yeah, Jack Brooks is always chairman," he said, producing a telephone and thrusting it into the speaker's hand. "Mr. Speaker, Chairman Brooks is on the phone for you," Monahan told him triumphantly.

"Hello, John, uh Jack," the speaker shouted into the phone, finally settling on the man's title just to be safe, "Mr. Congressman, how are you?" There ensued a lively conversation indecipherable to the average listener. But it was clear from the way the speaker stared at the papers on his desk that it was probably indecipherable to him as well. After a moment or two of this, McCormack signed off, "All right, John, 'bye."

That night, Howard K. Smith introduced me. I briefly laid out the insurgents' complaint that the speaker was too old and frail for the job, said the speaker had declined to be interviewed on the subject but had allowed us to watch him work that day and, without further ado, shut up and let the film run.

On those rare occasions when I have had the good sense to let the pictures and natural sound speak for themselves, it has always worked out well. For instance, one of the best interviews ever conducted of Ronald and Nancy Reagan was one in which Reagan never said a word. But I ran almost all of it on the air.

The interviewer was Emery King, then of NBC News. He was the lone network reporter standing in the outside press area when the Reagans came to the window at Bethesda Naval Hospital to reassure us that the president was, indeed, recovering from his colon cancer operation in the summer of 1985.

King shouted up, "How are you feeling?" The president put out his hand in a gesture of energy and smiled broadly.

"When are you going home?" asked King. Reagan shrugged elaborately, vigorously shaking his head from side to side.

"Is your throat sore, you aren't answering," said King. The president, who had recently had tubes down his throat, went through an exaggerated pantomime trying to explain it.

As King continued his "exclusive interview," there followed lots of gestures, nods of "yes," facial expressions of enjoyment from the First Patient. This went on for a couple of minutes. It was terrific. I ran almost all of it instead of doing my own commentary on the president's condition over the pictures. It turned out to be a clean kill. Both other networks used a few seconds of the pictures, all right, but neither used King's questions—not even NBC.

And on occasion, there are no words from anyone, just the pictures to enjoy. When the National Turkey Federation presented Reagan with his Thanksgiving turkey his first year, he leaned over to pet it and the bird began flapping so vigorously that for an instant it looked like the president of the United States was being beaten to death by a turkey wing. Reagan took it good-naturedly, but in succeeding years, the Thanksgiving turkey has been drugged before presentation. The "Just Say No" slogan does have its exceptions.

Pictures are what make television news such a powerful communications medium. It's the information people get from seeing things themselves through television that changes minds, not opinions expressed by television reporters. Television's influence comes from being able to bring the reality of the world to people who can't be there personally. We can't always bring you the latest pictures instantly, but with advancing technology, we're in a far better position to do so now than we used to be. In the old days, we would often have to tell the news of a breaking story and buttress it with a report previously prepared on a background subject that tied in with the latest news. Sometimes, of course, we didn't even have a background report ready.

I remember on a Saturday night in 1972, on Easter weekend, when the North Vietnamese began a major new and open invasion of South Vietnam, there was no way to get the story quickly, there being no satellite service from Saigon. I was then anchoring the *ABC Weekend Report* from New York and my producer, Stuart Schwartz, and I were desperately searching the shelf of "evergreen" pieces, hoping to find some picture story that we could tie in with what was happening. The shelf was bare except for an upbeat report on tourism in South Vietnam from correspondent

Jim Giggins. "Well," said Schwartz wistfully, "maybe you could report that thousands of North Vietnamese troops poured across the DMZ, then say brightly, 'What brings these tourists to South Vietnam? More on that from Jim Giggins.' " We restrained the urge, and all the audience got to see that night about the reality of the world was my face.

Despite the headaches and problems you run into in producing television reports, the fact is, that's part of the fun of being in this business—and of the rewards. I've always felt a little envious of but also a little sorry for print reporters, who work hard to get a story, write it on a piece of paper, then go home. It's exactly at that point that our work in television news really begins.

Chapter Ten

COVERING THE CANDIDATES

As a reporter who savors politics and other Washington stories, I enjoy covering campaigns. Oh sure, I complain about the hours and the time away from home and, when you're not traveling first-class with a president, the fleabag hotel accommodations and other inconveniences. But the truth is, I love it.

It may be demeaning for politicians to have to struggle through the snows of New Hampshire and elsewhere to get votes, flying in and out of hundreds of airports, fighting so much fatigue that they often tell the crowd they're glad to be in Sioux Falls when they're really standing in Omaha. And such marathon campaign activities may seem irrelevant to negotiating with the Soviets. But this testing through a long, arduous campaign is the best way I can think of to determine someone's ability to be president—short of actually seeing that person perform in the job. For that reason, I oppose a single national primary or even three or four regional primaries, designed to shorten the process. I want to see how the candidates conduct themselves in a long campaign, whether they can organize one, whether they can finance one, whether they can stand up to the pressure from the press, their opponents, their own staff, even from Mother Nature.

I once watched Jimmy Carter in early 1976 striding back and forth on the tarmac of the Manchester, New Hampshire, airport grinding his teeth in anger. He was trying to get to the little town of Berlin, in the northern part of the state to campaign. But it was snowing up north and the pilots were trying to decide whether they should take off or not. He was already forty-five minutes behind schedule.

"What's wrong, Governor?" I asked.

"I think the rudest thing in the world is to make people wait," he said, meaning the crowd gathering in Berlin to hear him.

Well, under this kind of pressure the pilots took off. We flew to Berlin in a snowstorm. The trip has gone down in the annals of campaign lore as the "white knuckle" flight. We were all scared to death. Well, not quite all. Jimmy Carter didn't twitch.

Facing the press is a trial by fire for a candidate who does not have the built-in protections of White House incumbency. Having to undergo the minute-by-minute scrutiny of reporters over an extended period certainly tests character.

In early 1976, Carter used to include in his set speech a litany of great Americans, among them George Washington, Abraham Lincoln, Franklin Roosevelt, John F. Kennedy, and Martin Luther King, Jr. Then one day he hit North Carolina and a predominantly white crowd and omitted Reverend King's name. That night on the plane, James Wooten, then of the *New York Times*, asked Carter as we all circled round, "Did you forget, Governor?"

Carter thought about it for a moment and then gave the "right" as well as honest answer.

"No," he said. "I didn't forget."

Another time, Carter stood on the tarmac in Houston, Texas, and tried to smooth over his comments in a *Playboy* interview about Lyndon Johnson. Democratic Party chairman Robert Strauss had warned him that the part of his interview in which he had said that both Johnson and Nixon lied to the American people was perhaps more damaging to him in Texas than his celebrated comment in the same interview about having "committed lust in my heart." And he *had* to win Texas.

Carter told the local press corps assembled at the Houston airport that the *Playboy* "summary" of his remarks were unfortunate. He was clearly trying to leave the impression that the Johnson reference had been taken out of context. I was standing to Carter's immediate right, and I had a copy of *Playboy* with me. I pulled it out, secured the candidate's attention in my own particular fashion (by shouting in his ear), and read the offending part to him in the presence of the other reporters and cameras.

"Did you say that or not?" I demanded. Carter looked at me with all the love of a king cobra in the instant before striking. He swallowed. "I did," admitted Carter.

Greg Schneiders, one of his principal aides, told me later he thought I had saved the campaign. "If we had left the airport still trying to pass it off as a *Playboy* 'summary,' our credibility would never have recovered," said Schneiders. What he meant was that candidates, like other human beings, may be forgiven for making mistakes, but if reporters and the public come to believe they twist the truth in an effort to get away with something, they are through. Carter himself recognized this. When people charged him with saying one thing in one part of the country and another elsewhere, he would reply, "Why, if that were true, one kid with a tape recorder could destroy my campaign." I've always thought of myself as a kid with a tape recorder when it comes to keeping the record straight on what candidates and presidents say.

These incidents from the Carter campaign are small ones. But they revealed a good deal about Carter's character. Once, through another small incident, I learned something about how Governor George Wallace of Alabama operated. In the spring of 1968, I went down to Alabama to cover Wallace's presidential campaign. My film crew and I went to an evening rally of his in a rural area near the little town of Eutaw. Wallace delivered his usual stem winder, raging against "pointy-headed" Washington bureaucrats and judges who wouldn't let school districts manage their own affairs. The "folks" whooped and hollered.

When it was over, Wallace, who in 1968 had not yet been paralyzed by a would-be assassin's bullet, stepped onto the edge of the platform and started shaking hands, as was his habit. We shot two or three minutes of film of the handshaking, then turned off the light and relaxed. After all, how many handshakes can you put in a ninety-second report? But as the line moved forward, my cameraman, Charles Jones, spotted a familiar face.

"That's Robert Shelton," he said, pointing to a nondescript man standing at the edge of the crowd. Sure enough, I recognized him from his pictures—Robert Shelton, the imperial wizard of the United Klans of America (the Ku Klux Klan to most of us). A moment later, Shelton got in line to shake hands with Wallace.

"Start shooting," I ordered.

Jones turned the light back on and started filming. Into the pool of light stepped Shelton, and George Wallace automatically grabbed his hand. They shook. Wallace's smile disappeared. Wallace's political aides froze. Here he was trying to project a less threatening image to the North, trying to shake charges that he was a racist, and ABC News had filmed him shaking hands with the imperial wizard of the Ku Klux Klan.

Wallace stepped away from the line and huddled with his aides and the Georgia state patrolmen who were on hand as bodyguards. Two state policemen came over to us.

"Let's have the film," one of them said to Jones.

"You have no right to do this, Governor," I told Wallace.

The trooper just reached over and grabbed the camera off Jones's shoulder and started taking the film magazine apart.

By this time, the crowd was moving forward toward us. The "folks" probably had no idea what it was all about, but they could see George Wallace on one side and those eastern liberal network people on the other, and the "folks" had no difficulty choosing sides. I would like to be able to tell you that I went down fighting. I didn't. I took one look at the crowd as they started to surround us and forgot all about the rights of property and the First Amendment. Jones, sound man Walter James, Jr., lighting man Judd Marvin, and I got out of there fast.

Yes, I would have used the film. But I would have pointed out that Wallace seemed as surprised as anyone to find himself shaking hands with Shelton.

Now, different people might conclude such incidents with Wallace and Carter and others convey different things, but no one would have had a chance to interpret them at all if those campaigns had been waged in television studios and through a few antiseptic appearances.

That's the way the campaign of 1984 was conducted, at least on President Reagan's side, and that's why it was the most frustrating experience I've ever had in covering politics. The Reagan people, led by savvy political tacticians like Stuart Spencer of the California consulting firm of Spencer-Roberts, White House chief of staff James A. Baker III, deputy chief of staff Michael Deaver, and campaign director Edward Rollins of the reelection committee determined early on that they were not going to put the president in a position where he would have to actually engage in the rough and tumble of a real campaign.

They intended, in the time-honored fashion of incumbency, to keep him "presidential," that is, above it all, and let whoever the Democrats nominated beat his head against the cold wall of White House indifference. That's a good strategy when you are managing a popular president in good times. But as a reporter, my job was to get around it if I could.

A reporter's job in a campaign is to challenge the candidate to explain and defend his views and to answer the charges leveled against him by his opponent. When I covered Carter I did it to him, when I covered Reagan I tried to do it to him. But in Reagan's case, the above-the-fray strategy got in the way.

In 1984, Ronald Reagan, candidate for president of the United States, did not hold a single full-length television press conference between the time he was renominated and election day. Instead, his campaign consisted of carefully staged events at which he surrounded himself with friendly partisans, who, along with him, acted out patriotic and religious themes for the television cameras. Anyone could see what was going on and, in case the audience had been struck by a sudden myopia, I repeatedly pointed it out.

During my report on his visit to the Grand Ole Opry House in Nashville, Tennessee, I put it this way: ". . . the president failed again today, however, to say exactly how he intends to reduce the deficit, if not through higher taxes. None of this talk about deficits and taxes and such is the essence of the Reagan campaign. The essence of the Reagan campaign is a never-ending string of spectacular picture stories created for television and designed to place the president in the midst of a huge throng of wildly cheering patriotic Americans. And today's occurred right here in Nashville at the Grand Ole Opry."

I then showed Reagan standing with Roy Acuff, listening to Lee Greenwood sing "God Bless the U.S.A.," while balloons and confetti showered down on them. I concluded: ". . . God, patriotism, and Reagan. That's the essence this campaign is trying hard to project."

Now, you might ask, If that's all that was going on, why keep putting it on the air night after night? Why not exercise news judgment and show the president only when he's actually doing something new? The answer is that we felt we had an obligation to show the president's campaign as well as his opponent's campaign, whatever it was. So we kept putting it on, and we kept pointing out what it was.

One day Reagan went to Bowling Green, Ohio, for a rally at the college there. The gymnasium was packed with brightly scrubbed faces and neatly dressed bodies, all with their American flags, all ready to hear from their hero. A couple of hundred yards away from the gymnasium, behind a rope line guarded by police, several hundred demonstrators pushed and shoved, shouting anti-Reagan slogans.

Now, it might occur to you to ask how come none of the anti-Reagan people had gotten into the gym to heckle him face to face. After all, everywhere Walter Mondale went, great numbers of Reagan admirers showed up to heckle *him*, sometimes disrupting his rallies to the point where he could hardly proceed. The answer is that the Reagan rallies were all tightly controlled and staged. The way you got in was to apply for tickets from local Republican organizations, and people who were not already true believers didn't get them. That day, I showed the two contrasting scenes, outside and inside, let people hear the "tough" questions Reagan was asked inside, beginning with, "Hi, Mr. President, my name is Becky Holster, and I'd like to say you look great."—"Thank you," said the president fearlessly—and concluded my report this way:

"The president's aides insist that this campaign is open and everyone is welcome. But with only a few exceptions, since Labor Day, only Reagan supporters have managed to get in."

Larry Speakes wrote our senior vice-president Richard C. Wald to complain about such "unfair" reporting, no doubt, I'm sure, just for the record rather than from real conviction.

But even though reporters made certain the public understood the nature of the Reagan campaign, that didn't help smoke the candidate himself out of hiding and into the public debate. The protection plan was too solid.

Just once the plan slipped up. It came about this way. So intent were his strategists on dispelling the idea that Reagan couldn't get along with the Soviets and might get us into war that when a meeting was arranged between him and then Soviet foreign minister Andrei Gromyko for late September 1984, Reagan came to the White House briefing room himself to announce it.

Reagan took a few questions. The first twelve questions in a row concerned the Soviets. That was natural and what the staff expected—and wanted. Then he called on me and I switched subjects.

"Mr. President," I said, "Walter Mondale has now tabled a fairly specific budget reduction plan and says it's only fair that you do the same before the election. Will you, sir, and if not, why not?"

Three hundred and thirty-nine words later, we had heard a lot about the subject in general but nothing that addressed my question directly. He said he had submitted lots of budgets in the past and he believed the deficit would be reduced by continued growth of the economy and by getting control of spending.

I tried again. ". . . Isn't it fair to spell out to the American people precisely what cuts you have in mind?" I asked.

"Yes," began the president, but sixty-nine words later he had gone no further in fleshing out that yes except to point again to the thousands of words contained in his *previous* budget proposals.

One last try. "So, if we take your last budget sir, and look at them, look at the specifics, we'll have your next plan?" I asked.

The president replied with eighty-five words, none of which was *yes*, none of which was *no*. Instead, he placed his hands face down in front of him, raised one and lowered the other, and said, "It's as simple as this: If that rate of increase in spending can be brought down, as we've brought it down already [down went the right hand], if at the same time, through economic growth, the rate of revenues begins to climb at a steeper rate [up went the left hand], those two lines have to meet [hands now even with each other] and where they meet is a balanced budget. And this is what our plan is."

All clear to me. If, when people later saw Reagan's next budget, asking for deep cuts in veterans' programs, child nutrition programs, Medicare pay-outs and the like, they were taken unawares, I don't see why; he had spelled it out as plain as the two hands in front of your face.

I probably wouldn't have pursued it further that day. But we'll never know. Because as the president finished his last answer to me, the questioning was ended on instructions from the White House staff. As the president was leaving the room, others tried to get in one or two more questions, but Reagan told them, "Save them for the next time." I shot back, "But we're not certain there's going to be a next time, sir." There wasn't until the morning after election day.

On the morning after election day, Reagan met the press briefly in a televised session and someone asked him if he would hold more press conferences now that the campaign had ended. "Look, I won," he replied. "I don't have to subject myself to . . ." At this point everyone laughed, but in truth the record shows he meant it.

By the time of the two big debates between Reagan and Mondale, it was clear to most of us that Mondale was going to lose the election. But political reporters aren't paid to go home before election day on the theory that the race is over. And the first debate did deliver a thimbleful of fuel for the Mondale campaign. A lot of Americans who watched what happened in Louisville that night were shocked by Reagan's halting performance. I said on the air afterward that the old champ had left the ring still on his feet, "but the legs seemed a little wobbly."

The fact is, to those of us who cover the president regularly and see him in various situations more often than the general public,

Reagan didn't look much different than he often does. Yes, he clearly grew tired at the end of the ninety minutes. After all, he was seventy-three years of age at the time, notwithstanding the general public view that he is perpetually only thirty-nine. But beyond that, the general fumbling with answers, imprecise expression of views, lapses into anecdotal material, and rambling syntax is typical Ronald Reagan.

Usually on television, of course, you see him reading a well-crafted script from a TelePrompTer. Or reporters like me, desperate to come in within the time limits set by the program producer, show you only the sharpest, most precise twelve seconds of an overall Reagan presentation. So the public was unprepared for what it saw at Louisville.

There was suddenly a lot of comment that the race might tighten drastically and even tip in Mondale's favor as a result of that first debate. I didn't believe it for a moment. There was a second debate coming up, and Reagan would have a chance to recoup based on the most lenient and forgiving of standards. No one was going to demand that the "old champ" actually *win* his next fight. The standard would be whether he managed to stay on his feet at all. By that time, contrary to the conventional wisdom that no one concentrates on a presidential campaign until after the World Series, I think most voters had made up their mind and the majority wanted to vote for Reagan if he could just reassure them.

"People will be watching tonight because of Louisville," I said on the Brinkley show round table on the day of the second debate, "to see whether the president stands up, makes sentences that make sense from the standpoint of not stammering and stuttering, and doesn't drool. And if he does that, then Mr. Mondale can win all the debating points he wants and the president can misstate all the facts he wants and the president will be perceived to have won and Mondale won't have much of a chance . . ."

That night in Kansas City at the second debate, Reagan, you'll recall, did not drool and went on to a smashing reelection victory.

The payoff in presidential political campaigns may be election day, but the real election year olympics for television has always been the nominating conventions. At the networks, gold medals are awarded for scoops. I've covered every major party convention beginning with 1964, and I've always enjoyed the competition on the convention floor for scoops.

I'll never forget at the Democratic National Convention of 1964, watching Sander Vanocur, then NBC's White House correspondent, interview President Johnson live exclusively on NBC. Vanocur, thinking ahead, had stationed himself in the box next to Johnson's, and when a helpful Secret Service agent looked the other way, had simply leaned over and started asking questions.

After what seemed like an eternity, Bill Leonard, then a CBS correspondent, later a CBS News president, came rushing up just as Vanocur was concluding. Desperate to get into the act, Leonard asked LBJ if he wouldn't wave to Roger Mudd, who was in the CBS anchor booth. That sounds silly, but as someone who has been on both sides of an interview scoop, I know how desperate you are to get back in the game when you've been beaten.

I sharpened my live interview technique on both local and national figures during my time at WTOP-TV. I noticed one thing over and over about beating the competition to an up-for-grabs interview. You had to speak early and aggressively. If you waited until you were called on or until someone came forward voluntarily, you always waited too long.

In 1972, I put that lesson to work at the Democratic National Convention in Miami Beach. George McGovern was nominated, and on the last night, he came to the podium, on which dignitaries of the party were seated, to deliver his acceptance speech. I was waiting with other reporters behind those seats. We all wanted to get the first interview with McGovern when he was finished but were being held back by a lone security guard, whose instructions were clearly to allow none of us on the podium to talk to McGovern.

At the end of McGovern's speech, I asked the guard if he would let me go on the podium to talk to Senator Edward Kennedy. "Sure," he said. "Go ahead."

I alerted our floor control room to the situation, and Howard K. Smith threw it to me live as I stepped onto the podium and walked up to Senator Kennedy, who was in the back row.

"What did you think of the speech, Senator?" I asked.

"A very good speech," he said.

"Thank you, Senator," I said, moving past him toward the front, still on the air.

Halfway up, I asked Senator Hubert Humphrey what he thought of the speech, never pausing in my forward motion. I think he said it was fine, but his exact words trailed behind as I burst through the front row and fell on McGovern, who was still waving and nodding to the applauding audience. The other networks went wild trying to find camera shots other than the podium as I proceeded to interview McGovern exclusively on ABC.

It was a scoop. It was also 3:30 A.M. and very few people saw it.

But as luck would have it, I got another, even better, chance to beat the competition a few weeks later at the Republican National Convention, which was also held in Miami Beach. Richard Nixon had been renominated, had delivered his acceptance speech, and had stepped onto a specially constructed ramp in order to shake hands with every single delegate in the hall. They lined up and started up the ramp to partake of this singular honor. I, too, started up the ramp until I was stopped by the staff aide guarding the approach.

"Where are you going?" he asked. I was wearing my press credentials and all the bulky gear that floor reporters used to wear. I had a battery pack around my waist, earphones on my head with an antenna sticking out, and a microphone in my hand. That guard knew exactly who and what I was.

"I'm going up to shake the president's hand," I told him.

"Okay, go ahead," he said with a smile, motioning me on.

My God. What a scoop was in the works! It was late, about 12:30 A.M., but not as late as with McGovern. I started trying frantically to raise Av Westin, who was the producer in charge of the control room that handled floor correspondents. As I inched forward, I grew more frantic, yelling into the microphone. At a convention, floor control must listen for signals from four, maybe six, maybe more correspondents, who have radio gear on. With the noise from all those correspondents coming through the speaker monitors at once, it's often hard to pick out the one person who really has something that must go on the air.

Finally, Westin heard me and wanted to know where I was. I told him I was in the line going up the ramp and within a moment or two I would be in a position to interview the president. He immediately started pitching this to the senior producers and news department executives, who make the final decision on what to program.

I got to the top of the ramp, thrilled about the scoop that was going to be mine, when suddenly I heard Howard K. Smith, our anchorman say, "And so, that wraps up our coverage of the 1972 Republican National Convention . . ."

"No," I screamed in Mrs. Nixon's face as she stood in line next to her husband. The dear lady shrugged back in alarm.

". . . this is Howard K. Smith, thanking you for being with us and saying good night from Miami Beach," said the voice in my ear.

I lurched forward into the imperial presence. Nixon extended his hand, and sixteen years after I had first shaken it back in El Paso, I shook it again. He looked at me, at my headphones and antenna, at my microphone. He did not look pleased and was clearly bracing for the misfortune he suspected was about to befall him. He had nothing to fear. I was so frustrated, so desperately angry, that I was no threat to anyone. I cannot now remember what one or two pro-forma questions I asked Nixon, but they weren't important.

I ran down the other side of the ramp intending to find the executive responsible for taking us off the air at my moment of triumph and throttle him. I never found out who was responsible. But I'm still looking.

Things finally worked out in 1976.

There stood Jimmy Carter in New York's Madison Square Garden, his acceptance speech to the Democratic National Convention as its presidential nominee just completed. Robert Strauss, chairman of the Democratic Party and the greatest political showman since P. T. Barnum, was dragging to the podium every Democratic official ever elected anywhere to share a moment in television's spotlight. The county tax assessor of Bernalillo County, New Mexico, could easily have been up there waving to the crowd.

I was standing on the press area of the podium platform with other reporters watching all this. Through my radio gear, I told floor control what I was going to do. Harry Reasoner called me in and put me on the air and I simply walked through the throng of governors, senators, and county assessors, stuck a microphone in Jimmy Carter's face, and asked him how he felt. It was shortly after 11:00 P.M., near enough to prime time to count. The other networks began trying to find some shot that didn't include me. They failed. Of course, they didn't have any audio from my microphone, which had one of those ABC plates on it, just to rub it in. Within a couple of minutes, Ed Bradley of CBS and John Hart of NBC came rushing up, but they might as well have been hours late for all the good it did them.

I will not insult your intelligence by trying to make you think that scoop was a landmark event in television journalism. It was not. The ABC promotion department put it in my network biography for a while, and I'm still trying to get all copies of the version destroyed so well-meaning people introducing me to speak don't continue to say, "And he obtained the first interview with candidate Jimmy Carter after Carter was nominated in 1976." But at that moment, for me and for ABC—which wasn't yet noted for getting there first—it felt great.

My last effort at this kind of thing came in 1980, at the Republican National Convention in Detroit. Ronald Reagan finished his acceptance speech, retired to the back of the podium, and fled down a stairway on one side of the platform. I came charging down the stairway on the other side of the platform, playing out cable behind me from a technician on top, who was pointing the electronic gear in the right direction to put me on the air. I was live and yelled something inane like "What are your thoughts now?" as Reagan swept by. He answered briefly in the same spirit of fervent nonsense: "I feel good, great," and was gone. Some scoop!

The days for that type of convention interview are probably over. Convention security forces, Secret Service or otherwise, train their people to keep us all at bay. But let's face it. If those days are over, not much is lost. The competitive pressure for live interviews on the convention floor often pushes reporters and producers into putting junk on the air.

The worst single interview I've ever conducted live was on the convention floor in Dallas in 1984. It was with Nancy Reagan.

I hate to say anything bad about Nancy Reagan for two reasons. First, I think you could look Ronald Reagan in the eye and call him anything you wanted, and as long as you were smiling, he'd just laugh. But suggest the slightest imperfection in his wife, and he'll go for you with fire in his eyes. Second, I like Mrs. Reagan. As I told her on *Air Force One* coming back from China in 1984, when she jokingly said she hadn't bought her husband anything at the Xian market because I hadn't given her the money, "I have always had a *yuan* for you." But her husband's wrath and my affection for her aside, this is a story crying out to be told.

Mrs. Reagan came to the hall one night, and all the networks were granted an interview, one after another. Diane Sawyer of CBS, Chris Wallace of NBC, and I lined up to take our turns.

Mrs. Reagan is difficult to interview under the best of circumstances. Unlike her husband, she is not at ease around the press and seems to be constantly on guard that she not be trapped into saying something she will regret. Furthermore, she may be a delightful conversationalist in private, but she does not display that side of her personality in public interviews. At least, not to me. At least, not to me that night. To be fair about it, it would have been difficult for anyone to make engaging conversation amidst the yelling and shouting that was going on in the hall around us. How anyone can collect his or her thoughts while several hundred delegates, marshals, reporters, and hangers-on are babbling away and a loudspeaker blares from the podium is a miracle. But as they say, the show must go on.

When it was my turn, I took as my opening text an interview the president had given to the *Washington Post*, published that morning. I said to Mrs. Reagan, "The president told the *Washington Post* that you and he talk things over, talk everything over, that he comes back from the Oval Office at the end of a day and sits down and says—what?"

"Whatever he wants to say," she replied.

I kept at it. "I mean, would he say, 'Nancy, I just got a letter from Chernenko today and let me tell you what he said'?"

"No, no, no," she replied, clearly alarmed by the prospect that I might wrench from her an admission that she had been masterminding the whole of East/West diplomacy for the past four years.

I refused to give up. "What sort of subjects, then?"

"Well, subjects that a man and wife would talk about . . . I can't . . . I don't . . . you know . . . subjects that a man and wife would talk about."

This interview was already lost. A smarter reporter would have replied, "I know exactly what you mean, I've often talked to my wife about the very same things," and would have then tossed it back immediately to Peter Jennings in the anchor booth. But we all sometimes throw good money after bad, so after a little more chitchat about what she and her husband did and did not say to one another, I waded into a new batch of verbal quicksand. I switched to the women's issue. In retrospect, that was ridiculous. Nancy Reagan, like her husband, is no feminist.

"One final question," I said solicitously, softening my voice in an effort to gain her confidence. "Ms. Ferraro is running on a ticket against your husband and George Bush *(it's always good to refresh memories about these things)*, she's a woman, though *(sometimes my grasp of the obvious amazes me)*. How do you feel about this. Do you have sort of dual feelings?"

"No, I think it's fine to have a woman on the ticket," she replied.

"Right, but do you feel a little—is there a little part of Nancy Reagan secretly pulling for her at least not to fall flat on her face?" I continued deftly, or at least desperately.

Now, Mrs. Reagan seemed to feel for sure that I was trying to make her say something awful. Perhaps a headline flashed through her mind, "Nancy Reagan Endorses Democratic Ticket on ABC; Distraught Husband Files for Legal Separation."

"Now, Sam," she answered. "That's a kind of 'when did you stop beating your wife' question, isn't it?"

"Oh, I didn't mean it that way," I reassured her, sinking into the quagmire up to my nose. "I meant simply that she's the first woman on a national ticket, and although you want your husband to win . . ."

". . . Yes, I do," Mrs. Reagan interjected forcefully, hearing at last something to which she could give her wholehearted endorsement.

". . . I thought there might be some little part of you that sort of said, 'I hope she at least makes a credible showing,' " I wound up.

Now even though I had not, as Mrs. Reagan apparently feared, *tried* to trap her into saying something wrong, in a strange way she was sort of boxed in. She clearly wasn't going to say yes to that, but she must have realized it would be terribly ungracious of her to say no.

"Well, I'm sure, I'm sure she will," she began. "I think it's opened the door to—as my husband said once—it's a natural progression, you know of women progressing in life and career and just as there was a woman on the Supreme Court . . ." Her voice trailed off.

Around us beat the cacophony of the public address system and the babbling in the hall. I stood holding the microphone out to her. She stood, looking vulnerable and a bit frightened, in awkward silence.

I put us both out of our misery. "Thank you very much, Mrs. Reagan. We've enjoyed talking to you." Back to Peter Jennings at last. Better late than never, I always say.

Not all conventions have been so filled with froth and slapstick. My first, the Republican convention of 1964, was pretty grim. Goldwater delegates had come to nominate their hero, and they were in no mood to brook or even hear any opposition. That was the convention at which overzealous security guards grabbed NBC's John Chancellor while he was broadcasting live from the convention floor. As they hustled him off, he left the air by saying, "This is John Chancellor, reporting from somewhere in custody."

I was on the floor of that convention when the delegates booed and hurled obscenities at Nelson Rockefeller as Rockefeller tried to speak.

"It's a free country, ladies and gentlemen," Rockefeller told them. The "bund" booed louder.

Does it sound to you like I didn't like the mentality of that convention? You are right. So I surely voted against Goldwater that November, didn't I? You are wrong. I voted for him. It's the only presidential vote of mine I've ever revealed, and I revealed that one unintentionally.

When the campaign was over, a group of us who had covered the Goldwater campaign, including the young fellow from the Copley News Service, Lyn Nofziger, were having a drink and talking about how we'd voted. Little did I suspect that Nofziger would go on to other work (press secretary to Governor Ronald Reagan, later assistant to President Reagan). Now, every time I appear before a conservative audience, someone brings up that vote and I have to talk about it. The fact is, over the years I've voted for both Republicans and Democrats, liberals and conservatives, for president and I have no regrets about voting for Goldwater. To this day, I believe he would have made a good president. But I do have a problem with political reporters talking about their votes. So I haven't done it since.

Political reporters love to sit around and retell these "war stories" of campaigns and politicians gone by. But what we spend most of our time doing is trying to figure out who will be the winners of tomorrow. More often than not, of course, we're just as wrong as everybody else.

Before the 1984 election, when people asked me who would be elected president, I would sometimes dodge the question by spinning out a humorous description of my own checkered history of covering only losers.

I would point out that I covered Goldwater in '64, McCarthy in '68, and Humphrey in '72. The audience would begin to get the idea.

"True," I would continue, "I covered Carter in '76, but he started that campaign fourteen points ahead and only won by half a point. If I'd had another week, I would have gotten him. You see what happened when I covered him again in 1980."

By this time, everyone listening knew I was making a joke of the whole thing and would laugh uproariously when I delivered the punch line: "You ask me who's going to win in '84," I'd conclude. "I'll be covering Reagan; he doesn't have a chance."

Ha. Ha. Until one day someone sent me one of those right-wing magazines. Exhaling fire and brimstone from every pore, the magazine predicted that the despicable left-wing press would do everything it could to defeat Reagan. "Why," said the magazine, "Sam Donaldson of ABC openly boasts, 'You ask me who's going to win in '84? I'll be covering Reagan; he doesn't have a chance.' "

I've always said right-wingers can't take a joke.

Chapter Eleven

ABROAD

Air Force One lifts off the runway from Andrews Air Force base, heading overseas. An hour or two earlier, a chartered wide-bodied jet has lifted off carrying the press corps making the trip with the president. The news organizations pay for the press plane, not the taxpayers, and it isn't cheap. When other trip charges are thrown in, ABC News often winds up paying one and a half times the commercial airlines' first-class fare to send each member of its traveling party overseas.

And why are we all going, anyway?

Because news organizations believe, correctly, that Americans want thorough coverage of their president whenever he's abroad. And for television, the world as a backdrop is a welcome change from the White House Rose Garden. What we are going for, usually, is not news of lasting importance. With the exception of the Carter trip to Vienna to sign the SALT II treaty with Soviet President Brezhnev and the Carter trip to the Mideast to put together the Israeli/Egyptian peace treaty, none of the presidential trips I've been on has produced any dramatic news.

Consider the Reagan-Gorbachev summit in Geneva in November 1985. There we were, thousands of us, an army of us, prepared to report the news. There was none.

Playboy magazine even sent First Son Ron Reagan to cover Sam Donaldson covering Ronald Reagan. I told Ron he could follow me around, even sit in the editing room while David Kaplan and I tried to whip the nightly mess of porridge into an angel food cake, but he would have to understand that he would occasionally hear curses leveled at his father's celluloid image when the video didn't work out right or laughter when his old man said something we thought particularly silly. As it turned out, Reagan *père* didn't say anything particularly silly, but he did lose the battle of the photo opportunities. The first loss wasn't his fault.

By the luck of the rotation, I was the pool reporter for the first meeting between President Reagan and Soviet leader Gorbachev. We were ushered into a room in which the two men sat facing one another, flanked by their aides and interpreters. They had seen each other in person for the first time just moments before, so you couldn't logically ask them how the meeting was going or whether one or the other had thrown in the towel on Star Wars. But you had to ask them something.

"What's your first impression of Mr. Gorbachev?" I asked Reagan. He started to reply when a walkie-talkie radio belonging to someone in the press pool suddenly blared forth, drowning out his answer. It was some desk man trying to talk to one of his reporters or technicians in the field. I was holding a radio in my right hand and instinctively grabbed my on/off button to make sure it was off. It was.

The president's answer having been lost for all time, I turned my attention to Gorbachev. "Mr. General Secretary," I said, "Andrei Gromyko once said of you that you have a nice smile but iron teeth—I guess meaning you're tough. What do you have to say about that, sir?"

That wasn't a profound question, only one designed to get the leader of all the Russians to say something. Gorbachev, through an interpreter, fielded that in a breeze, by opening his mouth wide and replying, "It hasn't yet been confirmed. As of now, I'm still using my own teeth." A knowledge of my place plus a life-long dread of discovering halitosis in my interviewees kept me from rushing over to peer at and probe Gorbachev's mouth.

I turned again to the president and asked him another question. He started to answer. The offending walkie-talkie radio started to squawk as if on cue, once again drowning out his answer. We, the press, were ushered out.

I was furious. I conducted a full field investigation. Every reporter and technician present in the room who had a radio swore it wasn't him. Whoever it was—and as Larry Speakes says, "They know who they are"—you lost Ronald Reagan that photo op, you dirty rat.

But from then on, it was the president's fault that he lost the battle of the photo opportunities. He seemed tentative to Gorbachev's expansiveness. He seemed reluctant to enter the public give-and-take, contrasted to Gorbachev's reluctance to shut up and go into the meeting. He seemed to be playing the role of Bud Abbott to Gorbachev's Lou Costello. And one afternoon, he let "Mr. G" hit a home run right past his nose.

Up the walk in front of the Soviet Embassy, scene of that afternoon's meeting, came Reagan, Gorbachev, and others, including White House chief of staff, Donald Regan. Now, Regan had been very injudicious. In a pre-summit interview with Donnie Radcliffe of the *Washington Post*, he had delivered his opinion that most women would not understand the important topics of the summit such as "throw weights or what is happening in Afghanistan or what is happening in human rights." Instead, said Regan, most women would rather read about "the human interest stuff of what happened . . ." meaning, he made clear, the various social teas and what-not featuring Mrs. Reagan and Mrs. Gorbachev.

It had taken the story two days to get to Geneva. Even though the *Washington Post* and the *New York Times* had both thundered editorially in righteous indignation over his remark, my trusty desk hadn't thought for two days to pass it along to me when I'd call in five times a day and inquire, "What's new?"

But eventually, I had the facts. So when the two leaders faced the press area, I asked the president whether he agreed with his chief of staff that women wouldn't be interested in the important topics of the summit such as throw weight. Regan looked icy. Reagan looked pained. Gorbachev looked confused.

Deprived of the convenient claim of misquotation because of Radcliffe's careful habit of bringing a tape recorder to all her interviews, Reagan said he knew Regan well and was sure he didn't really mean what it sounded like. At that point, Reagan had the perfect opportunity to switch gears and wax eloquent on his own enlightened view of the perceptiveness of womankind. He just stopped instead.

So I turned to his companion and asked, "Mr. General Secretary, what do you think women are interested in at this summit?"

Gorbachev's personal interpreter whispered a translation. But Gorbachev looked puzzled. He clearly didn't understand the background of what was going on here, and it made no sense to him that this fool behind the rope was now asking not about his teeth but women's views. But Gorbachev is no slouch, more's the pity for the safety of the West. Not content to remain confused, he gestured to Reagan's interpreter, William Krimer, who had been called out of retirement by the State Department to make this trip. Krimer, who has been to six of the last eight U.S.-Soviet summits, is simply the best.

Krimer whispered in Gorbachev's ear. As he did, you could see "Mr. G's" face light up. He sensed competitive advantage. It was like NBC's Andrea Mitchell suddenly realizing that Donaldson has been struck by an attack of laryngitis just as the president is walking by.

"My view," said Gorbachev through his interpreter, "is that both men and women in the United States and in the Soviet Union, all over the world, are interested in having peace for themselves . . . and for that they are interested in the reduction that we have . . ." and on and on and on as Reagan squirmed and Regan shot killing looks at that fool behind the rope line.*

* In the summer of 1986, Regan came down with another similar attack of foot-in-mouth disease. He said he didn't think the women of America would want to give up their jewelry from South Africa as might be required if economic sanctions were imposed on that country by the United States. He took a lot of flak for that and later I asked him why he kept putting his foot in his mouth when it came to women. He replied that he'd done it once over the Geneva summit, a second time over South African diamonds, and, he argued, "I'm sixty-seven years old. Twice in a lifetime isn't bad."

That night, when I did my report on ABC, I tried to even things up a bit by showing Gorbachev in the meeting that followed voicing what struck me as a sexist remark of his own. CBS's Lesley Stahl was the pool correspondent inside the meeting, and in reply to one of her questions, Gorbachev's ambassador to Washington, Anatoly Dobrynin, translated his answer to suggest that the women were getting a little pushy with their questions.

Over on CBS that night, Stahl was insisting that Gorbachev had actually awarded her a verbal medal for having the courage to ask such good questions.

All this is funny, you say, or a little sad, but certainly it is irrelevant. Why don't you speak of the substance of the summit? Well, in one respect, that one, chief of staff Regan was half right. There was nothing of substance to report. A news blackout had been imposed at the suggestion of Secretary of State George Shultz. I suspect that Shultz did that not because he truly thought a little news would scuttle the summit (a farfetched idea indeed), but because he understood that nothing much of immediate importance was likely to take place and a blackout would serve as a convenient cover to keep that fact hidden.

It is true, an overall discussion of the superpower relationship is always relevant, and we did a lot of that on the air during that period—from chewing over missile strengths to examining that old geopolitical maxim "He who rules the heartland commands the world." But my job is to try to tell you "what's really going on here," and if the answer is "nothing much," there's no way I can pretend otherwise. Besides, one of the principal things going on in Geneva was the playing to the world audience by both sides through the photo opportunities. The picture's the thing: Who smiles widest, who sounds more dynamic, who looks most reasonable.

If *you* don't think *they* don't think the picture's the thing, consider the most famous still picture of that summit . . . the one of Reagan on one side of the sofa and Gorbachev on the other, with White House chief of staff Regan hovering over the sofa back in between, making it look like he was the driving force keeping the summit on track.

Sure, it was Shultz and national security adviser Robert McFarlane who did the work in Geneva, and if credit is due they should get it. But it was Regan who decided which pictures shot by White House staff photographers would be released.

He who rules the heartland, hell. He who controls the pictures commands the world.

But even if there isn't big news produced on a presidential trip abroad, we need to give the president thorough coverage. And believe me, doing that is extremely hard work. The first long trip Jimmy Carter took abroad almost did me in. We started out by going to Warsaw, two days later to Teheran, the next day to New Delhi, two days later to Riyadh, the next day to Aswan and Paris, two days later to Brussels, then home. Whoever put together that schedule was nuts.

Carter got his usual amount of sleep each night, but I got only two or three hours. Here's why. When you go overseas, the time frame shifts. When it's air time in New York, 6:30 P.M., it's 12:30 A.M. the next day in Europe. You work all day covering the president, into the evening when he attends the state dinner in his honor, after which you sit down to edit your report for the evening news.

In the Orient, it's even worse. You're out of sync *ahead* of the U.S. by a full twelve or thirteen hours. You work all day covering the story and work all night editing it for the evening news, which goes on the air back home as the sun is coming up for another day of work where you are. When I'm in the Orient, I always begin the *World News Sunday* broadcast, which I anchor, by saying, "Good evening from [Seoul, Beijing, Tokyo], where it's already Monday morning."

So on that first major Carter trip abroad, I was learning how to cover a president abroad and stay awake long enough to do it. I was also learning that you need a lot of help from people who are familiar with the territory through which the president is passing. Fortunately, when we landed in Poland, I got it from Pierre Salinger.

Pierre Salinger, President Kennedy's press secretary, since 1977 ABC's man in Paris and now chief foreign correspondent, is our "man for all seasons." Not only does he know everyone overseas, he makes me look good when presidents go abroad by generously sharing his information with me. I got my first helping hand from Salinger almost the moment Carter arrived at the Warsaw airport. The president got off *Air Force One* and told the crowd he had come "to learn your opinions and understand your desires for the future."

But that's not the way the U.S. State Department translator repeated it in Polish. He seized on the word *desires* and told the Poles that Carter had come to have carnal knowledge of them. Not only that—at another point, the translator turned "left the United States" into "abandoned" the United States, making it sound as if Carter had decided to defect to Poland. There were a lot of chuckles from the crowd over this lustful defector, but none of us in the non-Polish speaking White House press corps could figure out why. It wasn't long before Salinger got the story from his Polish sources. He passed it on to me, and I was able to beat my network competition in reporting the fiasco.

When Carter left Poland to continue his trip, Pierre Salinger stayed behind, and Barbara Walters, Ted Koppel, and I muddled on. In Iran, the division of labor was easy in the case of Walters and me. She went to such things as the New Year's Eve ball in the shah's palace, where she heard Jimmy Carter say there was no place he and Rosalynn would rather spend New Year's Eve; I stayed back at Iranian television putting together the report on it.

Koppel, who was our diplomatic correspondent at the time, and I had to work things out a little more equally. We always managed to do it. I would do a "here he comes, there he goes" piece, with just enough substance so you knew I wasn't completely out of touch. Then Koppel would follow on the air with the sagacious "what it all means" report. Using that formula, Koppel and his successors on the State Department beat, Barrie Dunsmore and John McWethy, and I have tripped our way merrily around the world many times delivering two reports where often one would do. But then, we all have to work.

And sometimes play. In India on that first trip, Walters and Koppel and I couldn't get over the fact that the then prime minister of India, Morarji Desai, drank a quantity of his own urine each morning for medicinal purposes. You can laugh if you want, but Desai was eighty years old in 1977 and, as I write this in 1986, is still alive. One night in New Delhi, we fell to talking about it as we drank a bottle of wine.

"Well, you know, it's like this wine," said Koppel. "It's not a great urine, but a good urine."

"Travels well," said I.

"A little on the heavy side," said Walters.

We doubled over with laughter. The Indian diners around us thought we were crazy.

I held my own against the competition during that first long trip abroad until I got to France. There I was beaten. We were all dead tired by the time we got to Paris, so the next morning, when Carter and French President Valéry Giscard d'Estaing took a train to Normandy to go to Omaha Beach, the ABC trip master, Michael Duffy, gave all the producers the morning off to sleep in. That meant that as French television beamed back the pictures of live events from Normandy, ABC engineers were recording them but no editorial personnel were watching. I figured that was okay. I would be there and see it all with my own eyes.

At the American cemetery, Carter gave a speech. Then it was Giscard's turn. He spoke in French. In the middle of his address, I slipped away from the other reporters and made my way down to the bluff overlooking Omaha Beach to join the small press pool waiting there for the two presidents to walk by. Soon enough, they came along and I saw it all.

On the return trip to Paris aboard Giscard's special train, the French served us the same great meal with eleven courses that the two presidents were eating. We were all so tired that Bob Schieffer of CBS and I took turns waking each other up to announce the next course had come and gone. We were so tired, in fact, that when Jody Powell came back to offer us a photo opportunity with Carter and Giscard, we turned him down. That is the only time that has happened since I've been in the White House.

Back at the edit room, relying on my notes and my memory, I called for the shots I wanted and proceeded to build a respectable report, which was relayed to New York via satellite before the other networks'. When my competitors' reports were ready, I relaxed back behind the ABC edit partition and listened to them being satellited.

The NBC story sounded pretty much like mine until, suddenly, I heard the unmistakable voice of French President Giscard, speaking in *English*, declare emotionally about the American landing on Omaha Beach, "Everyone knows Colonel Taylor's command—'The only people who are on the beach are those who are dead and those who are about to die—we must move.' All this, France remembers."

It was dramatic. It was moving. It was shocking that the competition had it. How could NBC have gotten Giscard to say it, and where? While I was turning over that question, CBS began relaying its report. Ye Gods, I heard it again. ". . . All this, France remembers," said Giscard to the CBS audience. I couldn't stand it. I tore around the partition and cornered Bob Schieffer.

"Where did you get Giscard saying that?" I demanded.

Schieffer seemed taken aback. "Why, at the cemetery," he replied.

"But he only spoke in French," I said.

"No, after he spoke in French, he repeated it in English," said Schieffer. "Weren't you there?"

Oh yes, I was there. I had slipped down to the beach. And everyone else at ABC was in bed. Believe me, from that day on I've tried to look quickly at everything available. And a good thing I do. One night in Geneva, during the Geneva Reagan-Gorbachev summit, my producer, David Kaplan, and I were going through all the pool material looking for routine shots of the two leaders and their aides around the conference table when we chanced across the famous pose of the two leaders leaning across the table shaking hands. No one had bothered to tell us it was there, if anyone at ABC knew it. Thank goodness we stumbled on it.

Reporters are not the only ones who sometimes stumble along on such foreign trips. Presidents have been known to, also. Lyndon Johnson once took a trip around the world without knowing exactly where he was going. In 1967, Johnson went to Australia to attend the funeral of Australian Prime Minister Harold Holt, who disappeared one day while swimming in the ocean. Some thought Holt might have been eaten by a shark. But once the funeral was over, Johnson simply ad-libbed his way around the world. He took off after a stop in Karachi, Pakistan, heading west with "no firm idea where he was going to land," as ABC's White House correspondent of the time, Frank Reynolds, described it on the air. Johnson would either land in Rome, if a meeting with the pope could be arranged on last minute notice, or simply go on to a refueling stop in Portugal. It turned out the pope was in, so Rome it was.

If a stop at the Vatican turned out to be good for Johnson, it wasn't so hot for Ronald Reagan. Reagan went there in 1982, during a European trip that had been overscheduled, leaving him, and us, insufficient time to rest. So he seized the opportunity to take a nap during his audience with the pope. As the president sat under the hot television lights listening to Pope John Paul II's welcome, Reagan fought to stay awake. He lost. Our cameras zeroed in, and that night we showed the presidential nap. Not only did we show it that night, we have shown it again and again and again because all the interesting, even ghastly, scenes of presidential deeds and misdeeds go into the tape library, where they are instantly available for recall and reuse. Sometimes I think if I see Jimmy Carter hugging Leonid Brezhnev in Vienna one more time, I'll scream.

But at least a hug is a sign of affection. The memorable picture we occasionally rerun from Bonn is anything but. It was at the economic summit of non-communist industrialized nations in Bonn in 1978 that one of the leaders let fly with a rude gesture seen round the world. At the conclusion of such summits, the leaders all gather to be photographed together. That year, they were to come out on some steps. Carter led the way, and spotting me in the crowd of reporters, said teasingly, "Where do you want us, Sam?" I began directing, calling for German chancellor Helmut Schmidt, who was delayed, to come out and take his place, suggesting to British prime minister James Callaghan that he move a bit to his right, and so forth. Everyone seemed to take it good-naturedly except Canadian prime minister Pierre Trudeau. He slapped the edge of his left hand sharply into the crook of his right arm, bringing his right forearm up smartly in a forceful and world-recognized gesture of rude defiance.

All the cameras were trained on the group, and that night on television in seven countries, Trudeau was seen giving someone a rude gesture. Modesty and my innate sense of good taste kept me from identifying the target. I really didn't hold it against Trudeau, but I must say, when I heard the report that Ronald Reagan, having taken enough of Trudeau's nit-picking during a later summit, threw his glasses down on the table and exclaimed, "Damn it, Pierre . . ." I gave three cheers for Reagan.

Reagan is given to an occasional mild expletive, and once in Tokyo he did it on camera. The president was taping an interview with four Japanese journalists while paying a state visit to Japan in 1983. The interview was being piped back to the U.S. network edit rooms. The senior Japanese reporter welcomed the president, and Reagan, reading from prepared remarks on the TelePrompTer, said he was delighted to be there. "I have received a letter from one of your countrymen," read the president, "Masayasu Okayum . . . [pause] . . . Okamura [Reagan was struggling with the name, squinting at the TelePrompTer] . . . Ah, *damn it!*" exclaimed the president, giving up in a glorious burst of frustration.

"Let me say that name again," asked the president plaintively.

Well, shut my mouth. There was much scurrying around outside of camera range. Whispered conversations, chairs being scraped, technicians either pushing equipment or running for the doors.

"Take two," said the president professionally.

The picture went dead for a moment, then came alive with the familiar happy, avuncular Reagan back stroking the name Masayasu Okumura with the dexterity of a native-born Japanese. But too late, folks. We had in our possession a videotape of the president of the United States in a moment of high vexation, an understandable vexation, saying, "*damn it*." Of course I intended to use it in my evening news report, not in dark denunciation of Reagan for cursing, but in a lighthearted way of saying, "See, even the mighty are human."

But Pierre Salinger, who was also on the scene, was aghast. As a former press secretary, he felt keenly that presidents shouldn't have to live in a glass house every moment, particularly when just taping an interview could be and started again.

"I hope you don't feel you have to use it," said Salinger. "I'm sure no one else will." I thought about it. I knew Salinger was wrong. But it was, after all, a very small thing. No important piece of information was involved, no high principle on which I must make my stand, and I do like Pierre. I didn't use it.

Naturally, NBC's Chris Wallace did.

"Didn't use it?" inquired Wallace teasingly the next day. "Why, I didn't realize how much of the old Donaldson punch was gone."

Damn it to hell, Mr. Okayum . . . Okamura . . . whatever your name is.

Visits to Tokyo always seem to get the juices flowing, sometimes in the most strenuous ways. In 1979, at the economic summit held in Japan, some of us fought a near pitched battle with the Tokyo police. President Carter had invited the press to come over to the U.S. Embassy to hear daughter Amy play the violin, but the police wouldn't let us cross the street. One of Carter's press aides, Randy Lewis, and I led the charge through the police lines. There was pushing and shoving and much yelling and screaming, and finally they let us through. Probably the reason they didn't smash us with their batons was the fact they didn't understand English and thus failed to comprehend that I was yelling such phrases as "Remember Pearl Harbor" and "Tonight, marine, you die."

The police in Tokyo are something. When Reagan went to an economic summit there in 1986, I was in the press pool that rode on *Air Force One.* When we landed, the Secret Service detail and the press went down the plane's back ramp and immediately ran into a flying squad of Japanese police, who refused to let us take up our accustomed place near the front ramp that Reagan would use. Their theory must have been that the president of the United States had allowed terrorists to board his aircraft and ride all the way to Tokyo with him and they were going to protect him from these fiends now that he was on the ground. The Secret Service finally got through; the press didn't.

I will say that it's not always foreign security forces who sometimes get a little overzealous. The U.S. Secret Service once held up the prime minister of Italy for a moment or two when he tried to enter his own palace in Rome to meet with President Reagan, who was waiting inside. And in Bonn, during an economic summit there, the Secret Service blocked off a street down which Reagan would shortly ride and wouldn't let French president Mitterand enter until Reagan had come and gone. In Beijing, the Secret Service put so many men around Reagan when he walked through the Great Hall of the People to meet Chinese premier Zhao Ziyang that you could hardly see the two leaders shake hands. The only people there were Reagan and his aides, Zhao and his aides, and the U.S. press corps. I wonder from which group the Secret Service feared an attack?

That trip of Reagan's to China in the spring of 1984 was one of the most interesting trips I've taken abroad with a president. I had never been to China. Going with Ronald Reagan made it doubly exciting. Here was a man who was almost an original member of the Chiang Kai-shek Nationalist China lobby. A man who, along with Henry Luce, Dr. Walter Judd, Anna Chennault, and others had denounced "Red China" for years while trying to persuade us that only Chiang Kai-shek, known as the "G-Mo," clinging there on Taiwan, was worthy of our notice. Now, here was that same man going to "Red China" on a friendship visit in 1984. I would have paid out of my own pocket for a ticket of admission to the show.

While the press pool was waiting in the Great Hall of the People for the president to appear for his first meeting with Premier Zhao Ziyang, the premier and other members of the politburo came over and talked to the U.S. press pool. I asked Zhao how he felt having in his midst a man who had been such "an ardent anti-communist" and had denounced Zhao's country for so many years "in the harshest terms." Zhao and the others smiled. "I think any politician with vision will see that it is an outmoded idea to distinguish nations for friendship or hostility on the basis of ideology," replied Zhao through an interpreter, adding with a sly smile, "I feel that President Reagan is aware of it."

The thought of Ronald Reagan paying no attention to ideology in deciding whether he liked a country or not was so mind-boggling that I was rendered temporarily speechless, and before I could recover myself enough to pursue it, the moment had passed.

The Chinese leaders, who have a way with words as we've already seen, charmed Reagan. At their first meeting, Premier Zhao told him through an interpreter, "Mr. President, after such a long flight you don't look tired at all, you look very energetic at your age and it's very rare."

"Well, thank you very much . . ." said Reagan, looking pleased as punch.

Zhao knew that when you have a good thing going, you press on. "People here say you look much younger than your age," he continued.

"As far as I'm concerned, the meeting has already been a success, thank you," replied the president. And it was.

The Chinese took him to Xian, site of the famous terra cotta warriors, buried so long ago by an emperor who wanted a mighty army to protect him in the hereafter land. The press corps was bused in to the central square at Xian before the president arrived. So we got to see the Chinese set up a fake marketplace. They set up tables, decked them out with all manner of goods, and installed neatly dressed "salespeople" behind them. Next, "customers" gathered around the tables waiting for the signal. When Reagan arrived, he found happy-looking Chinese buying and selling goods, paying money, making change just like they do in capitalist countries. The president borrowed some Chinese money and bought a few things. Of course, after he left, while the press buses were loading, the Chinese took down their market and disappeared. Reagan said later he was aware that things might not have been what they seemed, but the impression stuck in his mind.

In a small way, the press corps evened the score with the Chinese for their duplicity, however. When Naomi Nover, a little old white-haired woman who runs a shoe-string news service, tried to push her way into a reserved area at Xian and was stopped by a Chinese guard, Gary Schuster of CBS pulled out a dollar bill and thrust it into the guard's face. Schuster pointed at the picture of George Washington on the bill. He then pointed at Naomi Nover who happens to bear a striking resemblance to the father of our country from certain angles. The guard broke out in an embarrassed smile and, bowing low, waved Nover through.

The visit went very well. Reagan did not even seem to mind that on his way out of Beijing, the Chinese had thoughtfully routed his motorcade along the side of Tiananmen Square, where huge portraits of Marx and Lenin were displayed so that the cameras could show the presidential limousine gliding under a picture of Karl Marx. On the return flight, Reagan came back to the rear compartment of *Air Force One* to talk to the press, something he does so rarely. He was bubbling over with good cheer about his trip and told us that he and the Chinese leaders had agreed on many things. After landing in Fairbanks, Alaska, the president continued this love affair, singing the praises of, and these are his exact words, "this so-called Communist China." Wow! So-called? Roll over "G-Mo," times have changed.

Traveling abroad with presidents is usually hard work, but there have been moments of bliss. Reagan took me to Bali, and Carter took me to Guadeloupe. And it was on Guadeloupe that I scored my most unusual scoop, the roast pig report, thanks once again to the good offices of Pierre Salinger.

In the cold January of 1979, the big four Western leaders repaired to the warm French Caribbean island of Guadeloupe to examine the thorny issues of the day. They also took the opportunity to examine the vacationers on the nudist beach below the open-air thatched-roof hut in which they held their working sessions.

There sat Carter of the U.S., Giscard of France, Schmidt of Germany, and Callaghan of Britain. Unfortunately for him, Callaghan drew the seat with its back to the beach. Later, I was told that the others had to constantly call his attention back to the business of the moment as he twisted around for a look at the happy vacationers *au naturel.* But this bit of gossip came my way later. At the time, we were all hungry for news and there wasn't any.

Now, mind you, in a perfect world I could report to New York that there wasn't any news on Guadeloupe and all the reporters, producers, technicians, couriers, and hangers-on sent there at great expense could go out for another swim. This is not yet that perfect world, however, and I knew we had to report something and probably at the top of our news broadcast. Enter faithful Pierre Salinger who, as a French resident, was in his element. He had discovered the private residence where the leaders would dine that night. He had learned the menu. Roast pig. Not only that, he had persuaded the host to let ABC News come by for an exclusive look at the oven in which the pig would be roasted.

We went. We saw. I conquered. NBC and CBS were beaten that night by an exclusive report on the roasting of the presidential pig. Another clean kill, if you will, no offense meant by that to the pig.

You learn a lot of things traveling with presidents. But you clearly aren't seeing countries as they really are, only as their leaders want the president of the United States to think they are. For instance, when Carter visited Nigeria in 1979, the government suspended public executions on the beach just below Carter's hotel for the duration of the trip, an understandable public relations move, I'll admit.

But despite the whitewash, a lot comes through—the poverty in some places, the anti-American attitude in others, the warm feeling for us in still others. And you can't travel abroad without coming to a stronger appreciation of our dominant yet uneasy place in the world. Consider this bit of byplay in Nigeria:

Said Donaldson playfully to a Nigerian army major as we all waited for *Air Force One* to land: "Give us your oil, your oil, we've come to get your oil."

Replied the major to Donaldson, flashing a big, toothy smile, "Okay, give *us* your bomb."

On second thought, Major, keep your oil.

Chapter Twelve

WHEN THINGS GO WRONG

When Frank Reynolds slammed his palm down on the anchor desk on March 30, 1981, the day President Reagan was shot, and snapped, "Let's get it nailed down, somebody. Let's find out!" he was exhibiting the best instinct of our business. I understand how some viewers might have cringed at the intensity of Frank's outburst. But surely no one can criticize his demand that the information we pass along to the public be exactly right.

That was a day on which it was difficult to keep things straight. It's always like that in a crisis.

Frank and I had been at lunch at Mel Krupin's Restaurant, next door to our bureau, which was then located on Connecticut Avenue. I looked at the clock. It was 1:40 P.M. Reagan was giving a speech to Robert Georgine's AFL-CIO Building and Construction Trades Department at the Washington Hilton at 2 P.M. It was going to be a "nothing" speech, and I was tempted to go back to the bureau with Frank and talk some more, but you can't be the White House correspondent and not cover the beat.

Roone Arledge used to nag me about the way I spent my time, asking why didn't we send some bright newly graduated journalism major to the routine events to take notes so that I could spend my time tracking down really important stories or producing in-depth television reports. Arledge hasn't raised that proposal once since the day Reagan was shot.

I got to the Hilton in time to hear Reagan's speech. We had two camera crews there, one set up on a tripod to photograph the president head-on, a second to roam through the ballroom getting reaction shots to use in editing the report. The second cameraman was Hank Brown, his partner carrying the videotape machine, Harry Weldon. I told Brown that when Reagan finished, I wanted him to stay on until the president left the room. I told him I would go upstairs and save a spot for him on the rope line outside to get Reagan's departure from the hotel. "Get up there as fast as you can," I said, "but I want the pictures of the president leaving the room, and if you don't make it outside in time, I'll work around that." Brown got outside and into place on the rope line about thirty seconds before Reagan appeared.

I have often thought what might have happened to my career if he hadn't made it. Later, when the furious postmortems would have been conducted as to why ABC News had none of its own pictures of the assassination attempt, Brown would have had to say it was because I had told him to linger downstairs. Of course, Cable News Network didn't have its own pictures that day (it hadn't scheduled a camera crew outside), but that didn't stop CNN; it just "lifted" ours off the air and used them as its own. No one at ABC knew it until a week later when a CNN producer friend of mine, Wendy Walker, told me how nice she thought it was for ABC to give its permission for them to use our tape. Permission, hell. Walker wasn't aware of it but it was pure theft.

When the president came out of the special VIP doorway, surrounded by Secret Service agents and staff, I was standing on the rope line about fifteen feet away, behind which cameras, reporters, and the general public were packed. John Hinckley, Jr., was there also. It was not a designated press area, so press credentials were not required in order to enter.

As the president moved toward his limousine, Michael Putzel of the AP and I started throwing questions at him concerning

Poland and the growing fear that the Soviets might move to crush the new Solidarity workers' union.

Reagan turned his head toward us and may or may not have been about to answer. At that moment, Hinckley started shooting.

POP! POP! . . . I knew instantly it was gunfire. And though I realized it was coming from my immediate right (Hinckley was about six feet away from me), there was never any question in my mind who the target was. So until the president had been propelled into his limousine by Jerry Parr and Ray Shaddick, the Secret Service agents walking on either side of him, I never took my eyes off Ronald Reagan.

I saw no evidence that he had been hit. No blood, no outcry, no sudden slump or twitch of the body. The videotape shows he grimaced when the slug struck his chest, but as I watched it in person, his slight change of expression looked like surprise. I was aware that others had fallen to the ground and that a lot of people were piling on top of someone just a few feet to my right. But I kept watching the president.

The instant the limousine door shut and the car began to move, I ran for a telephone. As I turned, I took a mental snapshot of bodies lying on the sidewalk. I thought I saw four, but couldn't be sure.

There was a bank of pay phones against a wall fifty feet inside the hotel's lower lobby. But as I crashed through the entrance, I saw a private phone on the Gray Line Sightseeing Tour desk just inside the door. I grabbed it and called in. The ABC operator, Mary Faux, connected me to the special number that rings on all phones in the main news department editorial areas. "This is Donaldson, and this is no drill," I said. I'm sure I sounded agitated and a bit breathless. And my first ad-libbed telephone report taped for replay was not a model of perfection. I reported:

> Here at the Washington Hilton, shots rang out as President Reagan was leaving the hotel and about to enter his limousine. At least one person was hit and fell to the sidewalk with blood coming from his body. It was not the president. I don't know whether the president was hit. I do not believe he was. His car left rapidly under police escort. The shots were fired by someone in the crowd of people

> watching the president depart. Five or six shots rang out. It sounded like a pistol shot. At least one person has been hit and fell to the sidewalk. I do not believe the president was hit, but I'm not certain. His car drove off rapidly.

The president had been shot at approximately 2:26 P.M. That report went on ABC radio at 2:30. It was the first report of the shooting on radio or television. And, of course, I had gotten several things wrong. But news like that can't wait for the end of the story. You report what you know as soon as you can. When someone shoots at the president, you can't wait until you have all the details confirmed.

When I ran back outside, I saw three people lying on the sidewalk. What had happened to the fourth person I thought had gone down? He turned out to have been the president's military aide, Lt. Colonel Jose Muratti, who was carrying the nuclear attack codes (it's called the football, because the codes are contained in a soft leather bag that looks like an oversized football). The codes are always carried by one of the military aides and go with the president everywhere. Muratti hit the ground instinctively when he heard the gunfire. Unhurt, he got up an instant later and ran for the motorcade just after I had run for the telephone. The control car picked him up.

The scene was chaotic—Hinckley being subdued against the retaining wall, a Secret Service agent, Bob Wanko, was waving an Uzi machine gun in the air, advance man Rick Ahearn and others bending over press secretary James Brady trying to stem the blood.

The first thing I did when I got back outside was to tell our camera crew that we had to get the videotape back to the studio immediately. Brown and Weldon had already dispatched it. We had a courier, Larry Smith, routinely waiting at the hotel. Weldon had given him the tape and said, "Go." Even though Smith had been knocked to the ground in the rush to get at Hinckley and his back had been injured, he jumped on his motorbike and sped away with the tape. We were the first network to get the pictures on the air, thanks to Brown, Weldon and Smith.

Next, I started interviewing other witnesses. I soon found a man who said he had seen shots fired from the grassy slope above the retaining wall. I told him he was dead wrong, that there had only been six shots fired, and *I knew* they had all come from the same location on the rope line. Why is it that grassy slopes or knolls turn up at such moments in the human mind?

I found a White House press office aide, David Prosperi, who told me that it was his information that the president had not been hit and was on his way back to the White House.

After the authorities had taken Hinckley away (the authorities were so rattled that they first tried to put him in a patrol car whose door they couldn't get open) and after the wounded men had been taken away, I returned to the studio and was rehashing the event live with Frank Reynolds when someone handed him a note. He read it and reported that late word from the hospital said the president indeed had been wounded and was to undergo surgery within the hour.

I've seen the videotape of that instant and of the look on my face. I was flabbergasted, embarrassed, and angry. I had been careful to say in my report that while I hadn't seen any evidence of the president having been hit, I couldn't be certain. But when Prosperi seemed to confirm my observation, I had wiped the thought from my mind. Now, to discover I had been wrong all along and had misled our audience, well, I was horrified.

I went to the hospital immediately and stayed there for the rest of the day. That meant I missed the action in the White House press room when Secretary of State Haig came out in a state of high agitation and agreed with a questioner that, yes, he was in charge there. But I've always believed the place to be when you are covering the president is where the president is, particularly if he's been shot.

At one point, Marion Barry, Jr., the mayor of the District of Columbia, emerged from the hospital and I asked him what he knew. Barry told me the talk inside was that Reagan would pull through, but that Jim Brady was gone. Would he say that on camera? Absolutely not, said the mayor. Well, if he wouldn't, I certainly wasn't going to.

A few minutes later, Bob Murphy, then our top desk man in Washington, now a vice-president of television news coverage in New York, called me to say we were under great pressure to announce Brady's death. The other two networks had already done so. Could I confirm it? I told Murphy of my conversation with Mayor Barry, but we agreed that wasn't confirmation.

ABC was the last of the three commercial networks that day to make that awful blunder and report, erroneously, that Brady had died. We finally did it because we thought we had confirmation from two sources, one on Capitol Hill, the other at the White House. But I think the lesson speaks for itself. At such times, wait for an official announcement.

Take Dallas. The late Merriman Smith of UPI saw attendants lift President Kennedy out of his limousine at Parkland Hospital. Smitty saw the massive head wound Oswald's third shot had produced. Moreover, Secret Service agent Clint Hill told him Kennedy was dead. But Smith's bulletin was absolutely correct.

FLASH

Kennedy seriously wounded perhaps seriously perhaps fatally by assassin's bullet

JT1239PCS

Smith pointed you in the right direction but was not about to make the leap into the kind of finality that we all did that day with Jim Brady.

Some people criticized Reynolds unmercifully for his sharp demand on the air when he heard the correction to the death report: "Let's get it nailed down, somebody. Let's find out." But I tell you, Frank was right to care, right to react that way, right to be angry at us for having misinformed our viewers on this matter, and right to say it on the air.

One more footnote on the day. When the president was safely out of surgery, the attending doctors at George Washington University Hospital held a press briefing, and along with the good news about the president, one of them said something that was dead wrong. Dr. Dennis O'Leary, the hospital spokesman for the president's stay, said that Reagan was "at no time in any serious danger." That proved to be incorrect. A few more minutes' delay in getting help and Reagan most probably would have died. He almost went into shock in the emergency room.

I'm not going to pillory Dr. O'Leary if he didn't have the facts, but if that statement was made primarily to reassure the public even at the breach of truth, then it should never have been made. I feel strongly that people have the right to know the truth about everything affecting the public interest. We can handle it. What we can't handle is the difficulty of trying to decide what's the truth and what's not when officials, whether presidents or doctors, speak to us. The chances are, in this case, however, even the doctors hadn't had time to evaluate everything. Fast-moving news events are difficult enough for people to handle under the best of circumstances. Shocking news numbs ordinary abilities to comprehend, evaluate, and report.

Here's a story that proves that from the day President Kennedy was shot. I was sitting in the Senate gallery watching rather dull proceedings when a press aide scurried onto the floor and started whispering to Senator Spessard Holland. Holland hurried to the rostrum and whispered to Senator Edward Kennedy, who was presiding at that moment. Kennedy stiffened, scooped up his papers, and rushed off. Holland took his place. Meanwhile, the aide with the news had quickly made the rounds of the senators present, including Mike Mansfield, Everett Dirksen, and Clifford Case.

What in God's name was going on? I leaned over the balcony and broke the rules of the press gallery by talking to a senator on the floor. "What's happening?" I asked Case. "Cannon has been shot," was the reply I thought I heard. Extraordinary. Senator Howard Cannon, the Nevada Democrat, shot. I ran out and almost collided with Senator William Proxmire, who was going into the broadcast gallery for an interview. "Cannon has been shot," I cried out. Proxmire did a double take as I ran off. A moment later someone made me understand it was President Kennedy. Strange how the mind refuses to function properly in a crisis, I thought.

Weeks later, Proxmire told me, "You know, it's strange how the mind plays tricks on you sometimes. I could have sworn you told me it was Cannon who had been shot."

"That is strange," I agreed, too embarrassed to confess the truth.

Months later, I did confess what had happened. To Senator Case himself. "You know," I told him, "I was so shocked by the news that I thought you had told me *Cannon* had been shot."

"I did tell you that," said Case. "That's what I thought I'd heard."

Usually when reporters get it wrong, however, it's for much simpler reasons. Sometimes it's because their sources of information tell it wrong.

During the early phase of the Senate Watergate hearings, I reported that James McCord, one of the Watergate burglars, had told the committee in closed session that Harry Dent had helped plan a campaign of dirty tricks against George McGovern in the 1972 election. Dent, a former Nixon White House aide, protested. I stood by my story. My source had been a senator, a member of the Watergate committee. And whether Dent had planned dirty tricks or not, I was convinced that McCord had said he had.

Dent brought a lot of pressure to bear on our news management, who, in turn, put the heat on me to make sure I was right. I asked other members of the committee about my story and at first they refused to say anything either way. The committee had taken an oath of silence. Finally, the vice-chairman, Senator Howard Baker, told me I was wrong. McCord had never fingered Dent. I retracted the story on the air. I didn't make an excuse. I said the story was incorrect and I regretted the error.

I have no idea why the committee member who was my source told me that. He claimed later he hadn't, that he had simply been speculating about Dent's possible involvement during the same conversation in which he had told me something about McCord's testimony. Hogwash.

But in the end, it's the reporter's reputation on the line when background sources are wrong. That's fair. Why should the public have to sort through the "who struck John?" of the source chain any more than I want to hear excuses from the plumber when the drain continues to stop up?

Sometimes, of course, we get it wrong because we just don't know as much as we should about a subject. The White House is a particularly tough beat in this regard. Pentagon correspondents concentrate their attention on defense matters. Space correspondents on space. Economic correspondents . . . You get the idea. White House correspondents have to try to know something about it all. One day the story there can be economics; the next, foreign policy; the third, farm legislation; the fourth, arms control; and so on. I sometimes feel that the old saying He's a mile wide but an inch deep was coined just for me.

Occasionally, reporters are wrong because they learn things too quickly. That sounds silly. But here are two examples.

John Scali was so well connected when he came back to ABC News after serving as UN ambassador under Presidents Nixon and Ford that on the day in 1975 when a top official of the U.S. mission at the United Nations received a report that Spanish dictator Francisco Franco was dead, only Scali got hold of the information. Being a careful reporter, Scali called a top official at the White House, who confirmed that the report had been received at the UN. Scali called the U.S. Embassy in Madrid and talked to a top official there, who told him the embassy had the same information. He went on the air and reported that Franco was dead.

Unfortunately, the flash to the UN and the word to the U.S. Embassy in Madrid were wrong. Franco was gravely ill, all right, but lingered for another six weeks while Scali twisted slowly in the wind.

Then there was that awful Saturday morning in August 1972, when I confidently went on the air with the story that George McGovern would select Lawrence O'Brien to be his new vice presidential running mate. A few days earlier, Senator Thomas Eagleton had left the ticket after disclosure that he had been treated in the past for depression, and McGovern had to find a replacement. ABC assigned one reporter to each of the most likely prospects. I drew O'Brien, the former Democratic party chairman. I already knew some of his close aides, and I started working them like there was no tomorrow. I would call them ten times a day, and consequently developed an excellent source in the O'Brien camp.

McGovern sounded out Edward Kennedy. No go. He approached his old friend Hubert Humphrey. Nothing doing. He asked Edmund Muskie. And Muskie went off to Maine to ponder and to consult his wife, Jane. But Muskie had promised a public answer that Saturday morning.

You can imagine how thrilled I was when late Friday night my excellent source in the O'Brien camp told me that McGovern had called O'Brien and said, "Larry, I don't think Ed will do it. If he doesn't, I'll call you immediately." The *you* was heavily emphasized, according to my source.

At nine-thirty the next morning, Muskie went on television to say he wouldn't do it. I called the O'Brien suite. "The champagne corks are already popping here," I was told. "We expect to hear from George any moment." That was good enough for me. I went on radio saying that I had learned McGovern would now turn to O'Brien. And just to make sure I could never climb out of the hole I was digging for myself, some evil genie made me add, ". . . and there are no ifs, ands or buts about it."

Time passed. McGovern did not call. The Mutual Radio boss called the ABC Radio boss to say the Mutual reporter at Sargent Shriver's house was saying it was Shriver. The ABC Radio boss laughed at the Mutual Radio boss, so much confidence did he have in his man Donaldson.

I was sitting on a couch in the lobby of O'Brien's apartment building undergoing a near terminal case of nervousness when the elevator door opened and my excellent source walked out.

"Did McGovern call?" I demanded.

"Yes," said my source. "He just did. It's Shriver."

At least Franco died eventually.

If the mistakes we make in this business are usually our own fault, the same cannot be said for the embarrassments. There are plenty of embarrassing moments that you can't do much about. When Barbara Walters found herself giving the lowdown from Camp David while a large goose flapped its wings and honked away right behind her, there was nothing she could do about it. Things are always going wrong in this business to produce serious, sometimes job-threatening embarrassments.

One time on WTOP-TV in the sixties, while showing a bunch of anti-Vietnam demonstrators shouting and carrying on in front of the White House, I picked up the anchor phone and shouted at the director that he had done something wrong, admonishing him with a mild curse to get with it. Unfortunately, the sound man opened my microphone in the confusion and my ranting went on the air, curse and all. Believe me, I was scared. I just knew when we got off the air the boss would be on the line demanding to know why I had cursed on the air and telling me to clean out my desk. But the call didn't come.

The next day, my boss, John S. Hayes, came into the news room. I quaked. "I just don't know whether it was the right thing to do," he said. "We got a hundred calls from people complaining about our letting those hippie demonstrators yell curses on the air. I guess we were right to do it, though."

"It was a close call, I agree," said I, mopping my brow. "Thank you for supporting our decision."

You'd think people would learn that a "dead" microphone should be treated with the same caution as an "unloaded" gun. But then, we would not have been treated to President Reagan's joking declaration that he had just outlawed the Soviet Union and the bombing would begin in five minutes, or his announcement that having just seen *Rambo*, he knew what to do the next time someone hijacked one of our airplanes. Reagan is not alone in not having learned this lesson, however. The rest of us are just as bad.

Once, NBC's Emery King was standing on the White House lawn ready to do a live two-way with Connie Chung in New York, who could be heard rehearsing the opening of NBC's early morning program *Sunrise*. Chung rehearsed welcoming everyone to the program, then rehearsed asking King why Reagan might not want to go to the Philippines to see Ferdinand Marcos. She did it once. She did it twice. She did it a third time, after which Emery King playfully replied, "How should I know, Connie?" Uh-huh, you guessed it. King was *on the air*. No one had bothered to tell him that this time it was no rehearsal.

During the 1977 inaugural parade, when my field producer told me the anchorman would be calling me in any moment, I let him know in no uncertain terms how I felt about that. "Tell them I have nothing to say," I responded forcefully. As it turned out, I had told the world—my microphone was open. But I actually got a plus out of that one. The *Washington Post* television critic of the day, Sander Vanocur, who is now ABC's senior political correspondent, was so taken with such candor that he praised me in his column the next day and recommended my approach.

Sometimes, of course, when you can't think of anything to say you must say it anyway. Nature abhors a vacuum, and networks can't stand dead air. Consider the time in March 1968 when I anchored one of President Johnson's speeches on ABC Radio. Another Vietnam speech. An easy assignment. I'd been ad-libbing about Vietnam for years. But the speech ended on another subject.

". . . I shall not seek, and I will not accept, the nomination of my party for another term as your president," said the old wheeler-dealer in a surprise ending.

Over to you, Sam.

I started to talk. Fortunately for my professional honor, no transcript exists of my attempt to make sense out of the amazing news Johnson had delivered. Roger Mudd, commenting on CBS, had the wit to tell his audience that he'd like to think about it overnight and come back the next day to discuss it. Mudd, of course, was only kidding. None of us in this business has the luxury of thinking about it overnight. I often say—only half in jest—that the rule must be to get the mouth in gear and hope that the mind will follow. If you wait until your mind produces just the right thought, you'll often sit mute.

On another occasion, I wish I had been able to sit mute. It was a night when I had only one scrap of news but had to keep telling it over and over. And that produced my most embarrassing experience on the air.

One Sunday night in New York in 1971, I was working on my script for the eleven o'clock *ABC Weekend Report* when a space flight to the moon got in trouble. Suddenly, we received a report from Cape Kennedy that the astronauts were experiencing a serious problem trying to lock their command module into the top of their lunar landing module. They were already launched into their trans-lunar trajectory, heading toward the moon, and if they couldn't lock, they wouldn't be able to land on the moon.

I did a quick bulletin from a flash studio just off the newsroom.

We began to mobilize. Unfortunately, our first team was out of position. Frank Reynolds and our space expert, science editor Jules Bergman, had covered the launch of the astronauts that morning at Cape Kennedy. They were still in Florida, but all the remote facilities enabling them to go on the air had already been packed up.

The ABC Sunday night movie was coming up and it was a blockbuster: *Hombre*, starring Paul Newman—sure to have a huge audience. Bill Sheehan, then the senior news vice-president, called from his hotel room in Florida and ordered us to do a quick on-camera bulletin at the start of the movie. Us meant me and Dick Sprague, an expert from Grumman, the company that made the lunar landing module. We raced across 67th Street to the basement studio and got ready, but just before we were to go on the air, the control-room producer informed me that the crisis was over. NASA had just flashed the word that the astronauts had locked successfully. There were no further details.

Well, the astronauts' crisis may have ended, but mine was just beginning. We went on the air with our bulletin. I told the audience fairly smoothly that the problem had been corrected but we had no details. I turned to Sprague, who, using wooden models, explained that the command module had to be turned around in space and its nose probe fitted into the hole in the drogue of the lunar module, at which point locking pins had to snap shut. Sprague said that apparently, that had finally happened, but he had no details.

Now, both of us had told the audience everything we knew, and it was time to get back to *Hombre*. But there is a hard and fast rule in this business, and that is that those of us on the air are in the hands of our producer. The producer is in charge of the broadcast. The producer tells us when to go on the air and, most certainly, when to go off. Not one peep had I heard in my earpiece from my producer since he had told me the crisis was over, just before going on the air. So I rather haltingly repeated what I had just said about the incident. Still, nothing in my ear.

I turned again to Sprague, a slight shine of perspiration popping onto my forehead. "Now, Dick, you say that probe has to lock in the hole in the drogue?" I inquired. Sprague looked a little puzzled but, being a good sport, replied, "Well yes, as I said, the probe fits here in the hole in the drogue like this, then the locking pins snap shut around it here."

While he was saying that I noticed that in the gloom behind the camera someone was waving something at me. I started squinting at it, trying to make out what it was. There sat Sprague on the right side of the home screen pointing to the hole in the drogue, while I squinted off the left side of the home screen at persons or things unknown.

By this time, the television audience was surely stirring, aware that something was going on here that wasn't right, but not sure what. There was more to come. I finally made out what was being waved at me. It was a sign, hastily written by hand, which said, "Jules on the phone." Yes, of course, they wanted me to talk to Jules Bergman now and get his expert opinion about the hole in the drogue. I looked around. This couldn't be happening to me. There was no phone to be found. I looked under the anchor desk. No phone. Sprague, of course, had finished his latest retelling of the hole in the drogue story. He looked under the desk with me, although he had no idea what we were looking for. But as I said, he was a good sport.

The man with the sign began waving it frantically. The control-room producer must have thought he had a mutiny on his hands. This correspondent Donaldson was refusing to talk to Bergman on the phone. The sweat was now pouring from my brow. But if necessity is the mother of invention, panic is its father. I explained to the *Hombre* audience what was happening. "They're asking me to talk to Jules Bergman on the telephone, but I can't find a telephone," I declared.

Presto. Within seconds, as Sprague and I sat there mumbling something about the drogue in the hole, I mean the hole in the drogue, a hand from the gloom thrust a telephone onto the anchor desk. I reached for it. It was a three-line phone and there were two lights flashing. Which one was Bergman? And who was on the other line, dare I find out.

I stabbed line one. I had guessed right; it was Bergman. "Tell us what you know, Jules," I shrieked. "Well," said he, speaking from Bill Sheehan's hotel room in Florida, "I don't have any details, but I can tell you that the probe of the command module must fit into the hole in the drogue of the lunar module and . . . *zzzzz*." At that instant, the line went dead.

Not a word spoke the producer. No raven croaked from above the studio door. The camera stayed on, sure enough never blinking. Dick, clutching his models to his breast, looked upset. I was horrified. I could barely talk. I wanted to talk, but the throat muscles wouldn't work right. "Aak, aak," I croaked, resembling more that legendary raven than a smooth-talking television reporter. I committed high treason. I took myself off the air. I just said, "That's it, there isn't any more to say. Now, back to *Hombre*." I'm sure the audience murmured, "Nevermore."

Later, I got a letter from a viewer in Colorado conferring on me what he said was the *cement bicycle* award of the year. I have no idea what that is, but I'm sure I deserved it. There is a rule in the business that when you're terrific, no one is watching, and when you're awful, the whole world is glued to its set. Naturally, *Hombre* produced the second highest rating of any Sunday night movie that season. I like to think I had something to do with it.

Finally, embarrassing moments are not the exclusive property of those of us who report the news. Those we report about have their share as well, including presidents. Ronald Reagan suffered a terrible indignity one day without even being aware of it at the time. It was the day he was presented with three fine Lippizaner horses from the famed Vienna Riding School in a ceremony on the White House South Lawn.

There stood the horses facing the president. There stood the president facing the horses. There stood the press corps and cameras off to the side, dutifully recording the event. The president began a speech accepting the gift when suddenly the press corps realized that the horses were involuntarily exposing their male members.

Now, for those of you not born on a farm, I must tell you that the portion of a horse's anatomy we are talking about here is really quite extraordinary. I mean, we are talking about several feet. We are looking at horses that, to the casual observer, have suddenly grown a fifth leg.

All the television cameras were quickly directed at the horses (reporters being among your most ardent casual observers), the close-up zoom lenses working overtime, as Reagan intoned, ". . . and we have only seen just a tiny bit of what they actually do in their exhibitions, partly due to the soft ground here . . ."

The president, whose forward vision of the offending sight was obscured by the natural forelegs of the horses, couldn't figure out why a loud, sustained ripple of laughter was rising from the press area. Later, a videotape of everything was made up and given to Larry Speakes to show the president in private. I'm told he roared.

Chapter Thirteen

THIS WEEK WITH DAVID BRINKLEY

David Brinkley is over the line—the one that separates those in this business who are valuable because of what they *do* from those few who are valuable because of who they *are*. Brinkley is a force. When he announces in his distinctive twang, "Hello, we're all here, welcome to our Sunday show," he does something for ABC that no one else can match.

Brinkley didn't want to leave NBC News, where he spent thirty-eight years. True, he wasn't doing much and wasn't in the mainstream of that news operation at the end. But he would have gladly spent the rest of his working days there if it hadn't been for the cold shoulder given him by William Small, a news executive who had spent years at CBS News but, after losing out on the top job there, had been hired by NBC to head its news department. CBS and NBC styles are totally different and Small didn't seem to appreciate Brinkley's.

Roone Arledge was smarter. He had been kicking around ideas for a new Sunday talk show to replace *Issues and Answers*. Arledge decided to go to a full hour and pattern the new broadcast after the tried and true *Nightline* format. That is, a set-up piece on the topic of that week's program, then interviews, with a strong personality as host. About that time, Brinkley put out the word that he was fed up with Bill Small and NBC. Arledge snapped him up, primarily to bolster our election coverage. Brinkley had never lost the top ratings for a convention or an election night in all the years he was anchoring at NBC. The new Sunday show seemed the ideal place to park him in the meantime. Dorrance Smith, who had served previously as my White House producer but was now the executive producer of my half-hour Sunday night news broadcast, was put in charge. Smith whipped together the elements, and the first *This Week with David Brinkley* program went on the air on November 15, 1981.

The first broadcast was a disappointment, primarily because the scheduled guest, budget director David Stockman, didn't show up. Days before November 15, the now famous *Atlantic* article, in which Stockman admitted they had cooked the budget figures and didn't really know what they were doing with supply-side economics, hit the stands. Stockman begged off the program.

The next couple of Brinkley broadcasts weren't a whole lot better. Then, thanks to Arledge, the program hit pay dirt with Libya's Muammar Qaddafi. It was a time when the papers were full of stories about Qaddafi hit squads headed for the United States. So Arledge called Smith around 1 A.M. on Saturday at home. "Why don't you interview Qaddafi," Arledge said. Smith thought it was probably impossible, but you don't say something like that when Arledge comes up with an idea, no matter how cockamamy it sounds. And a good thing Smith didn't. With only a few hours' notice, Lou Cioffi, ABC's United Nations correspondent, was put on a plane headed for Tripoli in the hope that Qaddafi would agree to an interview. He did and, as they say, the rest is history. Qaddafi denied he had sent hit squads to the United States and called President Reagan a liar and all sorts of other names. Reagan may have called Qaddafi a barbarian and a flake in the years since, but Qaddafi certainly started it that Sunday on the Brinkley program. His appearance was the talk of the town and the banner headline in the next morning's *Washington Post*. The program was made.

There have been other remarkable moments, notably the Brinkley show's involvement in the downfall of Philippine President Ferdinand Marcos. On November 3, 1985, Marcos was our guest via satellite from Manila. He was facing stiff opposition to his regime both at home and abroad. During the interview that day, George Will told him some people in Washington were wondering if he might not be willing to move up the date for elections. Will put it to him directly, ". . . Is that possible, that you could have an election earlier than scheduled?"

Marcos answered without a pause. ". . . I announce that I am ready to call a snap election."

There was a piece of news! Senator Paul Laxalt, who had gone to Manila the month before to confer with Marcos at President Reagan's request, told me later he had suggested to Marcos in a phone call a few days before that he might want to announce new elections but wasn't sure he was going to do it until he heard him say it on the Brinkley show.

The Reagan administration's attitude about the election was put into focus two weeks before it occurred by White House chief of staff Donald Regan on the Brinkley show. I asked him what the United States would do if Marcos won reelection through fraud.

"Well, we'd condemn the fraud [but] you'd have to do business with [him]," said Regan.

Marcos did try to steal the election but it didn't work, thanks to two powerful members of his entourage who joined his opponent, Corazon Aquino. They were defense minister Juan Ponce Enrile and chief of staff Fidel Ramos, who promptly holed up in a military camp expecting to be assaulted at any moment by troops loyal to Marcos. That is where we found them by telephone one Sunday morning in February of 1986.

We put them on the air over the telephone and some of the back and forth with David Brinkley was, under the circumstances, priceless. Consider:

MR. BRINKLEY: I believe Lieutenant General Ramos is there with you. Would he give us—would he give us his view on this question, what will happen if Mr. Marcos—

MR. ENRILE (by phone): You can ask him your question: I'll pass the telephone to him.

MR. BRINKLEY: All right, fine. General Ramos—

LT. GENERAL RAMOS (by phone): Mr. Brinkley, this is General Ramos.

MR. BRINKLEY: How are you this morning?

LT. GENERAL RAMOS (by phone): Fine. I feel fine.

MR. BRINKLEY: Good.

LT. GENERAL RAMOS (by phone): How are you?

MR. BRINKLEY: Very well . . .

I thought any moment they would ask about the wife and kids and exchange weather reports.

And, again, consider this exchange:

MR. BRINKLEY: The defense minister. Mr. Enrile. I have a question for you. Do you hear me? Who has the phone now?

LT. GENERAL RAMOS (by phone): Just a moment, please.

MR. BRINKLEY: Thank you.

MR. ENRILE (by phone): Hello, Mr. Brinkley.

MR. BRINKLEY: Mr. Minister, it appears to us—

MR. ENRILE (by phone): I'm no longer minister. I am ex-minister.

MR. BRINKLEY: Well, all right. Ex-Minister, ex-minister Enrile.

MR. ENRILE (by phone): You can call me Mr. Juan Ponce Enrile.

MR. BRINKLEY: All right, that'll be fine.

And so it went. Amid chaos, the threat of imminent military action, and great uncertainty, the two besieged men in Manila answered our questions with civility and the best example of grace under pressure I've seen in a long time.

Both these examples of remarkable Brinkley show moments—Qaddafi and Marcos, et al.—show how important the behind-the-scenes work of booking guests is to the success of the interview programs.

Those of us on the air take most of the bows for the program's success. But the underlying reason we're successful is that the Brinkley program airs interesting and timely topics discussed by authoritative guests. Asking the most penetrating questions in the world won't get you anywhere if you aren't asking them of the right people.

Dorrance Smith solicits our views, particularly Brinkley's, each week on possible topics for the next Sunday. He consults with the top executives of the news division, more often than not with executive vice-president David Burke who has a keen sense of what people beyond the Washington beltway are interested in. Smith gets our principal field correspondent working on a setup piece that will lay out the background on the subject for our audience before the interviews begin. Jack Smith, who currently fills that role, does a masterful job of making complex subjects understandable and interesting. We have been fortunate that his two predecessors, John Martin and James Wooten, possessed that same ability. Meanwhile, Veronique Rodman, the "booker," is lining up potential guests. There is often fierce competition among the Sunday talk shows for the same guests when the week's topic is an obvious and overriding one.

On the Sunday before the 1984 Democratic convention in San Francisco, Rodman had lined up Bert Lance, the man Walter Mondale had selected to be the next party chairman. But late Saturday night, Lance, under fire from party forces who didn't want him in that spot, canceled. Smith and Rodman called some interesting people, including Mr. Democrat himself, Robert Strauss, and he agreed to come on. But we didn't have any of the key players, such as Senator Gary Hart, who was scheduled to appear on CBS's *Face the Nation* with Lesley Stahl. Both programs were originating that Sunday morning from the same sky booth network complex in the convention hall, so Smith told Rodman to call Kathy Bushkin, Hart's press secretary, and ask if Hart would come across to our booth and be on the Brinkley show after he finished with Stahl. Since the Brinkley program runs for an hour, we would still be on the air after Stahl was through. Hart did it. And on the news wires, we took a lot of the play away from *Face the Nation*.

Stahl was furious. She yelled at Rodman, accusing us of having played a dirty, underhanded trick. To this day she cold-shoulders Smith when their paths cross.

I see Stahl's point. I would probably be as angry as she if the situation had been reversed. But after all, Gary Hart didn't have to do it. I think if anyone should be blamed in this episode, it's him, not us.

The next time a Ferdinand Marcos announces to George Will on the Brinkley show that he intends to hold an election, or some politician you dislike gets put on the hot seat by me, remember, none of it would be possible without the behind-the-scenes staff, especially the executive producer. Murrow had his Fred Friendly, *60 Minutes* has its Don Hewitt, and the Brinkley program has its Dorrance Smith—although he makes it look so easy that Roone Arledge was once heard to remark that the Brinkley show just seems to produce itself.

What the Brinkley show didn't have to begin with was Donaldson. I was not an original member of the group. The original setup included Brinkley, George Will, America's premier conservative columnist, and a third seat, which was to be rotated among various journalists from both inside and outside the company. But the rotating concept wasn't working, and Smith knew it.

I began to appear more and more in the third seat until one day, about two months after the program debuted, Smith told me to show up every week until further notice. I've stopped waiting.

At first, Brinkley and Will weren't pleased by my participation. They are both gentlemen, calm and deliberate in their questioning, and they thought I was too pushy and asked questions that were occasionally too harsh. You could feel a tension among us at first when I pushed someone hard. But Brinkley never tried to tell me I couldn't press my questions—he's too good a newsman for that—and within a few months we began to work better together and form a team.

David Brinkley is the leader. George Will is the intellectual. I am the district attorney. The combination seems to work. Because of David and his gracious manner, no one leaves offended. Because of George no one gets away with delivering fuzzy arguments. Because of me, no one gets a free ride.

All right, *one* time I gave a free ride: I failed to ask a single challenging, provocative question of leaders of feminist organizations on a program about the New Bedford rape case, the one in which a woman was assaulted on a pool table in a bar while other customers allegedly cheered the assailants on. I'd gotten burned when it comes to women's issues once in Idaho, when, covering Jimmy Carter's raft trip down the Salmon River, I interviewed a young park ranger named Judy Fink. On the air, I labeled her a "rangerette." Switchboards at ABC affiliates all over America were swamped with protests. The next day I did another interview with Ms. Fink and she saved me by indignantly insisting that rangerette was her proper title and she resented the complaints. But ever since, I've been very careful about offending women. So on this particular Brinkley program, I didn't demand that our female guests defend their assumptions about the case, as I should have. I'll challenge presidents any day, but taking on half the world is asking too much.

Other than that time, however, I think I've always pressed for answers. Here is an example from March 1986. The guest was Senate majority leader Robert Dole of Kansas.

MR. DONALDSON: Talking about money, what about Paul Volcker, whose term is up next year? Would you like to see him reappointed to the Fed?

SENATOR DOLE: I, I think he's been very effective.

MR. DONALDSON: Well, would you like to see him reappointed?

SENATOR DOLE: Well, I don't make that appointment.

MR. DONALDSON: You don't, but would you like to see him reappointed?

SENATOR DOLE: It's all right with me.

MR. DONALDSON: Wait a moment. I think you're—that's terrific—it's all right with you.

MR. WILL: How do you think he got to be majority leader of the Senate?

MR. DONALDSON: I'm going to ask a final try. Senator Robert Dole, Republican of Kansas, would you like to see Paul Volcker reappointed as chairman of the Federal Reserve Board.

SENATOR DOLE: I think it'd be a good idea.

Like I always say, if at first you don't succeed, try, try again. On other occasions, Dole can be most direct. In November 1986, I asked him if he believed Lt. Col. Oliver North had organized the diversion of money to the Nicaraguan contras from the sale of arms to Iran without higher authority. "Even Ripley wouldn't believe that," shot back Dole.

In 1982, questioning the candidates in the Illinois gubernatorial campaign, I asked incumbent James Thompson if he was a "crook," as his detractors were alleging, and challenger Adlai Stevenson III if he was a "wimp," as his opponents were charging. Both said no.

I asked Secretary of Defense Caspar Weinberger if he, as the whispering campaign suggested, was anti-Semitic. Weinberger, an Episcopalian whose grandfather was Jewish, answered no, that would make very little sense in his case.

When I confronted Secretary of State George Shultz with the accusation leveled in a widely circulated news story that he was anti-Arab, he was even more direct: "Come off it," snorted Shultz.

I once pressed Shultz to explain why no one within the administration had been willing to take any direct responsibility for the lapse in security that made it possible for terrorists to blow up the U.S. embassy annex in Beirut. This, after terrorists had previously blown up the embassy itself and a U.S. Marine compound in similar fashion.

Shultz got angry and sputtered that if somebody's head had to roll, "I'm willing to have it be my head anytime anyone wants, because I certainly feel responsible, absolutely, and I take that responsibility very seriously." He *was* the secretary of state and it was an embassy annex under his charge. Maybe he was being unfair to himself, but at least it was a direct answer. Actually, we've had good luck with Shultz on the Brinkley show. He once told us rather proudly that the United States had put Qaddafi "back in his box where he belongs" after a show of naval force in 1983, and that is perhaps the most remembered Shultz quote to date.

Incidentally, I followed up the death of our marines in their barracks in Lebanon in 1983 by asking three clergymen, who appeared on our program at Christmastime, whose side God was on when the young fanatic drove his truck under the building and blew it up. He thought he was performing God's will and would go to heaven for having done so. None of the clergymen gave a very good answer to that question and seemed uncomfortable that it had been asked.

I once suggested to then Secretary of the Treasury Donald Regan that the inaccuracy of the administration's forecast of economic conditions should make him humble.

"I'm never humble, Sam," said Regan.

I was so pleased by such frankness that the only thing I could think of to say was, "Neither am I. I don't recommend it." Perhaps that gave Regan the idea that he'd found a kindred spirit. A few years later, when called on to speak at the Gridiron dinner, an annual press roast, he joked that people asked him why Sam Donaldson can be so abrasive and overbearing. Said Regan, "Well, tonight I can reveal for the first time; Sam Donaldson is my son!"

The toughest guest we've ever had in the sense of getting answers to our questions was undoubtedly the Israeli soldier-politician Ariel Sharon.

Let me state right here that I think Sharon has been a harmful influence within the Israeli government. I think his policies, particularly in regard to the 1982 invasion of Lebanon, have hurt Israelis and a lot of other people as well. But as an interviewer, what I think of a guest's views is beside the point.

There are a lot of guests with whom I have strong personal disagreements on issues, but if they forthrightly answer the questions, I join in treating them courteously and count them as good guests. But Sharon never came to the Brinkley program to answer our questions. He came to make speeches on subjects of his own choosing, that's not so different, to be fair about it, from a lot of our guests. But Sharon was particularly tenacious in that he would deliver his views in a relentless run-on sentence that never stopped, making it extremely difficult to jump in with a question. Often, he would bring along maps, which he insisted on showing the television audience, to prove that Israel is a small country, surrounded by hostile neighbors, a country whose defense requirements are great and difficult. Well, that's a legitimate point, but not the only point we wanted to talk to Sharon about. But usually, we would get very little chance to talk about anything else before the time ran out.

Brinkley and Will are not good at interrupting people. They know it should be done when we are running out of time, but they are both such gentlemen that they cringe from barging in and cutting off some windbag in mid-sentence. They usually seem grateful when I do it. Of course, I then get the letters telling me how rude I am and inquiring why I can't be like that nice Mr. Brinkley.

In August 1982, in the midst of a fierce war he was directing in Lebanon, Sharon was once again our guest. And I was determined we would ask him some pointed questions about it. After he had made his case that Israel was a small country, difficult to defend, and was clearly intending to make it two or three more times, I interrupted him.

"General," I said, "you have a record of insubordination . . ."

He stopped talking.

". . . and I want to ask you about a specific act . . . I want to know if that last twelve-hour bombing of Beirut, which killed so many people, was authorized by your government or whether you did it on your own?"

Sharon shot back that he had never been insubordinate and that the bombing had been a cabinet decision. That came as news to the cabinet, we found out later. When we went off the air, Moshe Arens, then Israel's ambassador in Washington, told me he wanted to punch me in the nose for what I had said to Sharon. I wasn't quite certain whether he was kidding or not. But I was certain that Sharon was not pleased. "I will debate you on television," snapped the general. "I will debate my so-called insubordination on television, and we will see who is right."

For once, I rose to the occasion.

"I may be dumb, general," said I, "but I'm not so dumb as to debate you. Surely you know far more about your insubordination than do I."

Sharon's been back on the Brinkley show since, but he's left his maps at home.

Another tough guest from the standpoint of getting specific answers is the Reverend Jesse Jackson. Reverend Jackson does not bring maps, but like a lot of strong-willed, dedicated people, he brings a packaged litany concerning the events and causes of the day in which he is interested and he tries to deliver that litany without great regard to the specific question asked. In July 1984, Reverend Jackson, having just returned from Cuba, where Fidel Castro had released some political prisoners to him, was our guest. I asked him to respond to the charge being leveled at him by Reagan administration officials that he had been duped by Castro into becoming a propaganda tool. "Is there anything to that?" I inquired.

Reverend Jackson started off by saying that when Russia invaded Afghanistan, Mr. Reagan's response was that we should blockade Cuba (Reagan was not even president at the time). He then proceeded to talk about our need, as he saw it, to reestablish trade with Cuba.

I interrupted to ask, "Will you address my—"

Reverend Jackson plowed ahead.

I interrupted a second time to ask, "Well, will you address my question directly?"

Now, Reverend Jackson swung into a list of positive signals he perceived from Castro, such as exchanging ambassadors, dealing with the Contadora process on Central American peace, and reunification of families.

I interrupted a third time to ask, "Would you address my question directly? Do you think there is anything to the proposition that Castro was simply using you in an attempt to inject himself into the American political process?"

"I do not," answered Reverend Jackson, finally. Such small and undramatic triumphs sustain reporters over the rough times.

Not everyone dodges questions. My favorite straightforward answer on the Brinkley program was delivered by Washington super lawyer Clark Clifford.

"It is said around this town that a couple of years ago, three years ago, you pronounced a judgment on Mr. Reagan that he was nothing more than an amiable dunce," I told him. "Have you changed your mind?"

"No. No," Clifford replied, ". . . I still feel it."

I think when people come on the Brinkley program, they're fair game for any question of public interest that involves them. Our guests are not people unschooled in the ways of public life or television. They are almost invariably people who have fought hard to win positions of public trust and who claim to be serving the public interest. Either that, or they are professional people (businessmen, economists, writers, professors) who wish to advance their ideas and theories. And they should not be spared tough questioning. Most of them expect it.

We once had Frank Borman, at the time president of beleaguered Eastern Airlines, on the program and I began a round of questioning by observing, "Mr. Borman, I hate to beat up on you, but you're here—"

"—You're not beating up—" interrupted Borman, a bit too soon.

"Well, I'm just about to," I informed him.

"All right," said Borman.

And away we went on the subject, as I put it, of "why don't your personnel on the Eastern shuttle tell the passengers the truth when there's going to be a delay?"

I said most of our guests expect tough questioning; I didn't say they liked it. In the summer of 1984, Bert Lance, Jimmy Carter's ill-fated budget director, the same man who stood us up in San Francisco at the Democratic convention a few weeks later, was on the program. As Democratic Party chairman in Georgia, he was thought to be a kingmaker in the '84 election.

We asked him the appropriate questions about current politics, then, as time was running out, I said to him that if most Americans remembered him at all, it was as the budget director in the Carter administration who had resigned because of accusations that he had allowed himself large overdrafts at the Calhoun, Georgia, bank that he headed.

"Do you have any overdrafts today?" I asked. Lance said, "No," adding with a sorrowful tone in his voice and a hurt look on his face that he had hoped I had forgotten about that, but he was sure that I hadn't.

One of the techniques people use to escape the consequences of an uncomfortable question is to make it appear that the questioner is off base or viciously unfair in bringing up the subject. I got a lot of mail from people who told me how rude I had been to embarrass such a fine man as Mr. Lance. When the word came a year later that Lance was under investigation by federal and state authorities for new irregularities in his banking practices, including personal overdrafts, I thought about sending a copy of the news stories to all those who had written me to complain. Of course I didn't. But to borrow a phrase from Larry Speakes: You know who you are.

I believe you have to press guests on the Brinkley program when they don't answer the question or answer in a way that does not conform to the facts. Mind you, everyone has a right to his or her opinion; that's why we ask people to come on the show, to give theirs. But no one has the right to get away unchallenged with stating opinion as fact.

Attorney General Edwin Meese III came on the show once and complained about the executive order then in force requiring contractors doing business with the federal government to hire minority workers. Meese said the order required "quotas," and he argued that it should be changed. The order does not require quotas. Quotas are, in fact, against the law. The order requires that goals in hiring be established. Now, some feel that goals lead to the same rigid hiring practices as would quotas, and that is certainly a legitimate point to debate. But that is not what Meese said. Here is the way the exchange went:

ATTORNEY GENERAL MEESE: . . . what I am opposed to, what the president is opposed to, and what I think the majority of the American people are opposed to, is by saying, "Okay, we don't have enough of this race, we're going to discriminate against you because you don't meet our quotas." That's what's wrong.

MR. DONALDSON: Do you know of any law that requires a quota?

ATTORNEY GENERAL MEESE: Right now—

MR. DONALDSON: There is none.

ATTORNEY GENERAL MEESE: —the practices of the Federal Contract Compliance Office do talk about—

MR. DONALDSON: They don't require a quota.

ATTORNEY GENERAL MEESE: They do. They talk about those kinds of quotas, or at least they've been interpret—

MR. DONALDSON: They don't require one, Mr. Attorney General.

ATTORNEY GENERAL MEESE: Mr. Donaldson—

MR. DONALDSON: You're hitting a straw man.

ATTORNEY GENERAL MEESE: Mr. Donaldson, they have been—what they require there is so poorly worded, in the opinion of Bill Brock, the secretary of labor, as well as many others, that they have been subverted into quotas in carrying out the federal contracts, and that's what's wrong.

Okay, "subverted into quotas" if you think so, but there is no *requirement* for quotas and that's all I wanted Meese to acknowledge.

When it was over, some people, including one of our news executives, let me know they thought I had been rude to Meese. I disagree. Our program is not a forum on which people can say anything they want without being challenged when they have misstated something.

Of course, it helps when I have the facts straight myself. Lord knows I try to, and Lord knows I sometimes don't. Unfortunately, it's not just the Lord who knows it when that happens. Everyone watching does, too.

Once, on a program on arms control I told two different guests, Senator Sam Nunn and then national security adviser Robert

McFarlane, that President Reagan had said he thought the Soviets had a three-to-one advantage over us in every weapons category. I asked them to comment. I made it clear I didn't think the president knew what he was talking about. Shortly after we got off the air, it was made clear to me it was I who didn't know what he was talking about.

A friend at the White House called to say I had badly misquoted the president. Oh sure, I was close. The president had said he thought the Soviets were ahead of us in every category of weapons systems, conventional and nuclear. But he had not said they had a three-to-one advantage. And being close in the news business isn't the same thing as being right. I sent Reagan a note the next day telling him I was sorry I had misquoted him, that I purely "hated" to be wrong, but I had been and that I would correct the record on the next Brinkley program.

The next Sunday, during the round table discussion I replowed who said what, said I still thought the president was wrong in his view, but that was no excuse for misquoting him. I wound up looking into the camera and saying, "I was wrong, I correct it, and I apologize to the president for misquoting him."

When the broadcast was over, Reagan called me to say he had seen the apology and appreciated it. I thanked him for calling. It was a gracious thing for him to do, but such gestures are in character for him. When Bill Plante of CBS had an appendectomy, Reagan called him to wish him well. And when my engagement to my wife, Jan, was announced, he called me to wish me well. "You know what the song says," said the president. "It's better the second time around." I did, but I didn't have the heart to tell him it would be my third.

Curiously enough, another time I got in trouble because I was defending Reagan. On a program about Americana with noted writers Garrison Keillor, Toni Morrison, E. L. Doctorow, and William Kennedy, Doctorow claimed that Reagan had said he thought people who sleep on grates often did so by choice. I jumped in, using my best "not through the Iron Duke" manner to tell him that the man who made that statement was not Reagan but Attorney General Edwin Meese. "Let's be fair," I chided in my most supercilious fashion. "Oh," said Doctorow, obviously chastened. "I thought it was the president."

And, of course, it was.

So I wrote Doctorow a letter. I told him how embarrassed I was to call myself a White House correspondent and get something like that wrong and how sorry I was that he had to suffer in public from my ignorance. I got a nice note back from Doctorow thanking me for the letter but informing me I was still getting it wrong, that it wasn't he who had made that comment on the program or had had such an exchange with me, but William Kennedy. So I wrote a letter to Kennedy telling him I was going to keep at it until I got it right, but that if he wasn't the one, to simply pass along my note, making a chain letter out of it, and we'd all get rich.

I find that I make most of my mistakes when I believe I know something for sure. When I'm in doubt, I double-check it. When I inadvertantly write something wrong, like Senator William Kennedy instead of Edward Kennedy, a lot of people are there to correct it. But when I know I know, watch out. You'd be surprised how many times in writing this book I've been certain of a conversation or date, only to find on checking that I wasn't right. Then again, maybe you wouldn't be surprised.

But on the Sunday before election day 1984, I had the facts right in questioning Vice President George Bush. I think it was the toughest round of questioning I've conducted on the Brinkley program.

Bush knew it was coming, not because anyone had tipped him but because he's a pro and he understands there's going to be heat in the kitchen. Furthermore, Bush has known me for a long time. I first covered him when he was elected to the House of Representatives in 1966. Bush once tried to explain to the Soviets at a meeting in Geneva in 1982 that there was this reporter back in Washington named Donaldson who, if he were there at the time, would not give anyone a moment's peace.

I didn't give Bush a moment's peace that day, and I must say, he gave as good as he took. Here is a transcript of the fiercest round.

MR. DONALDSON: Mr. Vice President, Mondale said yesterday there is a deep character flaw in this person [Bush] that is apparent to the American people, and he cited a number of instances . . . one of the things he cites are the ugly personal things you and your people have said about Geraldine Ferraro. You said you'd kicked her ass.

VICE PRESIDENT BUSH: Now, wait a minute—

MR. DONALDSON: Your press secretary called her bitchy. Go ahead.

VICE PRESIDENT BUSH: I didn't say that.

MR. DONALDSON: I don't want to interrupt you. Go ahead. What did you say?

VICE PRESIDENT BUSH: Well, I've never said it in public! Let me just recite—

MR. DONALDSON: You did, Mr. Vice President. It was recorded on a news camera which was there, and you knew it was there.

VICE PRESIDENT BUSH: Which was eavesdropping in a conversation. If you want my opinion, I was whispering into the ear—

MR. DONALDSON: Well, you were in public, with the press around you.

VICE PRESIDENT BUSH: Well, if I'd wanted to say in public the statement that I have never repeated—put it that way—I would do it. You've just said it in public. And a lot of other people have—

MR. DONALDSON: I was quoting you, sir!

VICE PRESIDENT BUSH: —and you see signs all over the place. I'm not denying that I said it to that person, but I am denying I meant it for public consumption. And leave out me for a minute. My wife felt the same way, and then to have an opposition campaign in desperation try to rip her into some kind of a conspiracy is absolutely, patently absurd and grossly unfair, and anyone, I hope, that knows me and I hope knows my wife know that we would not participate in such—but it's a meaningless thing.

MR. DONALDSON: Well, I didn't bring up your wife—

VICE PRESIDENT BUSH: And what—may I finish?

MR. DONALDSON: Certainly.

VICE PRESIDENT BUSH: The point is the American people are not fooled by it. If they were, why would every poll show me head on head moving ahead and her going down if it had been so offensive or there had been such a visible flaw of character? Sam, there isn't. And there's no change in me for better or for worse. I may be the same kind of guy that I was, and it hasn't changed a bit.

MR. DONALDSON: Well, I didn't bring up your wife, but I did bring up your press secretary, Mr. Teeley, who said of Ms. Ferraro, "She's bitchy." Why would he say that?

VICE PRESIDENT BUSH: But you didn't bring up Tony Coehlo, who used exactly the same word in saying what she shouldn't be in the debate. Exactly.

MR. DONALDSON: If he were sitting here, I would bring it up.

VICE PRESIDENT BUSH: Well, you'll have a chance then for that, but you're not going to get it from me.

It had been a tough round, and I thought it particularly deft of the vice president to try to put me in a position of criticizing his wife. You will recall that Mrs. Bush had said Ferraro was something that rhymed with *rich*. Later, she said the word she had in mind was *witch*, but a lot of people thought she had another word in mind instead.

Bush was particularly sensitive about his debate with Ferraro, after which he had used the "kick a little ass" phrase. I had watched that debate on television and commented on it on ABC immediately thereafter. Alone, I believe, of all the network people who commented immediately, I had called Ferraro the winner. Bush brought this up during my questioning of him on the Brinkley show, saying he thought he had won the debate, but adding, "Sam, I don't want to get too personal here forty-eight hours before an election, but your analysis was quite different, as I recall."

It was an uncomfortable moment. My instinct is to slug it out toe to toe when I'm talking to someone and our opinions differ, just as George Will and I do on the Brinkley round table each Sunday morning. But it seems to me that isn't my job as a questioner, in which my opinions are of no consequence and only the guest's are. So I contented myself with replying, "I happen to think Ms. Ferraro did very well. But your analysis of the debate is certainly acceptable to me."

But if that was a rough-and-tumble exchange with Bush, here's one I had the next summer with Governor Mario Cuomo of New York. Cuomo didn't like the president's tax reform proposal. He particularly objected to the elimination of the deduction for state and local taxes since that would hit New York taxpayers who itemized deductions particularly hard. But to keep that deduction would mean the loss of billions of dollars in revenue under the new reform proposal unless some offsetting provision was adopted, so I asked him how he would make up that lost revenue.

Cuomo said it had taken the president months to come up with his plan and it would be unreal to ask him to come up with one of his own now. I asked him if he was attacking the president's plan, didn't he have an obligation to put forward his own ideas about how the revenue would be made up. Sure, he replied. Give him a few months and he'd come up with a better plan. Since he didn't have one at the moment, I asked him why we couldn't assume that maybe his alternative would be to raise the rates again or hit the middle class again in order to subsidize those who deduct state and local taxes. Cuomo replied that he was sure one could come up with a plan that contained real fairness.

"But you don't have it for us this morning, right?" I asked.

Cuomo got angry. "Of course not!" he replied. "Do you want a plan written in seven minutes on ABC television when it took them months and months to correct their own? That's ridiculous, but not surprising." Later, Cuomo called one of our top news executives to complain that I had been unfair to him. The executive pointed out that I had questioned Treasury secretary James A. Baker III, who was on the same program but on the other side of the issue, just as fiercely. Cuomo took the point.

I've spent a lot of time talking about the questioning on the Brinkley program, but the feature that is often the most interesting for me is the round table discussion. At the round table, George Will and I and a rotating guest commentator give our views in what Brinkley often refers to as a "no holds barred, almost anything goes" free-for-all. Jody Powell, Tom Wicker, Hodding Carter, Mary Ann Dolan, Morton Kondracke, and Robert Maynard are among our regular guest commentators. Brinkley mixes it up with us when he chooses, but generally presides.

We get together an hour before air time on Sunday mornings and talk about the topics we want to discuss. On the theory of "let's not leave it in the locker room," we don't actually discuss them in the advance meeting, but it's pretty clear from our records where we stand.

I was very troubled at first about my participation on the round table. I am an honest, careful reporter and I try to keep my personal opinions out of my daily news work. But I wondered whether people would believe that when they saw me delivering a tough report from the White House after hearing me deliver a very strong personal opinion on the same subject on the Brinkley program. I finally concluded that people would understand the different roles and, more important, would believe that I understood them. After all, Bill Plante and Chris Wallace also have strong opinions. Any reporter who does not would be so ill-informed or uncaring that you wouldn't want that person to cover the news. In a sense, knowing what my opinion is actually gives you a better chance to gauge whether I keep it out of my news reports. I'm satisfied I'm not compromising my integrity or credibility with viewers by performing the dual role of reporter-commentator, and I think most people agree with that.

Once having chosen the topics, we all try to think a bit about what we want to say. Will makes notes to himself, mostly phrases he wants to use, I believe. I just think a bit about where I want to come down in the argument and about some illustrations I might want to bring up, but I don't put any of it into words in advance.

Sometimes, of course, this gets me in trouble when I can't think of just the right word or phrase when I need it. I experienced a terrible blackout shortly after the story of Reagan's Iranian arms sale broke when we were discussing the fact that many people were clamoring for Reagan to fire top officials in his administration. Someone brought up the fact that Reagan hates to fire anyone; he shrinks from the task. I jumped in to observe that if he couldn't,

I'd bet Mrs. Reagan could, "She's the smiling mamba," I said forcefully. Boy! Did the the roof fall in on me on *that* one. The White House East Wing, where the First Lady's offices are located, rocked with indignation. I hadn't meant to call Mrs. Reagan a snake. I had only meant to say she is tough when it comes to her husband's welfare and if she perceived that some of his aides had been disloyal or inept, she had the backbone to strike them down hard. But, of course, that isn't the way I had put it. So, I wrote her a note of apology. To apologize on the air would have simply repeated the libel. These lapses of mine aside, the beauty of the Brinkley round table is that it is spontaneous. And it can be tough. Will knits his reasoning together so well that if you accept his initial premise, you can't find a chink in the armor of his logic through which to penetrate. Then, too, Will will hurl two quotations from Locke, one from Gladstone, recite from the Federalist papers, and wrap it all in some folksy saying such as "Nellie kicked the cow." Awesome.

I usually just argue, using basic reasoning, sometimes emotion, and always, I hope, verve. It seems to work. I probably get as many letters telling me what a jerk the writer thinks Will is as he gets saying the same thing about me. I trust we aren't hearing from the same people.

I disagree with Will on many subjects. But that does not prevent me from liking him. I enjoy arguing politics and issues and I don't take offense when others press their views. Every year since they've been in Washington, Ronald and Nancy Reagan have gone to Will's suburban home for dinner. And often I've stood outside in the cold in the press pen waiting to hurl a few questions at the president when he leaves. The first time that happened, it seemed to embarrass George. So I yelled across at him, "It might be easier on everyone if you invited me to dinner inside rather than have me waiting outside [a variation on a famous saying of Lyndon Johnson]." So far, Will has ignored my suggestion.

I thoroughly enjoy working on the Brinkley program and hope it continues. If Roone Arledge comes to me tomorrow and says, You have to give up everything you do for ABC News but one thing and you get to choose that one thing, it would be the Brinkley program I'd keep, hands down.

Chapter Fourteen

FAME

It is possible to get a big head in this business, to begin to think that you are universally admired. It is possible, but only until you open the day's mail.

A woman from Waterford, Maine, writes: "You are rude, insensitive, crude, debasing, autocratic, unfeeling, judgmental, condescending, superior and stubborn."

A man from Hemingford, Nebraska, reports in: "The election is over and in spite of your herculean efforts, the 'Old Champ's' legs were not knocked from under him. Your liberal bias and editorializing has been rammed down the American people's throats for long enough."

An entire church congregation in Skidmore, Texas, advises: "Our church is in prayer for all the hostages and President Reagan. We stand united for you and Dan Rather to take the next plane for Siberia."

How do I feel about getting such letters? At first, it bothered me a great deal. We all want approval, and as Shakespeare said, "If you prick us, do we not bleed?" But over the years I guess my skin has toughened. I believe fundamentally in the right of people to criticize, even when I'm on the receiving end, and I understand criticism goes with my job.

I bring people the news, often of things unpleasant. Moreover, I challenge government officials and other public individuals who are admired by the viewers. If you believe passionately in Ronald Reagan and his policies, it is more than a little disconcerting to hear a reporter suggest he's done something, anything, that is less than a hundred percent perfect.

I am forever getting letters from the "true believers," who do not wish to take me to task for an error (they cite none) or a deliberate distortion (they allege nothing specific) but simply implore me to get off the back of "the best damn president this country has ever had."

I pay close attention to letters that point out an error I've made. When I "closed" the New Orleans World's Fair six months early on my Sunday evening news broadcast because I misread the wire copy, I replied contritely to each one of the letters from New Orleans taking me to task. When in a fit of mental lapse I spoke blithely of Martha Curtis, George Washington's wife, I groveled abjectly in responding to those who put me down as an ignoramus, after pointing out the name was Custis. And when viewers make a calm and reasoned argument that I've been unfair, I think about it. Sometimes I concede they have a point and try to mend my ways. But the "true believer" who simply rails against me and my kind gets my attention (I personally read every letter) but not a response.

Often, "true believers" will attempt to conceal where they're coming from because, I suppose, they think their criticism will be more effective. They'll write, "I didn't vote for Reagan, mind you . . ." or "As a lifelong registered Democrat . . ." before they flay me alive for being so mean to that nice man, but then they almost always reveal where they're really coming from by telling me how much they despise "sloppy" Tip O'Neill, "slimy" Walter Mondale, and every other prominent liberal they can think of.

Now, mind you, for the four years of the Carter administration I got letters telling me how mean I was to Jimmy Carter and how much I was detested for being "unfair" to him. But interestingly (and understandably) enough, it was not the same people who found me terrible then who find me terrible now. Shortly after the presidential change in 1981, I began getting letters like this one: "What has happened to you? You used to be a good reporter who asked tough but fair questions. But you've become a mad dog the way you treat President Reagan, always attacking him for no reason." I got about an equal number of letters from people who said they hadn't been able to stand me during the Carter years but thought that I had begun to "mature" now that I was holding Ronald Reagan's feet to the fire.

Not everyone is angry when they see me getting on Reagan's case, however. Some people are delighted and write me letters of lavish praise meant to spur me on to fiercer attacks. They begin their letters with high compliments for my work (a foolproof way to get me to read on, I assure you), then swivel quickly into a vitriolic, sometimes abusive, denunciation of "that Grecian Formula grade-B cowboy." Frankly, I toss those letters into the same pile with the ones that call me a "mad dog" for my "vicious" attacks on Reagan. Of course, some people who despise Reagan are not complimentary to me. They see me as part of the "too little, too late" bunch when it comes to "exposing and destroying" that "idiot in the White House." They accuse the press of molly-coddling "old Bonzo," and because I am sometimes mentioned in dispatches from the front as being "tough" on Reagan, they jump to the chance to tell me how much of a "cream puff" or "sell-out artist" I really am. After all, they seem to believe, if the press, particularly Donaldson, were really doing its job, Ronald Reagan would long ago have been swinging from a high tree on the Ellipse.

On an ABC *Viewpoint* program in 1984, a program that lets a studio audience put reporters on the spot, the talk got around to presidential coverage and a young man rose to ask me a question. I knew what he would ask, some variation of "How come you're so nasty to the president?" I was ready with my answer, which I've given thousands of times, portions of which you find spread throughout this book. Instead, he asked, "Why is the press so soft on Reagan and why do they accept everything he spits out?" and I spent the next minute and a half sputtering. Sometimes it's hell to have to think up new answers.

That young man, and others like him, do have a point. The press, myself included, traditionally sides with authority and the establishment. For every truly tough question I've put to officials, I've asked a dozen that were about as tough as Grandma's apple dumplings. Most of my critics, however, don't take the point of view that the press is too soft, so with your permission, I'll scramble back on familiar ground and return to debating them.

The hardest thing for some people to understand, or at least agree with, is that reporters are not there to sing the praises of any particular president. We are not there to automatically attack him, either. But in performing the "oversight" function of trying to find out and report what's really going on at the White House, inevitably more of the mistakes and problems get spotlighted than the triumphs. I mean, when things are going right, hooray! No corrective action is needed, the public is being well served without having to bestir itself. It's when things are going badly—that is, when the news is bad—that the public ought to be told without delay. Some people apparently would rather not hear any of the bad news, however. A woman in Atlanta, Georgia, writes: "Why is the press under the delusion that they [are] another branch of government, established in the interest of the people to keep the government honest? President Reagan, in contrast to the media, gives us a good dose of accentuating the positive."

This feeling that we ought to be cheerleaders engenders no greater passion in some people than it does when it comes to U.S.-Soviet relations or, for that matter, the subject of communism in general. I've got boxes of letters accusing me of working for the communists, being in the pay of the Kremlin, advocating the overthrow of the American way of life, and generally behaving like "a gutless, yellow commie rat," to quote one of my recent correspondents. Some such letters are written in crayon, but most aren't. Another detractor addressed his envelope simply: "Sandinista Sam, Washington, D.C." I didn't mind that so much but I must say I was rather put out that the post office department unhesitatingly delivered it to *me*.

Listen here, folks. I served my time in the army (a fact that always seems to infuriate the "right-thinking" Americans who complain about my patriotism). I pay my taxes so the MX can be built, even though at this writing we still have no idea where we're going to put it. And I know which side of the barricades I'm going to be on if the nuclear whistle blows. In the meantime, however, my job is to try to uncover the logical contradictions or covered-up mistakes in our own policies toward the communists.

But if I have my critics among the general public, I also have my critics in the public press. I think it may not be the best use of our time for reporters to write about each other, but that view has not deterred some of my colleagues from, in the action coda of the artillery man, "finding me, fixing me, and firing!"

The first big "shelling" I took was from Ken Auletta in the now-defunct *More* magazine. Auletta had come on the Carter campaign in the fall of '76 to write about the press. Of course, in the pursuit of this mission he did not bother to tell any of us, or at least not me, who he was or what he was doing. In the piece he wrote about how Carter was making a monkey of most of us, particularly of the television reporters. Auletta made fun of the suit I wore and carried that criticism forward metaphorically by commenting on my "garment center personality" (I trust the good workers around 34th Street won't take offense). Finally, he quoted "one of the little people who rides in the back of the plane" as saying I was the "biggest asshole on the face of the earth."

Wow. Some high honors you'd just as soon not have. Particularly did that hurt because while I won't insult your intelligence by claiming perfection, I don't make it a practice of throwing myself on the "little people" of this world. I felt a little better, however, when a couple of weeks later Jody Powell called me in and said he'd been thinking about it and he thought he ought to let me know he had given that quote to Auletta, at least he was one of those who had. "Little person who rides in the back of the plane" indeed.

In the same genre, Judy Bachrach took a chunk out of my hide with a 1979 piece in the now-defunct *Washington Star* (you notice, they do pieces on me and fold right up). It was titled, "ABC's Bad Boy in the White House," and, among other things, accused me of biting women, sporting a "wardrobe spun in polyester heaven" (there seems to be this preoccupation with my clothes), telling a group I had expressed intimate designs on the First Lady, and acting crazy even without a drink. That piece hit the stands during a period when the news department management was making some sharp assessments on roles and missions for senior correspondents and my wife was in the process of throwing me out of the house. It did not do me a world of good in either realm. Bachrach seems to think she has found a good thing, however. I appear regularly in her pieces as a bit player and always fall into the orchestra pit. During my recent bachelorhood, she wrote a piece in the *Washingtonian* magazine entitled "Washington's Lousiest Lovers," within which there was a box signed by a pseudonym listing me as one of Washington's eleven lousiest lovers. I was described as "boorish and a bully to boot."

How would she know? My friends, I assure you Ms. Bachrach has no personal knowledge of my skills or lack thereof in the department she claimed to be discussing, and such is my feeling toward her that if she and I find ourselves the last two people on the face of the earth, she will acquire none.

Columnist Pete Dexter, then with the *Philadelphia Daily News*, once wrote an entire column denouncing me for my crudeness and rudeness in asking Senator Gary Hart to do his Teddy Kennedy imitation during a television interview. The only thing was, it was Roger Mudd who did that on NBC, not me, but we never want to let such details get in the way of the duty to expose those we don't like.

Then there was the piece about me in the *Washington Post* by Stephanie Mansfield. It opened by depicting me as standing in my kitchen, pounding the table, shouting at her, and demanding of my wife that she produce the garlic instantly for the Caesar salad I was whipping up. That certainly makes a catchy opening, but does not square with my recollection of the facts. How could anyone believe such things of me?

Aside from the opening, the article was favorable, I'll admit—except, of course, for the headline. The bulldog edition of the *Post* was delivered to my feverish hands the night the article appeared and I was much relieved to see the headline "TV's Toughest Talker." That is complimentary. It set the tone for what would follow. I was so pleased. You can imagine my unhappiness when I woke up the next morning to see that overnight, someone had changed the headline, so the vast majority of *Post* readers were treated to my picture and the accompanying words, "Big Mouth of the Small Screen." Oh well, easy come, easy go, I always say.

Aside from personal letters and mention in the press, being on television brings me personal encounters almost everywhere I go. Years ago, I got used to people running up to me in the street shouting, "I know you, I know you, you're . . ." Here they would grope for a name (Dan Rather, Ted Koppel, once someone called me Ed Bradley), while I would go into high-gear prayer that the light would change and I could make my escape. Whether they know my name or not, they often say triumphantly, "I see you every night on television." I've never figured out a perfect response to that. When they say, "I see you and I like you," "thank you" is appropriate. When they say, "I see you and I despise you," an answer also comes readily to mind, although so far I've been able to restrain myself from delivering it. But to say only "I see you . . ." this presents a problem. Mark Weinberg of the White House press staff, when told "It's good to see you," replies, "Thank you, it's good to be seen." But that seems a little too flippant. So I usually content myself with replying, "I hope you continue watching."

Oh yes, it's flattering to be recognized, and for the most part, people are decent about it and after a word or two are willing to respect my privacy; I have absolutely no quarrel with them. But there are some people who seem to believe that if they recognize me, however inexactly, they are doing me an immense favor never before bestowed by humankind and insist that I respond by giving them all the time and attention they desire. They will want to tell me their life story, critique my work or the president's, haul me over to that table of sixteen in the next room of the restaurant and introduce me to each of their friends seated thereat or in some other way command me to devote my time to them. And if I insist on running off with some lame excuse such as "I'm on deadline" or "my fish is getting cold," they will get all huffy and say in a loud voice so I'm sure to hear it, "Well, I always heard he was an arrogant, pompous ass."

Once, while I was browsing through the record department of

a suburban shopping center store on a Saturday morning, unshaven and garbed in old knock around clothes, a woman who recognized me literally drove me from the building. "What are *you* doing here?" she demanded. I tried to come up with a soothing answer but could think of nothing better to say than "I'm buying records." Had I had the wit to reply that I was conducting an undercover investigation for a television report on record fraud, it might have been okay. But "buying records" proved to be totally inadequate—worse, to her it proved to be offensive. She seemed extremely upset by the fact that the reporter whom she always saw dressed in white shirt, blue sport coat, and red tie, and usually clean-shaven, or at least, through the magic of makeup, apparently so, was out in public dressed like a bum. She kept at me, demanding to know why I was looking the way I was, buying records in a cheap suburban store, until I made my escape and ran out the door.

Then there are the times I go on the road with the president and, as part of the press pool, go into an auditorium before he enters to be met by people yelling and screaming not at the president but at me. I'm pleased to report I get as many cheers as jeers from most crowds, but there are exceptions. On inauguration night in 1984, I traveled around with Reagan to all the inaugural balls and at one, the youth ball if memory serves, a mighty *boo* went up from the Reagan youth when I came in with the press pool. The president was right behind us and may have thought his loyal troops had mutinied. I considered taking my revenge by showing the booing on television in accurate juxtaposition with the president's entrance but stayed my hand in the name of professionalism.

There is the reverse, beneficial, side of being recognized, such as when head waiters give you a table without reservations or airline counter managers upgrade your ticket to first-class without being asked. I try not to ask for special favors or trade on celebrity status. When I call Washington restaurants for reservations, for instance, I ask if they have a table for two or four available at 8 P.M., and if they say, no, I thank them and hang up and if they say yes, I then give them my name. I don't accept special "deals" on merchandise or free trips or other personal privileges that I feel are being offered me because of my television status. Why do I believe in such strictness, some might think foolishly?

I don't think it's really fair to trade on position, that is, to go to the head of a line when the only differentiation comes about because I'm seen on television and someone else isn't. Not only is it not fair, but I'm a firm believer in the adage that if you begin to believe your own press clippings about how important you are, you're lost. Of course, I'm not an absolutist on this. If the head waiter does recognize me and gives me a good table, I don't demand to be seated in the kitchen simply because I'm a latecomer. And if a remote acquaintance who happens to be the chief lobbyist for the American Railroad Association sends over a bottle of red wine at Christmas time, I drink it right down.

Having said all that, I confess I once tried to use my position for special advantage, but God must have been watching and kept me from plunging into sin despite my best efforts to do so. It came about this way. One Tuesday in the summer of 1985, I got a call that my daughter, Jennifer, who was on a trip to Europe, had been struck by a motorcycle as she crossed the street in Athens. She was in the hospital with a shattered leg. Any parent would have been worried sick and would have tried to figure out how to help. But I was not just any parent. I knew important people, and by God, this time I was going to use them. I wanted Secretary of State George Shultz to pick up the hotline to the U.S. Ambassador to Greece and order that all available U.S. medical forces descend on my poor daughter's bedside while a U.S. medevac transport plane be readied to retrieve her battered body back to the motherland for expert treatment.

I don't have Shultz's direct dial number, but I had Bernard Kalb's, who was then assistant secretary of state for public affairs. "Bernie, it's Sam," said I when Kalb came on the line to hear my story about my daughter's desperate need. I didn't spell out exactly what I had in mind for Shultz to do, but I let Kalb know most emphatically that I needed help.

"Of course you do," said Kalb, full of sympathy, being a father himself. "Miss so and so, get me the name and phone number of the info officer in Athens," I heard him sing out to an assistant.

Well, I would have felt a little better if George Shultz was going to call, but if Kalb thought he had the necessary clout, it was all right with me just as long as it all got done. "I've got it," said Kalb. "Here's the name, take it down, and here's the number. Don't forget to dial the country code before the number and good luck."

So the one time I tried to swing my weight around, it got me a telephone number that is also in the Rolodex at the ABC office. I will say this, though. The embassy people in Athens gave my daughter first-class attention until I could get there. For that I'm grateful, no matter who made the call.

In closing these thoughts about the notoriety and fame that go with being on television, let me hasten to assure you that I am aware that not everyone knows me. Recently, I was invited by a good friend to a small dinner party in honor of a Famous Author, whom I had not previously met. Not wanting to come off as a bumpkin, I studied up on her and her latest works. And when we were introduced, you could tell we were simpatico. We got on well; I was even seated at dinner on the Famous Author's left. Midway through the meal, and approximately two and a half hours into the conversation, she began telling us of her visit to the Philippines in the days just after Ferdinand Marcos's removal. She said the Philippine people were very grateful to the American media for the coverage, "particularly grateful to you, Bill," she said turning to me.

I knew I was in trouble, but hoped it would pass. It did not. She warmed to her task of passing on the thanks of a grateful nation. "Everywhere I went, they sang praises to Bill Plante. Bill Plante, Bill Plante, that's all I heard," said the Famous Author, raising her voice above the din at the table and fixing me with an admiring gaze. What could I do?

"Thank you," I said with what I hoped was appropriate modesty. "We all do what we can."

Chapter Fifteen

PERSONAL

One Saturday morning in mid-January of 1980, I left home in Great Falls, Virginia, and drove to a real estate office I had picked out of the Yellow Pages. I was looking for an apartment. My marriage of sixteen years was over.

Two months earlier, just four days after the U.S. Embassy in Teheran had been seized and just as ABC News was gearing up into its exhaustive round the clock coverage of the Iranian hostage crisis, my wife, Billy Kay, sat me down and informed me she wanted a divorce. I hadn't realized things had gone that far. Sure, I knew she was unhappy, that we weren't getting along, that the love and tenderness had gone out of our marriage. But I was unprepared for it to end.

I had been married once before, when I was twenty. That marriage had also ended in divorce, but the circumstances were different. My teenage sweetheart of the moment, Patricia Oates, and I had gotten married one Friday night in Juarez, Mexico. Why? Who knows. We were in love and it seemed like a good idea at the time. We were both immature and somewhat out of control, and certainly unprepared to accept the responsibility of marriage.

Eight months after our son, Sam, was born, my teenage sweetheart left me. I was in the army by that time, and when I came home from work one day, there was a note on the refrigerator informing me wife and son could be found at Mama's. Patricia had lost interest in me. Young Sam had it tough for many years, but to his credit he pulled himself up by his boot straps and has carved out a fine career as a psychologist.

But this time it was different. Billy Kay and I had been married since 1963. For the first few years while I was at WTOP-TV, with more or less steady hours, things had gone very well indeed. We had three children, Jennifer, Thomas, and Robert. Life was good. But when I joined ABC, things began to change in the classic sense that I put my work first, devoting my time and energy to it in single-minded fashion. Obviously, there are trade-offs for that kind of commitment—in family relationships, friendships, and the other rewarding ways people spend time. I don't look down my nose at reporters who want to spend their energy elsewhere rather than climbing the career ladder. Indeed, I sometimes envy them for having balanced their lives better. But for me, when I came to ABC, I put the blinders on to almost everything but hard work. Billy Kay, devoting herself to the home and family in the old-fashioned style, had nothing with which to take up the slack of my inattention.

It got worse in 1976, when, covering the Carter campaign, I was on the road or in Plains, Georgia, almost all year. I tried to shuttle the family down to Georgia throughout the summer. But even there, I was up at dawn to go down to the peanut warehouse and spent most of the day roaring up and down the Georgia roads in pursuit of the First Peanut Farmer. And it got worse during the years of the Carter presidency, as I tried to follow the rule I had set for myself: When Jimmy Carter did anything, anywhere, anytime that the press could cover, I personally would be there. That rule certainly worked in helping to establish my place in the ranks of White House correspondents. But it also helped to establish my place in the ranks of ex-husbands. Don't misunderstand me. I'm sure there are other things wrong with me than my interest in my work. And I know I'm not entirely to blame for the break-up of our marriage; it's seldom just one person's fault.

When Billy Kay sat me down and told me it was over, I asked for a few days before I had to deal with it, "just until this hostage crisis is over," I said. She agreed. So I took up residence on the couch. Days stretched into weeks. This was getting ridiculous. Two months later, with the hostage crisis still going strong, I finally looked up that real estate agency, found an apartment, and moved in. For the first week in my new place, like the fox trapped by the hounds, I "went to ground." I didn't want to see anyone, talk to anyone. I just wanted to think about things, listen to music (I didn't buy a television set for eight months), and adjust to being alone. I was depressed, but knew that life would go on. You remember my motto: Never give up. I wasn't about to give up then. I thought that I would simply plunge into my work even harder as a compensation and a therapy. But just the opposite happened. Oh, I kept up with what I needed to do and earned my pay. But I found I was more interested in laying out a new routine and a new private life for myself.

I grew roses on the balcony. I tried to have fresh flowers on the table each week. I kept the apartment clean without any help, even making the bed each morning before I left for work. I devoted every Saturday night to my children, cooking dinner for them. That's still true to this day, although as young adults they are free to come over or not, just as it fits into their plans. I only ask that they let me know in advance. My son Tom would come over often to play tennis with me. I used to tell him that I was one of the world's best tennis players. "Jimmy Connors has never beaten me," I would tell him. Being the good son that he is, he would just smile. And every once in a while, Tom would let me have a set or two. Good, strong sons do that for their aging dads, you know.

Tennis is fun, but let's face it, there is more to life than that. I began to date. I particularly began to date Jan Smith, a young woman in her mid-twenties who had worked at ABC before going to Kansas City to take a job as a television reporter for the NBC station there. For the next three years, I single-handedly supported Trans World Airlines and Kansas City's Alameda Plaza Hotel. Reagan would go on the road, I would have to drop off to edit a television report for that night, then, in the phrase I made famous around ABC, I would "make my way back slowly across country." All roads back led through Kansas City.

As you have perceived before now, this courtship, of course, was not one in the classic boy-meets-girl genre. I was keenly aware of the age difference of twenty-two years and was constantly turning its implications over in my mind. I suppose it wouldn't have mattered if I hadn't been serious in my intentions, but I was. One of the most difficult moments of my life was the night I sought out an invitation from Jan's parents to meet them and explain this. They wanted the best for their daughter, and here came a man, twice divorced and with four children, who was twenty-two years older than their daughter. Why, I would have thrown the bum out of my house. But Jan's parents are extraordinarily wise and caring. They let me know they didn't like this courtship one bit, but they also listened and served me a good dinner.

All parents want the best for their children. But children grow up and ultimately must make their own decisions. Parents then have the choice of supporting them or rejecting them because they don't do things the way the parents would. I've seen enough of both kinds of situations to know that rejection can't possibly be the right course. It's tough. My own children are old enough to want to do things their own way now. How dare they! But I love them, and I'll always support them. So it was with the Smiths.

Another extraordinary supporter during that period was the Reverend Mark Anschutz, rector of Christ Church in Alexandria, Virginia. Jan, who has a deep sense of her Christian religion, naturally wanted to marry in church. I had not gone to church in years and was skeptical as to whether any church would want to get involved in marrying a two-time loser. We had a number of counseling sessions with the Reverend Anschutz, who sized us up and, along with his bishop, decided we both knew what we were doing and meant what we said. Three and half years after Billy Kay informed me that our marriage was over, Jan and I were married in Christ Church. Dorrance Smith was my best man. Jan's sister Jeanne was her maid of honor, her brother Rob was one of my groomsmen.

Jan is a terrific person who brightens everything around her. She is loyal and honest, and I love her with all my heart. Another of the things we have going for us is her career. She is a television reporter who is making it on her own. She, too, is in a high pressure job, with demands on her time and energy. When I can't get home by a certain hour because of work, it usually happens that neither can she. Neither of us is sitting around waiting for the other. It is not that one of us is going out meeting new people and doing interesting things while the other is staring at the walls. Jan has a vital interest of her own that extends beyond me. Jan and I talk about the stories of the day and the business, but not as teacher/pupil. I wouldn't dare. Furthermore, I told her when we got married that my name would be more of a hindrance to her in the business than a help. She uses her maiden name on the air and on most of her credit cards.

So, what have I learned from my own ride on the high-pressure roller coaster? For one thing, it wasn't the news business's fault I hit some bumps. I believe each of us makes our choices freely. I made mine unwisely. With a little more thought, I could have balanced things much better. What I've really learned is that some things are important and some things are not and the trick is to know which are which and apportion time and energy accordingly.

The other day, *Nightline* executive producer Rick Kaplan called to ask if I would anchor the program in Koppel's absence for one week while Reagan was at his California ranch in late summer. I told him I had made plans to bring all my family out to Santa Barbara for that week and I'd like to take a pass. Until recently, I would never have done that. I would have canceled the family plans and stayed in Washington to work. Now, my colleagues in the ABC booth at the White House take most of the night assignments. And for the first time in almost twenty years, I try to take two days off a week, except when major news stories on my beat are ongoing.

I still want to do more in this business, in fact I still would like to "have it all," whatever that means, but never again at the risk of losing my family.

Chapter Sixteen

QUO VADIS

What's ahead for ABC, the television news business, and me?

Leonard Goldenson sold the company in 1986, to Capital Cities Communications. I was sorry to see Mr. Goldenson go (at my level, we always called him Mr. Goldenson). He had been a wise and generous boss who clearly understood that the way to get the best out of people was to make them feel appreciated and secure, rather than constantly try to keep them off balance and in fear for their jobs.

I always thought Goldenson was a supporter of mine. He must have been or, given the heat he got from time to time from friends and stockholders because of something I had said or done, I wouldn't still be here. Once, during a time when I was getting panned by Reagan supporters over something or other, he told me, "Just keep on doing exactly what you've been doing." My appreciation of that was dimmed only slightly when I picked up Mike Wallace's book and read that Goldenson had used those exact words to him back in the fifties, shortly before Wallace and ABC parted.

The day after the ABC/Capital Cities merger was announced, Goldenson brought Capital Cities Chairman Thomas Murphy to lunch at our Washington news bureau. Most of us had never met and had barely heard of Mr. Murphy (the title goes with the territory).

We had all been frantically reading the news clips on Capital Cities, an organization famous for its "don't waste money" bottom-line approach. So when Murphy walked in, I was ready. "I've learned three things about you," I said. "First, that you often take taxis instead of limousines."

"That's right," said Murphy.

"Second, that you painted your first building in Albany, New York, only on the two sides visible from the highway."

"That's right," said Murphy.

"Well," I said, "that is not altogether encouraging to us who regularly line up at the trough of ABC, but there is a third thing. It is said you pay your key people very well."

"That's right," said Murphy.

"Terrific," I concluded. "Come in to lunch and sit right down by me."

The truth is, any organization that is as big and diverse as ABC can profit from some belt-tightening and some new blood. Of course, none of us wants our own belt tightened or the new blood to move into our office. But I've never worried about my job, and I'm not going to start now.

The biggest imponderable is how the television news business may evolve. There once was a day when the network news departments reigned supreme. If you wanted news on television from beyond the county line, you had to get it from ABC, CBS, or NBC. Now, not only can you get it from a dozen smaller networks and cable competitors, the stations affiliated with the big networks can get reports directly from the scene by down-link satellite. The anchorman in Omaha can introduce reports from Moscow, Tokyo, Atlanta, and Washington bought rather cheaply from someone else, so who needs Peter Jennings and Sam Donaldson?

The networks are trying to think up new types of programming to give affiliates and audiences something they can't get from other services. As I write this, theme broadcasts, which jump on a big story and develop it in great length and depth, seem to be coming into vogue. The problem with that is, it takes a big story to hold a mass news audience's interest. And big stories don't come along every night. Furthermore, the recent trend toward "soft" news, that is, features on diet, dating, and a neverending string of social diseases, has driven us to a sort of gresham's law of the airways, soft news driving out hard. Sometimes I think we are in danger of forgetting just what the primary network news function ought to be: to inform people about the important things that happen in the world around them that do or could affect their lives. I guess you can shove almost any story into that definition if you push and stretch enough, but clearly, it should probably mean more emphasis on arms control than on diet control.

I also think we sometimes lean too much toward the flashy and titillating in an effort to earn ratings. I'm not against ratings. And I don't preach some purist line denouncing entertainment values in television news production.

Howard K. Smith once told me he considers that the worst sin in television news is to be dull. At the time, I thought he must be wrong. Surely the worst sin is to get the facts wrong or distort or . . . But now I think Smith is right. He does not mean reporters should not hew carefully to all the principles of honest journalism. He means that after that's been done, if the report is so dull that no one watches it, you haven't accomplished a thing. So I'm for interesting television news presentations. But it seems to me that too often we put on a story or a feature or establish a department or go after an interview because we think we can promote it and entice a greater number of people to watch our broadcasts rather than because of an honest belief that it has an intrinsic news value.

I think in the final analysis, the way to win the network ratings war at the dinner hour is to put on the most responsible hard news program covering the day's top events. Despite the ability of local stations to obtain the raw material, my hunch is there will always be an appetite for a network broadcast of this description that features well-known, established reporters. Give me a good crew of professionals covering the hard news against a good crew of professionals doing a nightly single theme show or filling much of their time with highly glitzy and promotable irrelevancies, and I think I'd beat them.

Which brings me to me and my future in the business.

It's no secret I want to leave the daily grind of the White House beat. It has been a great experience and I'm grateful to ABC for giving me the assignment. It is a prestige beat, and naturally, I've enjoyed that. But life moves on and so should I. Something's wrong with the system if I hobble out to the North Lawn some night to report on the activities of President Amy Carter (who, I have no doubt, knowing the Carter clan as I do, will someday get there). Every time I go to Roone Arledge and tell him I ought to leave the White House beat, he's very understanding and asks me what I'd rather do. I then begin fumbling and mouthing generalities. The truth is, there are only one or two jobs at ABC better than mine, and they are filled by good people already. Still, the nagging feeling that it's time to move on remains.

People ask me, "Do you want to be an anchorman?" That question always reminds me of the old story about the politician who, when asked whether he's in favor of alcohol, describes alcohol's good points approvingly and bad points disapprovingly without ever taking a final position. So if by anchorman you mean do I want to give up the enjoyment of reporting from the field, watching news events first hand, being free to call a story as I see it without sometimes having to deliver a homogenized line of pap in the name of not offending the mass audience, why of course I don't want to be an anchorman. But if by anchorman you mean do I want to sit at the center of the effort, help shape a broadcast in the way I think it should go, leave my imprint on the overall product, and, to be honest about it, reap the rewards and honors that go with being at the top of my business, why, of course I want to be an anchorman.

The fact is, every one of us wants to use our experience and whatever judgment we've accumulated over the years in the job of greatest responsibility open to us. Every one of us wants to run something important rather than be a valuable but secondary player. Isn't that right, George Bush?

Still, I'm well aware that anchoring isn't a job everyone can do, despite the fact that Peter Jennings makes it look easy. I think the key to anchoring is to be yourself. Too often in our business, people on the air try to be something they're not or play roles designed only to please the audience. If they think the audience expects them to be sad; they're sad; if they think the audience expects them to be tough, they're tough. Walter Cronkite was so good, among other reasons, because you always had the feeling that you were seeing an uncontrived, honest expression of his thoughts and feelings.

If Cronkite choked up when he relayed word of President Kennedy's death, that was natural. If he said, "Go, baby, go," when a space shot lifted off, that was natural. We've all seen people on television who seem to be trying to re-create Cronkite's strength in this regard by expressing studied reactions. It's as if they think they must lead the audience in some predictable emotion. Or rally the nation as if they were some national symbol. I think those of us in television news should report and impart information. If we do it as human beings, enough of the right emotion will come through. But if we try to be emotional, folksy, whimsical, or tough for effect, the audience will know it. Television unmasks phonies, and that applies to reporters as well as politicians.

Having said all that about anchoring, I don't have to be in any one precise post to continue to enjoy this business and feel that I'm contributing something. I do have to keep running hard. We all have heard platitudinous speeches at graduation time about how the older generation is looking forward to the younger generation taking over so we can retire and take it easy. Untrue. May I say right here to Samuel, Jennifer, Thomas, and Robert Donaldson and all the other bright young people of this world, you'll have to drag me kicking and screaming off the stage. I will not go quietly (well, that's in character, isn't it?).

The other day, an interviewer asked me what the high point of my career had been. My first thought was to beat the fellow up. I told him a story instead. Many years ago, an ABC correspondent was interviewing an eighty-six-year-old woodcutter in Maine. "Have you been a woodcutter all your life?" the reporter asked. "Not yet," was the reply.

I trust the high point of my career hasn't happened yet, either.

ABC WHITE HOUSE TROOPS

1977–1987

I've worked with many fine ABC reporters and producers who have been assigned to the White House for various periods during my tenure. Some people think they all deserve medals for having had to put up with me. The best I can do for them, however, is to say thank you.

Correspondents

Ann Compton
David Ensor
Rita Flynn
David Garcia
Bill Greenwood
Bettina Gregory
Sheilah Kast
Susan King
Steve Shepard
Jack Smith
George Strait
Mike Von Fremd
Kenneth Walker

Producers

Bob Aglow
Les Blatt
Sam Brooks
Ed Harris
David Kaplan
Leo Meidlinger
Terry Ray
Dorrance Smith

Index

There are three names mentioned too often in this book to index: Ronald Reagan, Jimmy Carter and Sam Donaldson.